The TRIUMPH Book

Melanie Davis

ISBN 978-0-9846035-0-3
Library of Congress 2010930767

The Triumph Book published by Triumph Press
PO Box 863982
Plano TX 75086-3982
www.TriumphPress.com

Bulk quantities of this book can be purchased by contacting
Melanie@TheTriumphBook.com

Cover Design and Interior Art: Carrie Svozil
Proofreaders: Ronda Knuth and Laura Pasley
Interior Layout: Melanie Davis and Kouba Graphics, Inc.
10 9 8 7 6 5 4 3 2

Dedication

This book is dedicated to all of the noble souls who have departed this life, providing their loved ones, and all of us, with the wisdom, strength, hope and joy found in the pages of this book.

Contents

Acknowledgements

Carrie Svozil, graphic artist for *The Triumph Book* and supporter in absolutely every way, is the person I would like to thank first and foremost. I have relied on her countless times for ideas, direction and emotional encouragement. Carrie worked with me for two years, designing and creating all the logos and cover art, without being paid. *The Triumph Book* was created by the selfless contributions of people like Carrie!

If there is a champion of compassionate service, Lorrie Anderson holds that title. As a volunteer manager at a large hospice in Dallas, TX she has made the last months and days of life comfortable, even joyful, for hundreds of patients. The assistance and true friendship Lorrie provides is one of the great assets to my grief recovery work.

There are many bereavement coordinators who deserve my deepest gratitude. For providing advice at the highest level, as well as assisting this cause to move forward quickly, I would like to thank: Shaneka Booker-Bell, LMSW; Eden Summers; Angela M. Fredrickson, LBSW; Rev. Carol Stone, B.S; Janet Ihne, M. Div.; Sue Rafferty, LMSW; Keith A. Colley, B.C. and Rev. Dorothy Meyer-Levine, M. Div.

Ronda Knuth is a dear friend and expert story writer who freely gave many skillful hours proof-reading and providing valuable feedback as I pieced this book together.

Laura Pasley also contributed her valuable proof-reading skill as well as meaningful emotional support.

Connie Kouba, of **Kouba Graphics, Inc.** is a true God-send as she spent tireless hours laying out the book, making changes and providing expertise.... all without being paid up-front, during or for some time after the printing. "Just pay me when you can" is what Connie told me and I had to beg her to send me an invoice. This book could not exist without her generous gifts.

Lori Mercer stepped in at the eleventh hour, before publishing, bringing her incredible talent and skills to the needs of the website and marketing of *The Triumph Book*.

My husband, Steve Davis, and our children deserve the principal credit for standing by me, making untold sacrifices, remaining patient and believing in this endeavor.

Finally, and most importantly, God receives the greatest praise for providing every challenging experience and wonderful opportunity which has given me the knowledge I needed to make this book possible.

Triumph over Tragedy

Although many differences exist between us, there is one consistent and profound experience humankind has in common: we all will suffer tragedy or defeat during the course of our lives. Death, loss, sickness and other adversities will inevitably come to each one of us. With pain and hardship being a natural part of the human condition, it is interesting that our typical reaction is often shock, anger or confusion. "How could this happen to me?" is one of the first thoughts we have in response to tragedy. There is almost always a period of bewilderment and raw emotion when initially confronted with extreme difficulty or loss.

Having lost a baby girl to SIDS, I experienced this shock, followed by the grieving process. What I've learned is that loss does not have to leave you forever empty and deflated. Instead, a deeper understanding and compassion, as well as a capacity for great joy, can eventually co-exist with the void. I say co-exist because the longing for what was lost doesn't go away, and never should. It is this very yearning which fuels an increase of wisdom and understanding. It is amid suffering and adversity that our longest strides towards greatness can be made.

The death of my seven month old daughter, Brynn, stirred a deep feeling of compassion and concern for others suffering through loss; and from this heightened awareness of the pain of others, I have come to realize that, on the whole, our society does not understand or facilitate healthy grieving. Too often we become literally *stuck* in our initial response to adversity. The anger and confusion we experience when faced with a painful change can become the continual state of living and feeling.

I found healing from my own tragedy by helping others through their pain. This journey led to the development of a program designed to guide individuals through a writing process that helps uncover the purpose and meaning found in adversity. While creating this program, I discovered that the idea of purpose, gratitude or joy coming out of tragedy is often treated as audacious or unachievable. Some bereavement counselors, those specifically trained to help people through grief, even told me the idea of *overcoming* grief is questionable and a "hot" word which should not be used.

If the natural and widespread experience of adversity serves no purpose; if we cannot rise above the raw anger and pain of tragedy, then we are doomed to wallow in it, learning nothing from our misery. If happiness and joy only exist for those not *yet* touched by tragedy, then what hope do we have that life is anything but a crap shoot we play with fingers crossed that we won't become the next unlucky loser? Viewing life as a lottery of victim-hood and hopelessness is, of course, a dismal state of being. However, until we stretch our capacity to see beyond our tragedies and discover purpose, meaning and opportunities to serve others with our newly acquired abilities, it is exactly the condition we are choosing by default.

The exercise of finding hope and purpose often begins simply with a *belief* that *it is possible* to overcome heartbreak. This book was written specifically to give powerful examples of triumph over tragedy. Each story represents a sorrow of monumental proportion, such as a man who lost his entire family to HIV after his young wife's blood transfusion; a kidnapped and murdered daughter; the instant death of a new bride on her honeymoon, fresh flowers in hand. *The Triumph Book* is full of courageous people who have endured the fire of adversity and who have risen above those challenges to find purpose and joy in serving others.

Collecting and editing all of these stories impressed me profoundly. As readers of *The Triumph Book* we are given the luxury of learning from experiences, and their outcomes, which took the author of the story tremendous endurance, pain and life-education to obtain. The authors deliver wisdom to you in a few pages which took them immense time and energy to reach. The value of these messages is priceless.

Each of these stories was written specifically for this book with the intent to help you along your journey in life; whether you are in the midst of your own dark path, preparing for when the time may come, or wanting to help loved ones through their difficulties. There is a high level of humility and concern each author put into their writing. They carefully chose their words and message, with you in mind.

This was not an easy process for any of the authors. They had to relive their tragedies, making them come alive, in order for you to have the closest idea possible of how the authors felt as they endured, and continue to work through, their adversity. Through these selfless contributions, moving examples show that the level of joy achievable is directly proportional to the degree of grief endured. Just as with all polar opposites, the deeper the sorrow, the higher the potential for joy; and so this book will take you to extreme lows, but don't stop reading, because every story will reward you for going *there* with the author. The writers of this book will help you recognize that tragedy is simply a path to becoming a greater and more compassionate person than you were before. Their messages are full of hope!

If you are struggling to trust that purpose, joy and triumph can actually come out of tragedy, please read these stories. They will empower you to have faith when facing your own gut-wrenching challenges and, in turn, become an equally important inspiration to another fellow traveler on the path of life. Always remember, you are not alone.

One

Little Brynn

Author: Melanie Davis

When I purchased a journal on March 5th, 2001, I didn't know that it would soon contain so much sorrow; or that it would lead to great purpose and joy in my life. During pregnancy, on the day I receive an ultrasound to learn if I'm having a girl or boy, I keep a tradition of buying a diary. On this day in March, I was excited to buy one covered in flowers and to write of my discovery... that my third child was going to be a girl! I was buying a journal for a new little daughter, Brynn.

I wrote in this journal all through my pregnancy, carried it to the hospital for the foot prints to be put inside, along with a mother's first message to her baby on the night of her birth. I continued to record in this special book all of the cute and funny things I knew I would forget over time as my daughter grew.

The content of Brynn's journal is special to me, but not for the reasons I expected. The first part of the writing contains fond memories of Brynn's life, but the rest is a story of tragedy, sorrow, purpose, gratitude and joy. I had an audience in mind as I wrote: my children and posterity. I didn't want my costly life-lessons and wisdom to be wasted by not sharing them with the ones I love. I wanted them to gain from all I have been through. I now share some of my journal writings here with you. I hope that you may find value in Brynn's story and trust you will understand it is full of my faith, as I would want my children to be taught, for that is why I wrote it originally.

Brynn's Journal

7/3/01

Little Brynn, you were born yesterday evening. You barely cried at all; in fact, the nurse had to make you cry to help clear your lungs. Your daddy was wonderful. He read to me from a book series, *The Wheel of Time* by Robert Jordan, as a distraction because I had no painkillers. You came through what is commonly called "natural childbirth." Because I am a fitness instructor, the contractions felt more like circuit training and I actually enjoyed the process. I was having a great workout... until the end when I was given an episiotomy without anesthesia. If you heard me screaming as you entered the world, *I am so sorry*!

After you were born, too much moisture remained in your lungs (you just didn't cry enough!), so you were taken to the NICU for observation. I was told you would be there for four hours, but you came back to me after an hour-and-a-half. You are pink and beautiful. All the nurses who check on you exclaim what a cutie you are; and what a good baby. You don't cry much. Most of your noises are sweet little puppy whimpers and I have found it's very easy to make you happy when you do fuss.

Your APGAR score was 9.9 out of 10. The most amazing thing of all is that you have dark hair! I genuinely hoped you would, but I wasn't sure how possible it would be since Danny and Jadi, your brother and sister, are both blonde. But you do! That's my girl!!!!! I can't wait to know you better and watch you grow. But for now, I am oh so content to cuddle and kiss you!

7/19/01

Little Brynn, you are just over two weeks old and the mildest baby. You almost never cry, and when you do, it is brief. A few days ago the slamming car door scared you and you let out a frightened wail... but it only lasted five seconds. I am amazed at how little you cry. Much of the time your agitation (grunts and struggles) is easily resolved by holding you close or letting you sleep with me. You cuddle up and calm right down. It makes me feel so good to be *the cure* for your discomfort! Brynn, you are growing cuter every day and you haven't lost any of that wonderful dark hair, although I still wash it gently!

Danny and Jadi are in love with you and want to hold and kiss you constantly. Jadi frequently rubs crumbs in your hair. You are so good and patient with them! You make funny faces, but don't fuss or appear too upset. Danny likes to tell you energetic stories and sing silly songs. Through it all, you listen very calmly.

10/20/01

Little Brynn, you are growing chubbier and more animated. You are also quite a slobber girl and make playful bubbles around your mouth. Your new designation is *little bubble machine*. Lately you enjoy being put on a blanket to play on the floor. You like grabbing your feet. Tonight I noticed that your feet were both wet. You slobbered on your hands and rubbed it all over them. We had a good laugh with you as you beamed and were so happy with all the attention. You are fascinated with Danny and Jadi. You watch them closely. Tonight you stopped nursing and arched back as far as you could to see them playing.

Brynn, you are a good *smiler*. When you wake and I pick you up, you always give me big grins, even in the middle of the night.

10/23/01

Little Brynn, it was entertaining to watch you enjoy your first bowl of cereal tonight. You seemed to like it. You displayed your enthusiasm by puffing your cheeks and blowing raspberries at me, spraying cereal everywhere.

12/9/01

Little Brynn, you hum while you eat the foods you prefer. I've been giving you a variety of "unique tastes" lately and you make a funny, yucky face to everything new I offer. But then you proceed and eat it all.

You don't seem to need much sleep. You typically take one nap late in the afternoon and usually not more than an hour. For only five months old, that's not much! You're genuinely happy all the time and don't appear to need any more. You are also a highly picky baby about where you sleep. We were at Grandma and Grandpa Davis' for Thanksgiving and you would not take naps at all or rest at night. One night you only slept two hours. This went on for days, but when we arrived home, I laid you in your own bed and you conked out immediately, for the whole night!

12/27/01

Little Brynn, you were Baby Jesus for our Nativity, Christmas 2001. You didn't cry at all, even though we wrapped your arms and confined you to a make-shift-manger with mass chaos all around.

Brynn, you rolled over for the first time today! You were lying on a blanket on the floor playing. The rest of our family was distracted by the television. When I looked at you again, you were on your tummy. I asked your daddy if he helped you roll over and he said "No." So I remarked, "Brynn, did you roll yourself over?" You smiled with your tongue protruding, panting like a puppy and looking very pleased with yourself. You are only five and a half months old.

1/15/02

Little Brynn, two days ago you cut your first tooth and today your second one broke through. You have been moaning sorrowfully. You are an early teether, compared with Danny and Jadi. Danny was over a year old and Jadi was pretty close to a year. You are only six months. You have taken your teething very well for being so young!

Brynn, *you love Danny*! He frolics around, makes goofy noises, and you brighten right up.

Just last week you were able to sit up alone. You can't move yourself into that position, but once seated, you hold yourself securely.

2/13/02

A week ago this morning I woke at 6:15 a.m. as your daddy was preparing for work. I threw the covers off and felt an urgency to check on you. I rushed down the hall, feeling instinctively that something was amiss even before I entered your room. Once inside I fumbled with the musical fish bowl attached to the crib, so that its blue light would illuminate your bed. Then I discovered you lying face down with the covers well above your head. I grabbed you and raced into the brightness of my bedroom where I could see your appearance was not normal. I screamed to your daddy. As he held you, I lifted your eyelids and observed they were fixed and dilated. I felt sick.

Your blazing hot temperature had us frantically stripping off your pajamas and calling 911. The dispatcher conducted us through infant CPR, which I knew, but was too distraught to remember. It was an agonizing procedure to attempt as your body was already beginning to stiffen, and the panic in our hearts was rising. When the paramedics arrived, I rode with you in the ambulance to the hospital. The whole way I wanted desperately to pray that you would be fine, but I knew you were gone, and it wasn't going to change. Your daddy arrived at the hospital with Danny and Jadi as soon as he could. I had no concept of time, but eventually the hospital staff ushered us into the sterile room where your sweet little body lay in lifeless repose; we were delicately informed that you had died. I wasn't surprised. All I could do, as I kissed your soft forehead, was say, "This is going to be so hard!" and "What do I do now?" Knowing this would be the last time I kiss your little head, as I had done constantly throughout your life, made it all the more tragic.

We were required to interview with a homicide investigator because you died at home. We told Danny and Jadi about your passing at the police station while filling out a report in a "quiet room." Jadi stayed happy-go-lucky through it all, but Danny, as well as your daddy and I, had some very sad moments.

Before long, we decided on a few basic plans. Our family agreed we wanted to go to Carson City, Nevada, for the funeral and burial, where your daddy is from and your great grandparents are buried. Grandma and Grandpa Davis handled most of the arrangements, with your daddy helping. I stayed out of this process and was grateful.

Your daddy picked out the casket. It was white and small (30 inch) with white velvet lining inside and gold teddy bears on the handles of the outside. It came with a small white velvet blanket as well, but we decided not to put it over your body. You were perfectly beautiful and I didn't want to shroud the gown we dressed you in; so I kept the covering as a special reminder of you. The blanket is made of the same material with which your casket is lined. It is comforting to me, though perhaps a bit macabre, to be able to touch the soft velvet and know it is the same fabric your little body rests in today.

Many people called, visited and brought food as the word quickly spread of your passing. Our Polynesian friends were especially generous. The Bishop of our church brought the most delicious bakery goodies and a check for $250. Your Great Aunt gave us her grave plot in the Lone Mountain Cemetery, right next to your Great Grandparents. Grandma and Grandpa Davis paid for the casket and funeral. A week after your death, the fitness class I teach gave me a certificate from *The International Star Registry* and now there is a star in the Pegasus system named after you!

Grandma and Grandpa Davis and Hansen traveled together to the mortuary and dressed your body in the beautiful white blessing gown you wore shortly after your birth. The dress and bonnet fit you perfectly (it just happened to be a larger size than usual for a blessing gown, when you bless the baby at a few months old). I wanted you to wear this dress at your burial since there are beautiful professional pictures of you taken in it. I cherish the memory that you were smiling for me in all those images. My mom confessed it was extremely painful, and yet spiritual, to dress you that day.

When everything was readied, we all caravanned from San Jose, CA, where we were living, to Carson City, NV for the funeral and burial. Our van, with your body and casket inside, broke down in the middle of the Sierra Nevada Mountains and had to be towed into Reno. Seeing your casket through the rear windows as the tow truck pulled out of the rest area was surreal. My dad and brothers paid for the repair and, though it was a distressing and emotional experience, I felt deep gratitude for their generosity as well as their immense love.

A viewing was held in a mortuary the night before your funeral. This is when Danny and Jadi were able to say their goodbyes to you. I wrote what Danny (five) said, and also recorded in this journal the song Jadi (3) made-up for you.

DANNY'S PARTING WORDS TO BRYNN

Brynn, you are a very sweet baby and I loved you very much. When you died it made me very sad.

But I'm not afraid because I know I'll see you again someday. Brynn, it was a nice time having you. You were very cute and sweet.

I miss you very much but I remember all the times and I had fun.

You were very good.

Love Danny

JADI'S BRYNN SONG
(Sung beside the casket at the viewing)

I loved you because of her she loves me
And she is the one I love
And she is the most incredible
And I love to call my sister
—Jadi

6

I arranged a picture display on a table at the rear of the funeral home chapel and, after seeing you briefly in the casket, I remained at the back near the images of your smiling face. It wasn't you lying there across the room, instead it was a cold, lifeless, yet beautiful, porcelain doll nestled in a sleek coffin. Heavy makeup had been applied which upset Danny and Jadi. Apparently babies are delicate and don't preserve well for viewings. The open casket lasted a few hours with many dear family and friends attending. I dreaded this event because I didn't know how I would handle seeing you in a coffin. It helped immensely to stay in the back by the darling pictures of you alive.

The next day we held the funeral. My brother, your Uncle Martin, spoke. He did an exceptional job, but spoke so much about me, I felt like it was my funeral! He showed how I had trials and events which prepared me for this tragedy by sharing a pivotal experience I had as a child: My little hamster lay dying in my hands and I was distraught. My father, a big man of 6' 3" loved me so much; he attempted to give that tiny hamster mouth-to-mouth resuscitation. I'll never forget how he held her gently up to his lips and tenderly puffed air into her tiny mouth, because she appeared to be having trouble breathing. It may sound silly to talk of a hamster's death at your funeral, Brynn, but my father demonstrated immense love for me as he sped my hamster to the veterinarians, forcing them to open early, only for a pronouncement of death upon arrival. The lengths he would go to prevent me from sorrow were boundless. My father's comfort was every bit as warm and effective when you died because that is how he always cared for me. Your death showed me how much I am loved, and my brother's talk reinforced these feelings.

11/4/02

It is much later as I'm finally sitting down to write my thoughts and feelings about you and your passing. I attempted to write a few times before, but wasn't ready. That isn't to say I've been wallowing in grief. Actually, I've been amazed at how strong we all have been. I never would have believed I could get through something like this, let alone gain the positive I have from this tragedy. I do miss you terribly, Little Brynn, and sometimes the sorrow washes over me in great swells, but other times I feel stronger than ever in my life.

The day of your funeral, actually that morning, I felt myself growing sick. It was important to me to be healthy and speak the feelings of my heart at the service, as part of my own healing. It was, and always will be, an extremely important day in my life. I prayed the Lord would give me

7

health and strength just one more day; and He did! However, Danny was also becoming sick. In fact, he threw-up on me a few minutes before the meeting; and so I washed the front of my dress in the bathroom sink and spent the rest of the day a little damp and smelly. Danny was taken home to rest.

The chapel was full of friends and relatives, many who traveled great distances to be with us. My talk reviewed your brief sojourn on the earth and how you are an angel who was only visiting for a short time. I was able to read many entries from this journal and am deeply thankful I wrote them! As I read how you never slept, and were always happy, it became clear to me that you truly were an angel who seemed to know her time in this existence was limited.

It is a gift, how gently you died. I feel strongly that your death was not meant to be a hard trial to drag me down. Even on the day of your death, I felt a heavenly warmth and peace which told me that all was right. I had never known such direct and powerful comfort as I experienced upon your death, and it has continued to this day. I can honestly say I am not angry. People warned me I would be, but I'm not. I often feel sad because I miss you, but I also feel privileged to have you in our family and grateful for the time we were given... that you weren't taken any sooner. I am profoundly grateful for how softly you were called home to God. Of all the ways people lose their little ones, crib death is especially merciful, in my opinion. I hope to die in my sleep one day. Your daddy and I both responded similarly. It has helped me recognize how well-matched we are and has increased my love and appreciation for him, to see his strength and faith. He has never been bitter either.

I feel certain that you will watch over and help your siblings. In this world of chaos and misdirection, to know, and for my children to know, there is a special angel watching over them brings me great comfort and peace.

The day before you died, I picked you up from the child care center. You were playing there while I taught my fitness class. As I held you in my arms, you gave me a kiss on the cheek. Even the childcare worker commented on how sweet you were to give me a kiss as a little baby. I rejoice that she observed your affection, because it allows me to know I wasn't just imagining your demonstration of love. That small token of affection right before your death has come to mean everything to me.

The night you died, just before I put you to bed, you were sitting on my lap as I read a book. You kept smiling at me, trying to get my attention. I finally put the book down and played with you for a little while. We sat in front of a mirror and you babbled to the "other baby" while trying to touch the reflected hands returning your playful slaps and bangs on the surface. You were absolutely darling, enjoying this game immensely. When I put you to bed, you sobbed. You didn't want to be put down, but I let you cry yourself to sleep because that is what babies have to do sometimes, or so I thought to myself. You rarely wanted to be put to bed, or leave my side. Oh, if I had only known this would be the last time I could hold or cuddle you, I never would have put you to bed at all!

Your hands felt a little cold as I laid you down, so I tucked you in with an extra blanket. I have learned not to say *"what if"* or blame myself that you ended up under those stifling covers. It would be very easy to accuse myself and carry an oppressive burden of guilt for your death, or the discomfort that may have come because of my doting. I could easily lament that I didn't spend at least an extra half-hour with you, when you were wide-awake; enjoying yourself and the quiet time we had together. These are thoughts I have learned to reject, and not entertain at all. There is no purpose to them, as they don't change *"what is."*

I often think about how I would feel if roles were reversed... if it were you still here on earth and I was the one to have died under similar circumstances; I would not want you to spend your life sorrowing over the conditions of my death. I wouldn't want you to suffer in constant pain. I would wish you to experience joy during what is left of your mortality (knowing you will join me one day soon). I have learned to control my thoughts based on this scenario: *what would I want for Brynn if I had been the one to abruptly leave?*

I corral my thoughts tightly inside these boundaries and rarely allow myself to contemplate the moments I wish I could change, or the morning I found you dead. Instead, I think about what purpose your death serves; and it has been easy to find reasons and ways to make your death matter. The truth is, I have felt a great sense of purpose and "rightness" to your passing from the day you died. This has been one of the most direct reasons I have been able to heal.

My healing has been quick, and it is a miraculous blessing. Life was excruciating just after your funeral because we all became horribly sick. Danny and Jadi had the same high fever in their sleep that seemed to have been part of your death. Steve and I spent many nights fighting ferociously to cool them down. However, I never had any fear that the virus would take them as well. I know I was reassured. For at least a week we all laid around in a king-size bed, sick and crying, explaining, understanding, and healing together as a family. That affliction was actually a great blessing!

In the many months since your death I have found opportunities to share my knowledge of God's love and how life, and death, has purpose. One friend told me that through my experience she believes she too could endure things she never thought possible before.

Little Brynn, this is your purpose on earth, your legacy and my life's endeavor: to share truth I have come to know through my experiences, and to assist others in sharing their stories. By so doing, the world is made a better place, with greater compassion, understanding and meaning in all we do and go through. Your death has created this opportunity for me. I sense I am in a companionship with you. By strengthening others and helping them to know there is much hope and joy in life, even after a tragedy, I am giving your life meaning. It will have as much significance as if you had lived your whole life.

Already many occasions have arisen to share your story. I am indebted to you for giving me this ability, because as I reach out to others, I feel just as I did the day of your funeral; as if Heaven is very close.

Danny has handled your death with wisdom and courage beyond his five years. He is old enough to understand what happened and feel deep sorrow. I continually observe how profoundly he has been strengthened by this experience. He is highly sensitive to God's Spirit and says prayers which are full of understanding and yearning to do what is right. It is truly remarkable to listen to him articulate his feelings and desires as he seeks and finds healing. He will be a great leader and example to Jadi and our new baby because of who he has become through this adversity.

That's right! At this moment I am sitting in the doctor's office enduring a three hour glucose test, expecting a baby girl in January. This is another blessing. I would not be having another baby right now if you were here. It is a blessing because we will always have you to love in our hearts and now we have this baby to join us as well. We may even have another, and I doubt we would have a fifth baby if you were still here.

I look forward passionately to the day I hold you in my arms again. I know with intense and constant faith that I will. I am reassured this is true with a knowledge that begins to transcend faith; perhaps it is a reward for seeking the purpose in your death... and striving to live for this glorious day. But it is also the hardest part of my present condition; my own death and/or resurrection seems infinitely far away. Sometimes I wonder if I can possibly wait that long. We have numerous pictures of you placed throughout the house, but I only look at them briefly. Gazing too long brings deep pain because I miss you so much!

Sometimes I look at your brother and sister and find solace in the blessing of raising them; they are beautiful! Other times I watch them and wonder what hard things they will have to suffer. I know that we must endure pain and sorrow to be elevated and wake-up the spiritual potential within us. I believe this is the reason we are here in this sometimes painful and otherwise hopeless condition we call mortality. I hope and pray I will be able to prepare your siblings for the difficult days ahead of them, so they can feel the blessings and joys, as well as the sorrows.

7/29/03

Little Brynn, the cause of your death is no longer a mystery. You died from a Febrile Seizure. This is a genetic condition which occurs when you have a fever that spikes too fast and causes you to stop breathing. Your little brother, Carson, has this condition. Just last week, at nine months old, he passed out (eyes open) beside me from a fever which came on suddenly, with great heat.

Thankfully I was there, as was your daddy, to pick him up and work with him while waiting for an ambulance. He was turning blue, and the look on his face horrified me. I thought for a moment that I was losing another precious baby!

Another ambulance ride with my child hanging onto life was surreal. But this ride would end differently than yours. With an oxygen mask and the reduction of his fever, Carson returned to normal and despite being observed all night at the hospital, he never had another episode.

3/18/05

Two babies since your death, Natalie and Carson, I have been engrossed in raising your brothers and sisters! Carson has never had another seizure, though I am vigilant when he appears sick. As time has gone by, I don't dwell too much on sorrow, grief and loss from your death. I frequently entertain the concept that the only separation between you and me is the fact that I can't see you. I like to think you are still an active part of our family; that you witness our lives, and can be near us in spirit. Though I can't fully articulate the feelings, or how I know, but often I sense you are close to us.

Melanie and Brynn, six months old

I still feel blessed that you were taken quietly and quickly, of all the ways people lose their little angels. I truly don't think of this experience as a trial or curse. There is a heartbreaking tragedy in the loss of a baby; but the Lord has buffered, blessed and made my life interesting and wonderful with a move to Texas, and the gifts of two more children.

Actually, it is painful if I allow myself to think about your death in any detail, but I believe I've been blessed with the ability to seal it in a safe place in my heart, knowing all things will be made right one day. I continue to find joy in living, even without you here to touch and adore. Your daddy has felt the same. What a great awareness it is to know that we are only on earth a short time and can truly rise above every difficulty we face.

Because of experiencing the tragedy of your death, I have come to know that God lives and loves us. On two distinct occasions I *physically* felt a Heavenly Presence comforting me. It started at the top of my body and descended through me. It was brief but undeniably real. Through this experience, and the joy I continue to find **because of** this tragedy, I KNOW God lives. What greater knowledge can a person ever have in this life than to know God is real?

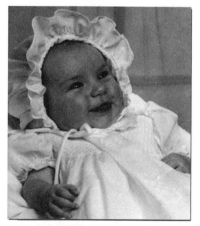

Brynn, three months old
Wearing the dress and bonnet
in which she was buried

Behind the Story

Three years after Brynn's death I published a beautiful hardbound storybook full of pictures and the writing from Brynn's journal that I wanted to safely preserve. Creating this storybook brought deep healing, knowing that my valuable life-lessons are recorded for my posterity and others to read. It is profoundly comforting to know Brynn will not be forgotten. We often hold onto grief as a means of ensuring our loved ones are remembered. Preserving Brynn in a beautiful book has allowed me the freedom to be at peace, with the assurance that future family and friends will know Brynn in the way I loved her.

The sense of meaning I felt on the day of Brynn's death has become clearer as I am able to share my book, her story and my continued hope with others going through their personal struggles. Often, when I am told of a family who has lost a child, I publish a copy of Brynn's Storybook and give it to them so they can read it and see how I got through something so difficult; and now I am also able to share my story in this book. Purpose and healing occurs every time I can share Brynn's Story.

The purpose of my life, and Brynn's death, continues to blossom as I find ways to help others overcome grief. This includes creating a program which assists people to write their grief story and preserve it in a way that allows their loved one to never be forgotten. In this same effort their life-lessons are also recorded for the benefit of posterity and can serve as inspiration for others going through their own adversity.

As part of the endeavor to support people through grief, I have compiled *The Triumph Book* which is full of examples from others who have endured severe tragedies and found greater purpose and meaning in their lives *because of* the adversity. This book is, in many ways, a continuation of Brynn's Story as I find my path and purpose by helping others share their own experiences widely.

Whenever I talk about this book, and give examples of the profound stories in its pages, I am frequently asked how I met the authors. For this reason I have decided to share an account at the end of each chapter called *Behind the Story*, explaining how I found the author, what they are doing with their lives now or other interesting information.

It is important to note that most of the stories in this book speak of God, or a Higher Power (and in some cases refer to a church or a belief system) who helped the writer through their adversity. The authors are sharing their experiences honestly and authentically, in many ways opening and exposing their souls, expressing how their stories unfolded, as well as those things dear to their hearts. It would be wrong for me to censor them for the sake of political correctness. While there are many different belief systems in this world, I hope that you, as readers, will recognize that this book demonstrates true principles which we all embrace: finding purpose and joy out of adversity; feeling compassion and serving one another in the spirit of love and charity. It is my desire that this book serve to show that despite our differences, we actually have far more in common. I hope that these narratives will be appreciated by all philosophies and faiths as a space where stories, as they happened and were perceived, can be freely shared and learned from.

With that said, please read on and enjoy with me the serendipity and miracles which formed this book.

Two

At Least We Were Married

Author: Terry C. Thomas, Ph.D.

Life can be good, so wonderfully good! We enjoy the best of times; reaching a pinnacle of achievement; and admiring the world spread before us. But, that mountain of joy can suddenly crumble to ash beneath our feet. We begin to fall. We fall deeper and deeper; perhaps as low as the depths of despair can take us, and then into the worst of times.

Stuck at the bottom and lost in the shadows of the valley; wouldn't it be great to turn back the clock? To get away from the horror and restore the life we lost? In my case, that will never be.

What if you could emerge with greater personal power and a new ability to experience even higher joy? I believe it is possible. I know it is possible. It happened to me; and, even though it was a hard-won battle, I succeeded.

The only way I can share my story is to turn back my own clock and experience what happened as if I were there again. You may grieve and perhaps a tear might even slide down your cheek as you read this story. But if I show you how you can always find a seed of purpose and joy hidden under your sorrows, I think you will agree it is worth the emotional price we pay to get there.

I cannot remember her last words before she dropped off into a light slumber. She was in the passenger seat of our car that Saturday evening after Thanksgiving. I noticed the sunset fading to dusk as I looked across her resting body. Our cute red VW Bug slipped along the highway. At last, we were heading south to Florida and on to Nassau; our eventual honey-moon destination. I couldn't help but think back to the day before. I could see by the glow in her eyes how happy she was. She was delighted when we walked into our room after the wedding. As she spied the bouquet of long-stemmed red roses waiting for her, I could see the joy on her face. In order to prolong her enjoyment, we brought them along on our honeymoon trip. They were now nestled at her feet in our packed car. I noticed some of the rosebuds tipping up and resting on her lap. She had fallen asleep. I thought about how Nancy was a romantic, just like me.

The passing twilight felt so peaceful. *"Honeymoon"* what a novel and strange word. The new wedding ring felt strange on my finger. I could not help but notice again the diamond on hers.

A misty rain began to hit the windshield as darkness fell quickly. Ah, the wedding! At last it had finally happened. It was blurry to me as it had passed so fast. Everyone said it was the grandest wedding they had ever seen. Nancy had thought about her wedding since she was a little girl; as most girls do. Not wanting to leave out anyone, Nancy asked nine—yes, nine—bridesmaids to stand with her in the cathedral-like church. Actually, as I look back now, that cathedral ended up having two dramatic services that week.

Any idea of family tragedy was as foreign to either of our families as a black hole from outer space crashing into the earth without warning. Good things happen to good people, we believed.

Nancy chose to attend a prominent southern university. It was there she came in contact with a campus organization related to church youth. She was invited to spend part of her summer training at their national headquarters on the West Coast.

She was not only sharp but well-liked. Her personality, her face and figure, radiated a natural beauty. I had briefly met Nancy during her summer training and had never forgotten her. It was a chance meeting later that triggered our attraction for each other.

It had been over a year earlier that, my eyes fell upon Nancy inside the elevator just as the door was closing behind her. I smiled at her, but something deep radiated within. I knew the other girls, but not the one that caught my eye. "May I ask your name?"

"Oh, I'm Nancy," she said, smiling as brightly as I did.

I know this person, I thought. It seems like we've been in love forever, like a wonderful déjà vu. That probably makes no sense. But things of love have nothing to do with the mind and logic; especially love at first sight.

"Where are you going?" I asked.

"Down to my room..." she replied.

"I'll walk with you," I said, and we quickly became more acquainted.

Little did I know that that night she thought about me as much as I did her: *Who was this girl?*

Who was this young man? Secretly, in her heart, she prayed she would meet me again someday. But later that evening, she and many other students departed for the airport and their scheduled flights home. She took something of me with her though, if only in her memory and in her heart.

This was apparently the end of getting to know the vivacious, elegant girl, and yet I knew that wouldn't be.

"Nancy," I remembered. "Her name is Nancy." I tried to think of other girls I knew named Nancy, but none came to mind. There was only this one *Nancy*.

I caught my breath and tried to remember what she looked like. All I could see was her pretty blue eyes and her subtle smile; that wry, cute, charming and honest smile. The smile that whispered, "There is more to me than you see. There is more than you can ever know, but you can begin the discovery."

Eventually, I located her last name and phone number. About a month after she had left, I called her dorm room. "Hi, you probably don't remember me, but I'm the guy you met on the elevator. I just wanted to call and say, 'Hi.' How are you?"

"Oh, I think I remember you," she said, but didn't let on how much she'd actually been thinking of me, too. She was guileless, so it was not easy for her to play coy. She had opportunities and invitations for dates piled high, but, it was this young man on the other end she was thinking about.

"Well, I was just remembering you and thought I'd give you a call," I said.

Author: Terry C. Thomas, Ph.D.

"I'm glad you did," she said. She was careful not to let on how glad she was.

Can you guess the rest? If you have a romantic streak to your nature, you might imagine their story like this...

Long distance phone calls increased with magnetic intensity. They met again; and again. They fell in the love they knew they had already fallen into. Nancy and Terry got married. They had a wonderful honeymoon and enjoyed a few years of just the two of them complete with travel. They had wonderful friends. And then children began to appear. Terry and Nancy grew old together, held hands, watched sunsets. They walked on enticing trails around little ponds and lakes, and remembered the wonders of their early life. One day in her old age, Nancy became ill and passed away. "Terry," she said in her final words, "I have always loved you and I love you more now than I ever have." His lips touched hers in a final, soft kiss. The family tried to comfort him, but within two months, Terry, as sometimes happens to lovers, died also.

Unfortunately, that's not how our story ended. We did fall in love, had a beautiful courtship and the thrill of being engaged. The day after the wedding, we were driving down the highway to our honeymoon destination as darkness was just falling. The passing twilight felt so peaceful. A misty rain hit the windshield. Nancy still rested beside me. My hands were on the wheel.

Suddenly, I saw lights racing up the highway from the opposite direction. A man who wanted to try out the speed of his car (I found out later) barreled up the highway in the opposite lane. Already going too fast, the pair of headlights swaggered from side to side as the car wavered on the slick coating of moisture covering the wet and oily pavement.

The lights were oddly mesmerizing, almost surreal. It was out of this world. In a shocking, sudden flit, still weaving back and forth, the lights turned toward Nancy and me. They climbed down into the median between the lanes, popped up from the shoulder with us in their sights and suddenly attacked!

It can't be! The lights leaped directly onto our southbound lanes; head to head, face to face, now eye to eye.

I was to see those lights in a slow-motion re-run parade through my mind's eye thousands of times in the bleak hours for months ahead.

That evening, with the harsh headlights upon us, there was no avoiding the nightmare. I barely released the gas pedal and my foot never reached the brake. There was no time; it was too late. In a flash, the headlights were but two feet in front of mine. They narrowed the gap and seemed to pause in mid-air as time stopped, then restarted in slow motion. *This cannot be happening.* Never before, nothing like this had ever occurred and I had no point of reference. *Stop. Stop. Stop. Stop this wild dream. It's an illusion; a bad, terrible dream. A nightmare!* Myriad thoughts raced through my mind in a fraction of a second.

I wanted to wake Nancy. "Nan—!" was as much of her name as I had time to speak. I remember saying it. She didn't wake up.

The headlights continued; just two horrible headlights, seemingly unattached to a vehicle. They looked like mean eyeballs, snarling to crush us. The headlights nearly met ours, as though reaching out for a butterfly kiss, and then nothing; nothing at all.

I see this playing out before me as if I am there again, as if I were going through this once more. That's how real it is to me and the impact this experience has had upon me.

I was knocked out, or so I thought, because I saw nothing else. My systems went into shock. My body was numb and paralyzed. It was beyond pain. Months later, I was shocked in a new way to suddenly remember everything as it had occurred. I was conscious after all and had seen and heard the whole experience.

"Where...are...we?" I struggled to ask the attendants. We were racing to the hospital and I became more aware of my immediate surroundings. I was in a dimly lit space in the back of the ambulance. "What day is it?" I asked. "Is it November 25th?" My mind focused enough to realize something terrible was going on. "We were married last night." I said. I looked up to see his facial expression turn to incredulous astonishment.

"Where is Nancy?" I muttered.

There was no answer. Rustling and whispering, but still no answer.

"How is my wife?" I ground out my request in a painful and breathless whisper.

"Your wife is all right," they finally told me. I desperately needed to believe she was okay, and the attendants realized that. At the scene of the crash, I had heard someone holler the truth, but I rejected it. I then buried it far down in the inner recesses of my being. Deep in my heart's subconscious, shock echoed in the great hollowness, but my mind overruled the truth and let me believe Nancy and I would be together again.

From a gurney in the hospital corridor, I looked up to see empty eyes staring at me from sad, quiet faces. People solemnly shuffled by single file to have a look at me. I felt like a spectacle; helpless and on a stage. Word spread and everyone wanted a look. No one spoke. They knew more than I did at that point. I was confident, thinking Nancy was doing well somewhere nearby.

Finally a highway patrolman returned and told me he had talked to Nancy's father. I'm still amazed at how my memory revealed with perfect clarity the names and numbers he needed.

The doctor told me he had spoken with my own father on the phone at Nancy's parents' home. I learned later what he'd really said. "If you want to see your son alive again, you'd better get here fast," he told my dad in no uncertain terms.

Something powerful came over me during those hours immediately after the crash. It was something difficult to express and even more difficult to understand. A wave of good feelings swept through me. Go figure. Of course it doesn't make logical sense; not to me, and probably not to anyone else. It was something I would have to rebound from; but, that would come much later.

Intuitively, I surmised from the somber attitude of those around me that this could be my last hour of life. But strangely enough, I knew that was wrong. I was filled with the knowledge that I had a great purpose to live. I saw with extreme clarity that my life had more living to it. It was not my time to die. This was as sharp as anything I had ever known. I had no doubt at all. Later, I would wish normal life was always like that, without doubts. But this was a unique moment, to say the least. It was an emotional feeling of joy, totally inappropriate to the reality of the circumstances. I was too stupefied to make it up. And too near death to be feeling emotionally elated. All I can say is that at that moment I had a strong feeling that God was close; and that made me feel powerful.

In the small surgery room, the green-gowned doctor stood on my right as they wheeled me in. There were three nurses or assistants who stood to the left. Surgical tools already in his hands, the doctor explained what was about to happen. I can't remember his exact words, but I do recall the tenor of his warm, welcoming, slightly southern-accented voice that revealed an awesome but humble confidence.

"Terry, do you know what we are going to do?" he asked.

"Not really." I replied.

The doctor began explaining, "We do not know how badly you are hurt. You've been in a head-on collision. We see multiple injuries on the surface. Your sternum bone is broken, and we'll be working on that. We don't know what we will find inside. We have to examine you, completely, and this could take hours. I spoke with your family and they are on their way." I realized later that this highly esteemed doctor was trying not to alarm me, but he did want me to know this could be my last moment of conscious life.

"We do not know if we can save you," I heard him say. His frank words did not affect me because of my inexplicable knowledge that I would not die that night.

But I knew differently from what he was saying. How I knew, I can't explain but I knew I would live. The joy of life reverberated through my heart.

"Can we have a word of prayer before we operate? For thanks?" I asked. My spontaneous request emphasized *for thanks* as best I could. My raspy voice carried an edge. I saw the doctor's eyes meet the nurses' eyes. I knew they thought I believed I would die; and that I needed a form of last rites.

Research tells us most people offer a prayer of some sort every day. I was not outside the majority. I had learned things about prayer and one is to give gratitude; no matter what.

One of the nurses moved her mask to wipe a tear. They all looked a bit uncomfortable at first, as if they were caught off guard. They shuffled. The doctor immediately became reverent.

"Yes, of course." He set down the scalpels, released his sense of urgency with a quiet breath, and looked ready to listen. No one said anything. It was up to me.

I kept it short, and they finally realized I was praying not from fear but from gratitude. Our shared reverence imbued that room with the spirit of thanksgiving, so timely on that November 25 night. Above all, I learned that gratitude—even in the worst of times—carried a healing quality which started from the inner soul and worked outwards. A prayer expressing thanks in any situation, as you can imagine, was not normal at a time like this. But that crash on the highway was not normal either.

After the prayer, it was "lights out" anesthesia for me. Next thing I knew, I was out of surgery. It was still dark outside and I looked up to see my own parents peering into my room from the doorway. I didn't know what was going on. Someone, perhaps my cousin, who had been my best man, must have driven them from Nancy's parents' house. I was alive and they were here to see it

The misty rain had passed when I woke up later that morning to bright yellow sunshine. The doctor was leaning over me. Physical sensations were coming back. I noticed pulleys and cords and chains holding me up by the chest and I could see other pulleys lifting up a leg and even one for each arm. It was the true cartoon caricature of a guy in the hospital. My face was even covered with bandages, but I had no way of knowing that yet.

I looked up to see the doctor's eyes carefully scanning my face. And then he started talking in a most gentle voice. He was, not looking me in the eye; but instead was examining the pulley attached to my chest area. I tried to watch his every movement.

"Terry, I'm sorry to tell you this, but your wife was killed in that wreck last night." I remember his soft voice; the tone, the expression, the calmness and his exact words; it was as if I just now heard them again.

He did it all so casually and so kindly; so matter-of-factly. I realized later that he was trying not to alarm me and put me back into shock. I think this is why I didn't have a lot of emotional reaction at the time. In fact, my bolts of emotions were to come later; gradually, for months. It came as my own body was healing and I could absorb it.

He kept his gaze on my injuries; moving his hands over them without pause. I was hearing something I already had known but had not admitted it to myself.

"Yes," I calmly responded. "I know." My memory of it was blocked, but, deep in my subconscious, I knew. I had seen although I believe shock had temporarily taken over. The doctor was kind for not shielding me; and, to bring the full truth to my attention. He knew I could handle it now.

But the full extent of what I really knew about that night took months to fully reach my conscious mind. It was painful, to say the least.

The day I returned to see the scene of the accident, my memory opened to expose the parts I had blocked. It was months later; shortly after I began walking again. Some people thought I shouldn't go back there, but I knew I had to see it.

Locating the exact spot was not difficult. Mile markers from the police report were accurate. As we stopped the car, my friends were concerned I might break down emotionally. To tell you the truth, by then I had learned to postpone emotional responses; or, to bury them for the time being. I was not worried.

"Terry," one of the girls said, "Are you really sure you want to see this?" We all felt a little trepidation, even though I also felt brave and ready. I slipped out of the car's back seat, which was difficult to do with casts still on both of my arms.

I traipsed along the shoulder of the highway and over to a little incline on the right. We were at the exact spot all right. There were still signs of the accident. Bits of small glass and metal parts scattered here and there. There were some rubber marks, but not much to go by. The grass on the hillside was brown and rusty where the other car had landed. Black oil marks still stained that area.

I considered how much had happened here. For the first time I began asking myself a question that was to nag me and grow louder over the next months. "Why?" That was the question.

How could any sense be made from this? I thought about the effects, bad effects, upon so many lives. *There we were in love, heading for more love and joy. Then, this horror happened at the very spot I where I am standing. Why? Isn't there supposed to be an explanation for everything?*

I'm sure others had already asked how sense could be made of all the pain people felt from this tragedy; but until now I had been so focused on my physical healing that I was just now getting around to this question.

Before I got back into the car, I discovered an orange piece of glass in the gravel that matched the color and shape of the turn signal from our totaled VW compact. The glass was small enough to fit into the front pocket of my jeans, so I picked it up, knowing I would carry it everywhere with me for a long time. Why? I don't know. Maybe I needed that connection to the scene; a connection to Nancy. This is the place where she had drawn her last breath.

"I'd like to stop in the little town up ahead and have a look around," I said as we got back in the car. My friends were okay with that. I felt a faint hope we would run into someone who had been there that night. Someone who might have remembered the accident and could tell me everything they knew. Was I in for a surprise!

We pulled into the local gas station just off the highway to inquire. I left the others in the car while I got out. "Hi," I said to the fellow working there. "Do you remember an accident several months ago out on the highway? Where the wife was killed and the guy lived? They brought the guy to the hospital here for ten days."

His face grew grim and his voice, terribly soft. "Yes, I do," he said.

"I'm the guy," I said. The fellow turned a pale yellow. He couldn't speak for a few seconds. As it turns out, he was part of the ambulance crew and had been one of the first persons on the scene. He was jolted, to say the least; speechless and stunned to see me.

"Are you really the guy?" His voice warmed. "Are you him?" I noticed he was staring, looking me over slowly. I nodded.

He reached over to the wall phone and called another guy who rushed over. As the second man approached the door a few minutes later, I noticed his pace slowed down. They didn't remember what I looked like any more than I them. After all, I had been lying down. I was all smashed up and they were working on me in dim light. But now they looked me over, still grasping that I was the young man.

By now my friends had walked in and we all stood around. What do you say at a moment like that? Everyone waited for me to take the lead. First, I said I wanted to thank them for all they had done for us. Being a curious and interested person; but not one to show a lot of emotion, I decided to ask a few questions.

"What did you see when you got there? Obviously, I was unconscious, right?" There was a pause. "What happened the way you saw it?" Still another pause, "How did Nancy look?" That was a tough question, one I hesitated to ask. I wasn't sure I wanted the answer to that one out of fear for what I'd hear. "How did I look at the time? What really happened?" I was not interrogating them. I was just trying to get information about the things I had begun to wonder about.

They did not want to talk about it; not really. Looking back, I don't think they had talked to anybody; not even each other, until that moment,.. It wasn't exactly dinner conversation. So, perhaps for the first time, they began to share what they had witnessed.

"You were not unconscious," the driver said. I was surprised at this news. "And you were mumbling."

"And Nancy?" I asked.

"She looked perfectly fine."

"Really, I'm so glad to finally know." I let out a deep breath I didn't realize I'd been holding.

"It was how she was hit that caused the instant death, but she looked fine." I felt like crying at that moment. It was the first time anyone had talked to me about it. Perhaps the first time anyone had talked about it at all.

"And I was knocked out?" I inquired.

"No, you were conscious," one of the men replied.

"What?" I said, startled. I was more than alarmed. Something awful was stirring inside of me.

"Really?" I asked again as if there might be a different answer.

"But my eyes were surely closed," I said in the form of a question, never expecting his reply. I was absolutely shocked at what he said.

"No, they were wide open. Your eyes were wide open when we got there and you mumbled, trying to talk, the entire time."

That was the trigger that began to unlock a chain of new memories. At that moment, a new world stored in my unconscious cracked open. I saw it all. I saw what I had shut out until then. My memory slammed into place, as it needed to do for me to emotionally heal. Things I had seen in actuality; such as the crowd of people standing around in a circle on the highway watching, the police car, the wrecker, car parts scattered all around, I had seen it all!— I did not realize I had seen until that moment as it paraded through my consciousness for the first time since the fatal night itself.

Standing there in the station that afternoon in my mind's eye; I saw the headlights of the other car in front of me, just as I had seen in dreams so many times for the past months. In those dreams, however, the crash never quite finished. But now I saw the headlights plow forward and continue into and through my car. Little did my friends and the ambulance attendants know that my memory was shaking loose as we stood there together. A new pain burned inside me. A long overdue, postponed emotion caused this ache. One part of me wanted to escape, to get out of there and quickly. The other part wanted to hear more details.

Granted, I didn't see everything all at once because the full story revealed itself to my consciousness over time, but this is what I saw happen that night. The details were sharp and vivid as they sprang to the forefront of my mind.

I saw the other car slide in front of me and pass through our car at a 45-degree angle, missing me but cutting through Nancy's side. It was a dullish white car—my mental vision saw it very clearly now. What an ugly sight, and I saw every wretched detail in slow motion. The vehicle looked massive to me, like a giant ship in the night merely sliding by.

The terrible clashing and crashing of steel resonated in my inner ears for the first time. I *had* heard it, I realized. And it was painful to remember. The screeching and crunching were bloodcurdling, followed by the sound of car parts splashing to the pavement all about. It was as if they fell from heaven, all those metal things crashing and splashing on the pavement. After that, there was silence for a moment, and then the subdued sound of a couple more pieces falling, the final few.

The night fell quiet. All was still. Nothing but an eerie blackness wafted about. My earlier thoughts of the sunset had fled. That sunset was gone now, too. No wind stirred, not even a slight breeze. Just dead silence. No one was there. No one. Not a car, not a person. Nothing moved. I, and I alone, really alone, was staring into the darkness, completely numb, no feeling. Now I remembered, and recalled that, at the time, my mind had been working; I was aware. I recall how sick I had felt to my stomach as the reality started to sink in.

It was still light enough that I could see the outline of car parts scattered across the pavement. I couldn't believe what I was seeing. I could not fathom what was happening. I just knew something beyond anything any of us had ever experienced was falling upon us. *This cannot be. O, my God, this cannot be.*

I thought of the honeymoon and instantly realized we weren't going to Nassau the next day. It had happened so fast, some other part of me believed this was just a bad nightmare and that we would still be on our honeymoon when I woke up. I believed what I was seeing and yet I disbelieved it, if you can grasp the contradiction. *It could not be!*

But it was real. We had been casually scooting along toward our joyful adventure of a dream honeymoon, but in a flash, I was spiraling into a bottomless hell of a seemingly no-return nightmare. Nancy was there, to my right, but we could not communicate. I didn't know it yet, but our relationship in this life was over. Done. In an instant.

I had heard a car approach from behind and screech to a halt. I couldn't turn my head much to watch as someone rushed from a car to Nancy's side of our car, and peered in. From the corner of my eye, I saw the look of horror on that face. To this day, I don't know who it was.

The person jumped back and began to yell out into the night, "There's two, and one's been killed. One's been killed. One's been killed. One's been killed. "I do not know how they knew."

I also saw the car that had struck us, resting on the bank to the right. I don't know how I managed to move my head. The driver, a tall, slender fellow, was moving around his car and appeared incoherent. He leaned against it and looked off into the distance. I later found out he had injured his ankle; otherwise, he was fine physically.

I saw the highway patrolman arrive. I saw the wrecker pull up and park ahead of our car, illuminating the entire scene with spotlights. It seemed to take hours. A crowd of people gathered in a circle and I later estimated dozens of cars had stopped by then. None could pass along the freeway going south.

As the team of rescuers gathered, I saw someone reach through the window into Nancy's side of the car. He looked her over and gently shook her shoulder to see if they could get her out. My head and face were locked into the twisted steering wheel and I could not move. I heard them say that they would leave this one for later. What everyone noticed when they removed her was she was still clutching the long-stemmed red roses; although I had never been able to turn my head far enough to see this myself.

"Yes, she is already gone," they said. "We'll take the other one first. He is still alive. He has a chance. We'll try to save him."

I also heard a voice jabbering. It was mine. I don't really remember what I was trying to say; which isn't unusual, I guess. People experiencing something of this magnitude would naturally just shove it into their subconscious memory and completely outside their consciousness.

Somehow, two or three guys managed to reach around me and slide me from the car. One worked around my legs for a long while. Another struggled to get an arm around my neck. A third fellow squatted and squeezed himself in close enough to get his arms under my lower body. They spoke to one another and coordinated their effort.

"I have him." Someone said. I can hear their voices clearly to this day in my memory.

"Okay, got him." And ever so gently they slid me from the front seat.

As I share this story with you, I see these things as if they are happening at this moment—all over again. It is more profound now because back when it happened, I was numb and going into shock. Now I am alert, in full health, and distance has allowed me to embrace it with greater objectivity.

The next thing I knew that night, I was in the ambulance riding to the hospital. I was awakening to a more conscious reality; yet not remembering what had just happened.

****

I did learn to walk again. My sternum healed in its rightful place, my broken arms mended. My smashed-up face and bruised legs eventually returned to normal. I did recover.

The general assumption back in those days was that if your body was healing, you were healing. Today, we know there's more to complete healing than just focusing on the physical aspect of the process. Our emotions, for example, make us who we are at any given moment. Emotions are real—from the joy, peace and love on the higher end to the lower-end feelings like anger, blame, and jealousy; a desire for revenge, defensiveness and bitterness. These are real "things" that are not physical, yet they have as much to do with pain, suffering and quality of life as the physical aspects do. While I received the finest of medical care for my physical self, I was left alone in this emotion-based pain, to probe—through trial and error—my way to healing on the inner level. We did not have the tools which are accessible today.

People tried to offer advice by saying things like, "Just trust in God!" I was already trying to do that. Or, "Get on with life as soon as you can." How could I do that when I was having more surgeries and new pains cropping up all the time?

Here is one piece of advice that irritated me: "There is a reason for everything, Terry." How could you ever find a reason that made sense of something like this? I think it was an effort to say something; anything, but it came across as a platitude. It is much better just to feel and express sympathy and empathy; which many people did, and it helped. But showing feelings is not always easy for many of us.

As months unrolled, my feelings were far from normal. TV was boring. Books were not easy to read. My concentration level was down. Much in the newspaper repulsed me. I discovered I had to be very careful about painful stories. If a story contained even a small amount of pain or suffering; my stomach knotted up. I would avert my eyes quickly or close the book or paper.

What was weird, I noticed, was that other people could sit and watch the grossest things and be unaffected by them. I felt I was normal and they were abnormal. But was it the other way around? I began to see each murder on TV or in the newspaper as an incredible loss of life for that person and many others in his or her circle. I felt a depth of pain intensely. The world was a violent place and we were standing by in a trance. I felt like an alien visiting earth and taking a look at how strangely humans treat each other. But I also knew I had to find a way to get back into life in the real world, even if reality left a lot to be desired.

I had no idea getting back into the "real world" could be so difficult or how many years that would actually take.

What kept me from being deeply depressed was something I had been exposed to, even though, like most people, I was not always perfect at practicing it. It was expressing gratitude daily. Like most people when they are faced with ultimate questions and harsh reality, I, too, began to think more about God. However, it was a new challenge to express gratitude when I would feel strong waves of debilitating grief or even an unexpected emotional storm.

Over time, I learned to look up at the wide universe and just say, "I don't know what to say thanks for, so I'm just saying thanks." Or, "I can't thank you for what is going on, or for losing Nancy, or what she is missing out on, or the pain her family and friends feel. I can't give thanks for how crappy I feel right now. But I just say thank you for something— for life. That I can breathe. That I have a place to stay." And this would start a flow of further gratitude. Then I would find more to be thankful for; things we take for granted, a chain reaction, life itself, people who care, and my faith.

Eventually, I found myself saying thanks for the time and experience I did have with Nancy. That was tough because I wanted more of that experience and felt deprived. I found sad feelings could turn to inexplicable peace, at least momentarily. Sure, I wanted to hold onto my grudge, sorrow and sadness; and, it wasn't easy to say, "I thank you for the time I had with this wonderful person and the experience I had with her. I even thank you that she realized the dream of her life, which was to be married. She was so happy." Many times it was not easy to say, like speaking through clenched teeth. But, once started, it usually got easier.

Like anyone, I had bad days. Please don't misunderstand me. I failed many times. But I noticed if I started down the path of thinking bitterly, I felt worse. This made no logical sense since we are trained to give thanks for good things and curse bad things. To discover the power of gratitude in the face of contradiction was a major discovery. I was never thankful for "losing Nancy." I just found a way to be thankful in the situation.

Sometimes I had to find a way to release anger. I learned anger was not bad if you got it out appropriately. I found that a good, loud, verbal explosion cleaned out latent feelings of anger that could have led to worse depression if stuffed inside.

For example, on a sunny afternoon several months after the accident I drove to the cemetery for one of my many visits. I found Nancy's grave and sat on the grass for some time. Fresh flowers had sprung up; even a dandelion here and there. No one was around; no lawnmowers, no visitors. The air was still. I was quiet inside too.

But I felt a strange, emotional anger sweep over me. With a spark of madness I stood up; talking, speaking louder, and then nearly shouting. I approached a nearby tree and felt like punching it. I did have enough sense, however, to know I'd probably break my fist. What I did, though, was to shout at God about the nonsense, the stupidity, the idiocy of the wreck and of Nancy's death, the split-second timing of the accident, and the emotional pain this caused people.

"I'm really mad about this. Where were you? I can't figure this out. Everything could have been so good for everyone. This stinks. I'm really mad. They say you love us and want us to have an abundant life. They say you are all powerful," I shouted with a fist up pointing at God. "Where were you?"

I never got an answer. But I had discovered I could talk to God face to face, man to man, and not get slapped around for it. This was entirely against my background. You just didn't talk back to God. But here I was. God became more of a friend to me through this experience. My intellectual side needed nurturing also. My brain was thinking more clearly and it needed to ask the question, *Why?*

The pain I felt for others as time went on– for Nancy's family and all their relatives, our friends, the kids from college, everyone—was nearly choking me. Why did Nancy die? And was there no justice, no balance, and no opposite sense of good to justify this tragic thing?

Several months later I finally reached the point where the emotional pain was just too crippling.

"Okay, God," I announced. "We need to talk again." I envisioned God as a type of sounding board. "I am not so mad right now; I am just preoccupied with how in the world you could be so good and still let this happen. No answer makes sense to me."

I began to realize that with God there was no answer to *Why*; at least that I would understand. I had to stop asking "why," and begin to ask "what— W*hat* was God doing?" "What could I do now?" I found it a better question. It dawned on me God had been there that night through all the caring people.

The last discovery I recall was absolutely amazing and is the most important for me to share with you because it healed me at the deepest level. I became more aware of my growing desire to help other people who had lost someone like I had. People were coming to me for help. *What else can I do?* I knew I was not the nurse kind of person, but there was something challenging I felt a desire to share our story and what I'd learned. I would have to sacrifice my privacy and give something from my life if I was going to share Nancy's life story to help others. It would be a tribute to Nancy and a way to offer something to others in exchange for what they had been doing for me. Sharing the story with a very large audience—with the world—could be all I would be able to give; and, the best I could give.

I also thought about how many people in other situations suffer unnecessarily because of grief and loss, and they don't know how to be helped and where to turn. What I had learned about the tools of gratitude, anger and letting go could be guideposts for many, many people who needed emotional healing. Telling our story in a book seemed like the most obvious way to reach the greatest number of people. At first I brushed aside the idea. Why? I was no writer. I had never published. But I couldn't ignore the thought. I had heard that writing your own story can help you; it can be a catharsis of sorts. I also loved enormous challenges—the bigger, the better—and for me, putting our story on paper was the most substantial challenge I'd ever considered in my life. I knew it would not only require developing a new skill, but also reliving the story and the painful emotions.

Late one night, I was restless in bed. You'll think me impulsive, I suppose; and, I can be. Wait until you hear what happened next. Strangely enough, like a bolt of lightning in the night, like a bonfire set ablaze once the kindling is in place, my emotions woke up. I was on fire with anticipation. I saw before me a book. This was not a "woo-woo" or supernatural vision, but something in my own mind over which I had control. My heart raced. In my mind's eye, the book was complete, finished. I saw hundreds of thousands of readers. Instantly I felt it would be widely read. I even saw the title; a title that was to become famous, *At Least We Were Married*. I kept repeating the title and wrote it down immediately so I wouldn't forget it. It had a ring to it, and it described how Nancy and I would feel if she could come back and join me and help me write it. I also saw the book's outline, chapter by chapter, and I noticed every detail of the first, short chapter, word for word.

I didn't wait. I got out of bed and jotted down the title and the outline. Then I stayed up and wrote the first chapter, short as it is. To this day, little of chapter one has ever been edited. It was sacred. I still sometimes wonder where it really came from; where this inspiration originated.

I experienced a by-product, an unexpected benefit, from describing my feelings using pen and paper. As I wrote, my own sorrows and emotional pains healed in a way they never would have; tucked as they were down deep inside me, because the writing got them out in the open to heal. It got to where it was writing for me, I was just pushing the pen. I became part of the audience, and while I wept through it, not to sound emotional, my tears began to wash away some of the hurt.

They weren't always full of sorrow; some of them were joyful. And sometimes they were both at the same time.

The true story I have shared with you remains with me. A person doesn't really get over it. You carry a scar. I do, anyway. I also cultivated the following tools to deal with the sorrow:

Feel gratitude. When things go badly, even tragically, find a way to express gratitude. It will change your life.

Get mad at God once in a while if you feel deprived. I found it better to get mad at the Big One, rather than people. He can take it, I learned. Again, may I impress on you I am still a learner of these things, and not perfect by any means.

Don't get twisted up in philosophical "Why?" questions that can never be answered. Get to the question *"What" can I do that's good about this now?*

Write the story of what caused the sorrow. Collect pictures, go through old letters, and then set them aside. You know, I never read my book once I finished writing it, at least until now. I had to let it go. You learn to deal compassionately with yourself if you are to be healthy, and how to accept what's happened; it was too painful to go back and relive again. Why keep picking at the scar? Even though I received hundreds and hundreds of letters from people sharing how the book had been so beneficial for them, it did at least as much good for me to write it and then set it aside. I was able to move past the story itself and the events it describes, and have a new and positive life with my memories of Nancy.

For me, and maybe for you, letting a tragedy like mine take you to a new and higher level of living is an ongoing process. Along the way, I hope you gain access, like I did, to tools you can pick up and use at any time.

Terry C. Thomas, Ph.D.

And while this particular tragedy is a scar that's healed, you'll always be able to see it. And that's okay. Triumph for me doesn't mean forgetting Nancy or the accident. I know that now, and I am not only comfortable with that wisdom, but I embrace it as well.

As I was writing my book, about a year after the accident, I asked someone, "Do you ever get over it?" That person had lost someone near and dear ten years earlier.

"Yes, you do. If you allow yourself, you can move to a happier, more abundant life than you've ever had."

And I have.

Behind the Story

After joining a business networking website, I created a profile sharing my endeavor to lift up those who are grieving with hope and purpose. I had the ability to advertise or seek, in a special section, something I needed. I decided to request any stories of overcoming adversity that could be shared in a book.

The second day I posted this need on the website, Dr. Terry Thomas messaged me that he has a story I might like to hear. His was the first story I collected and it was the beginning of a flood of amazing stories which led me to compile this book.

As a result of sharing his story, Dr. Thomas decided to re-release his book, written thirty years ago, *At Least We Were Married*, which sold half a million copies. I have had the privilege of reading his book and find it inspiring on many levels. I told Dr. Thomas that I will recommend his book to my children when they are ready for marriage because his book sets a positive example of beautiful, chaste and meaningful courtship; the kind which can lead to strong and lasting marriages.

Terry is currently working on a new book which shares the wisdom he has gained in the many years since this event occurred. To read *At Least We Were Married*, or learn more about Terry's latest writing, go to *www.AtLeastWeWereMarried.com*.

Three

The Gift That Changed My Life

Author: Ronda Knuth

Delightfully hectic are words that sum up life at Sunrise Senior Living at Pinehurst in Denver, Colorado where I live out my love on a daily basis. Phone calls, scheduling appointments, baking cookies, popping popcorn, braiding hair, moderating life and managing forty-million to-do's constantly popping on the horizon—it keeps me hopping. The day I received the gift that changed my life was one of those days.

A quick peek at the clock told me that it was almost lunch time, which meant it would soon be mail time. Scarcely would the carrier be out the door before eager residents, clamoring for their mail, would inundate the front desk. Sorting through the daily stack is rather mundane; what never gets old is the transformation on the face of someone getting a letter from home. There's nothing like it. Everyone needs to be reminded from time to time that they have not been forgotten.

One of the best decisions I ever made was to accept the position of Concierge at Pinehurst, a mere three minutes from my home. To be sure, there are challenges, but they pale in comparison to the good times. Best of all, in my humble opinion, are the hugs. I love this eclectic group of seniors. Interacting on a daily basis with an abundance of Grandpas and Grandmas has restored my self-confidence, and brought a measure of comfort to my broken heart.

As a family, we have experienced a great deal of sorrow in our lives. I have stood beside too many caskets; dried too many tears; cried too many of my own. During one three-year period, we said goodbye to a number

37

of family and friends who preceded us in death: twenty-one to be exact. Of those twenty-one, eleven were family. Of those eleven, two were bone-of-my-bone and flesh-of-my-flesh.

There are approximately 6 million pregnancies every year in the United States. Of those pregnancies, 600,000 women will experience pregnancy loss through a miscarriage and 26,000 will experience pregnancy loss through stillbirth. I had not considered those daunting statistics until I became one of *them*.

I don't understand this kind of sorrow. One mother carries her longed-for baby to term, dreading, yet anticipating, the difficult labor to come. When her work is done, she holds the fulfillment of her dreams tightly in her arms. She counts tiny fingers and miniature toes, and plants tender kisses on her baby's sweet nose.

Another mother labors in agony, torn, wanting the pain to end, knowing that when it does, the baby she has birthed will be lifeless and limp. She will hold, she will weep, she will unwillingly release.

One mother frets, not understanding the privilege of colic, sleepless nights, earaches, and runny noses. Another weeps for lost kisses, soiled diapers, first words, and skinned knees. I am that mother. I have cradled six precious children in my womb, but I cuddled only four of them in my arms. Only four shared my kisses. I tucked my nose into the softness and smelled the sweetness of only four. Six were mine, but two were gone before we said hello.

An ultrasound confirmed what the lack of movement caused us to suspect —our baby was dead. Not wanting to induce, the doctor advised us to wait for labor to begin spontaneously. So, we waited. We waited for one whole week. Mere words cannot describe the torment and agony of those days. My mother-heart tore in two.

The hours before delivery were long and painful. Unless you've been there, you cannot conceive the anguish of labor without the promise of life. The doctor predicted a speedy delivery, but he was wrong. The painful labor lasted for hours. When at last it was over, we held our tiny son in our hands and struggled to make sense of a loss that seemed so senseless. What possible good could come from this little one's death? He was perfect in every way, except for the umbilical cord wrapped around his right leg; and except for the fact that he was dead.

We named him William Andrew Knuth, but I called him Billy. A week later, I stood beside the miniature, satin covered white casket holding his body. I was numb with grief, spent to the very core of my being. If I survived, it would be because of the kindness of family and the grace of my God.

What to do with pregnancy loss was a mystery in those days. Some thought you should simply chalk it up to experience and move on, "You can always have another baby." Others were quick to offer pat answers designed to disallow the pain, "God must have needed another little angel." Even a brazen few suggested, "This is punishment for your sin."

I was not sure, based on their remarks, that I even had a right to cry. I had experienced a similar dilemma two years earlier when we surrendered another tiny Baby Knuth to heaven's care. This added grief was unbearable. When the hospital informed me that they had lost the pictures they had taken of Billy, I spiraled downward. Those pictures were the only tangible reminders I had of him and now they were gone. Nothing remained but a scant few memories. I clung to them, replaying them over and over in my mind. I was afraid that if I stopped remembering, my baby would be forgotten.

Finally, unable to assimilate the loss into my life, I gathered my sorrow, placed it in a pretty box with a bow on top, and carefully hid it on a shelf high in the closet of my heart. I shut the door and walked away. I made a conscious decision not to *go there* anymore. It hurt too much.

Pretending it did not matter, did not prevent my unresolved grief from exacting a severe toll. Depression became my constant companion. Years passed, eleven to be exact. I applied for and was offered the position of Concierge at Pinehurst. No one knew the depth of my pain, because I didn't tell them. Some days I did well to put one foot in front of the other. I was grateful for the diversion Sunrise offered. As long as I kept busy, I kept the dark clouds of despair at bay.

Then came a disquieting phone call from a friend in Ohio. "Ronda," she said, "I have a friend whose baby has been stillborn. I want to get her a gift. Do you have a suggestion?" Without warning, the closet door swung open, and all the painful memories tumbled out. I was surprised at their intensity and equally surprised at my ready response, "Get her a soft baby blanket. One she can cuddle with, and cry her tears into."

Instinctively, I knew that a blanket would be a tangible memento of that baby's brief life. There are many difficult aspects associated with pregnancy loss, not the least of which is coming home to a silent nursery and empty arms. Arms that should have nestled a newborn baby now hold nothing at all. Although I had not thought of it before, I knew the suggestion I offered was right. I knew that a soft, cuddly blanket would fill her empty arms—not with baby, but with something comforting. "If I'd had a blanket like that," I told my friend before ending the conversation, "I know it would have much been easier for me to grieve Billy's death."

Now, a week after that phone call, I sat at the front desk, waiting for the afternoon mail. I enjoyed the opportunity each day to greet the mail carrier. He had been delivering mail to my home for years, and now he was delivering it to my workplace. Usually our friendly exchange consisted of little more than a quick hello and maybe a bit of congenial neighborly news.

But this day it was different. He laid the mail on the desk, then turned and placed a parcel in my hands saying as he did, "I thought you might like to have this now instead of waiting until you got home."

I could hardly wait for him to leave so I could examine the contents of my unexpected package. "I wonder who this is from?" I thought. The return label indicated an address in Ohio, and in an instant, I knew, without even opening the box, what was inside. What I did not know was the impact it would have on my life for years to come.

I removed the brown paper bag wrapping from the outside of the box, carefully loosened the covering and peeked inside. The first thing I noticed was a piece of stationary folded neatly in two. Careful, lest it tear, I unfolded the paper and read the simple words it contained, "A blanket for William... for Momma. Trusting it's never too late."

Laying the note aside, I tenderly folded back the layers of crinkly, white tissue paper. Stifling a sob, I looked for the first time at the gift before me. With reverent awe, I extended a finger and felt the softness of a beautiful, pastel baby blanket. The downy blanket gave credence to the lives of baby Billy as well as Baby Knuth. It validated my losses and acknowledged the brief lives of my children. It seemed to whisper, "They haven't been forgotten." I wept blessed, healing tears.

In time I was able to do what previously had been impossible. I was able to release my babies back into the arms of God. Like Hannah of old, I could finally say, "... now I give you to the Lord." (I Samuel 1:28) So profound was my healing that I knew I had to share it with others and *The*

*Billy Project** was birthed. Whenever I learn of a grieving parent who has lost a baby through miscarriage, stillbirth or early infant death, I want to give them a gift like mine. Not just any blanket, but a soft crib blanket, one that should have snuggled a baby but instead comforts a mother with empty arms or absorbs the tears of a grieving father. And I always speak the words I wish had been shared with me, "it's okay to cry."

Some wonder, "Is it such a good idea to give a blanket to the parents after a baby has died? Won't it remind them of their loss?" My reply is, "Do you really think they have been forgotten?"

The ripple effect has taken blankets on a mission to soothe broken-hearted parents from the Bronx in New York, to comfortable Ranch Santo Margarita, California. They've winged their way to rural Humble, Texas, north to lazy Kimball, Nebraska, and even as far away as Germany. Other blankets have gone to a missionary, the wife of a popular talk show host, a sorrowing Lieutenant Governor and his wife, and a military couple miles from home. One mother wept when she received a blanket in memory of her son. One young mom told me, "If I close my eyes and hold the blanket to my cheek, for just a minute its tender softness feels like my baby's face next to mine."

What never gets old is the immediate transformation on the face of one receiving a comfort blanket. There's nothing like it. Knowing that their baby has not been forgotten is priceless. Every time I hug a sorrowing father or wipe the tears of a grieving mother, I am reminded of the healing that began in my own life the day

Ronda with Billy's Blanket

the mail carrier delivered my soft, pastel baby blanket. I am hopeful that through the gift of a blanket, they will begin a healing of their own.

Such a simple gift, yet it changed my life.

Behind the Story

I met Ronda Knuth as an associate in a National effort dedicated to educating the public on life-story preservation. Ronda and I teleconferenced and worked together across the miles, creating a program to raise awareness and teach people how to capture and preserve the stories of their loved ones. Many of the stories from those who have been coined *The Greatest Generation* (those who served and lived during World War II) are being lost at an alarming rate. If we don't take the time to capture the stories and life-wisdom of these important people, they will be gone forever.

Ronda is a true expert in this field and by working closely with members of *The Greatest Generation* in her profession at Sunrise Senior Living; she has been the catalyst for many valuable stories being preserved. Ronda often shares some of the most poignant stories she captures with me and I have come to appreciate her masterful storytelling.

As I began gathering stories for this book, I mentioned my endeavor to Ronda and asked if she might have a story to share. I already knew her writing is exceptional, and I wondered if there might be a fitting story she could contribute. I had no idea when I made this suggestion what profound experiences she had in her life! Ronda offered to provide not one, but two, important stories to this book.

I received this story just two days before what would have been the eighth birthday of my daughter, Brynn. In my religion, this is a special birthday and one I desired to honor in a meaningful way. It was a blessing to read Ronda's story just before this momentous day, as it gave my family an opportunity to do something we will always remember.

We have four friends who lost babies over the past year: a miscarriage, two still births and another baby who died the same age as Brynn (seven months old). As a tribute to Brynn, and a compassionate service to our friends, I took my four children to the mall and we went to *EVERY STORE* feeling each baby blanket, searching for the softest ones to give. When we had selected five blankets, four to give away and one to remember Brynn with, we wrapped them beautifully. Then we printed the story Ronda had just sent and delivered the blankets in person on Brynn's birthday to each family.

My children were excited to hand the gift to the mother who came to the door. It was deeply meaningful and my children still talk about this experience today. How wonderful it is to be able to teach children compassion, charity and love so powerfully! Even though it rises from the tragedy of infant death, it is not a small thing to instill this value in children while they are young. Many months later, we received the following thank you note from one of the mothers:

Dear Davis Family,

Sorry it has taken me so long to write this to you. It has been my greatest intention, I just have not found the best moment to do it! I wanted to tell your family thank you so very much for the beautiful gift you gave our family. It touched our hearts in so many ways, you cannot even imagine. On that same exact day, we had just gone to our first OB appointment for our new pregnancy to find out that it was probably not going to work out again. We have been trying for two years to have another baby with endings in heartache three times already. Even though those babies were never held, the bond formed for each of them from day one.

To receive your gift of such intense and unselfish love helped us on such a hard day. Your strength and testimony of your situation with losing a child has helped me to cope with mine and to know that Heavenly Father is not punishing me. It is part of His plan. As much as we cannot fully understand it at the time, people, like you, who can share their experiences and feelings openly, really help people like me, who prefer to hide and feel worthless when something happens.

I am so grateful to know you. I am so grateful Heavenly Father put you in my life so I can look to your example and find comfort in knowing we all have challenges and it is what we choose to do with them that makes us who we are. Thank you for sharing those openly. Thank you for helping me through my tough times!

Love R.

I was grateful to receive this message because it confirms my belief that as we share our stories, our sorrows and the life-wisdom we have gained, we can truly lift others out of their suffering. I have included this message, with permission, to give evidence of this assertion: Stories are powerful! In addition to receiving this note, we had other mothers who were given a blanket tell us that they made copies of the story and in turn gave blankets to other mothers they knew who were suffering. It has become a gift that continues to travel!

Four

Finding Brooke

Author: Cammy Wilberger

Everyone has a story to tell. Whether of pain and sorrow endured, triumph achieved or joy appreciated, our adventures make up who we are. Sometimes an experience is of such intense magnitude, it wraps its tentacles around your life and heart forever. May 24, 2004 was the day that changed our lives. I can still remember the exact moment: where I was, what the sky looked like, and how my body felt.

It was one of those bright, sunny May afternoons. The day was balmy with the hint of summer coming. Driving home from the school where I taught, I meandered through the countryside. About half way home, I called our daughter Brooke's cell phone just to see how her day had gone. She recently finished her first year at BYU and was working in Corvallis, Oregon cleaning apartments for the summer. She didn't like cleaning outside the apartments, so had not wanted to leave our Eugene home that morning.

The apartments were next to Oregon State University and their term wasn't over for a few more weeks, so the students had not moved out. While Brooke waited for the apartments to be vacated, she worked outside doing general cleanup. She was cleaning parking lot lamps which collected a lot of "disgusting spiders," as she put it. The week was planned out; she would come home from Corvallis Wednesday evening and accompany my class fieldtrip to the Oregon Museum of Science and Industry (OMSI) in Portland. On Friday she had an appointment for her wisdom teeth to be extracted. Her father was flying to San Francisco on business; it was going to be a busy week!

Brooke was an energetic, full-of-life young woman. With her first year of college completed, at nineteen she was bursting with hopes and dreams. We were glad to have her perky personality back in our home for the summer. After having six children, when Brooke left for school, our home seemed empty with only our youngest daughter (who was thirteen), my husband Greg and I. The rest of our older children and their families lived in Corvallis. All was well with the world and life was good.

Spencer, Brooke's next oldest brother, answered her phone when I called and after chatting for a minute I asked him "Where is Brooke?" He said they didn't know, but were trying to find her. Reminding him to not tease me, especially about things like that, "What do you mean you don't know?" I queried. He replied, "Mom, we can't find her anywhere and the police are here right now." Instantaneously, my heart stopped and breathing became difficult. I felt as if the world had dropped out from under me. My arms and hands were shaking, yet they felt numb and rubbery. Spencer just kept repeating "We don't know!" as I rapidly fired questions at him. I cried out that I wasn't sure if I could make it home and heard him shouting "Mom, Mom" as I hung up. Immediately I began reciting a favorite scripture from Proverbs, memorized years ago; "Trust in the Lord, with all Thine heart and lean not unto Thine own understanding...." (Prov. 3:5, 6) I cried and pled with the Lord to protect Brooke and help us find her.

Where do you turn when your world is suddenly upside down and you need to know what to do? Still panicked, I could feel a sense of calm coming over my mind. I had to trust in the Lord to protect Brooke. Methodically, I called and quietly asked Jessica to pack some clothes, as something had come up in Corvallis and we would need to spend a couple of days there. When I arrived a few minutes later she bubbly asked me "What's up?"

Middle school is such a challenging time and as I looked at Jessica, I wanted so much to protect her from what I wasn't even sure of; all that I knew is it wasn't going to be fun. I hugged Jessica and told her we needed to kneel and pray. Prayer was not new to us~ we had prayed together as a family that morning, and did so on a daily basis, but few of our prayers have been as heartfelt as those uttered at this time. Prayer became our survival tool. First, I needed the strength of Brooke's dad, but knew he was somewhere between Portland and San Francisco. I began trying to reach him. Not successful, I called our LDS (Latter Day Saints) Bishop's home and within minutes they were at our house. Then we left for Corvallis after another prayer.

My mind was racing with questions and my heart was full of fear. I was sure this could not be happening. I would wake up from the nightmare soon. When we got to Corvallis, I hoped they would have found Brooke, but that sick feeling in my stomach told me Brooke would not have gone anywhere without telling someone. Try as I might to visualize her going to lunch with a friend that had spotted her outside, it didn't make sense and that was not her way. It had been over six hours since they last saw her and she would never have been gone that long without letting someone know where she was going.

I called my daughter at the apartments and she numbly kept saying "We don't know mom, we are looking everywhere we can think of." Brooke's siblings had shouldered the initial panic and realization of what had happened. That immediate sense of loss was theirs to bear. I could see it in their young eyes. Parents are to be there for their children during a crisis, but here we were, all clinging together, wishing one of us could "fix it." One of them had been able to reach Greg before his flight had taken off and he soon joined us in Corvallis. Family strength is powerful and although none of us had any answers, we all worked together. We began gathering information and creating a flyer with Brooke's picture.

If something tragic had to happen, Corvallis was the right place to be! The Corvallis police department had been called when Brooke did not come in or have lunch with her sister. She and her husband managed the apartments Brooke was cleaning. Upon hearing the situation, the police quickly determined this was not normal and they came to the apartments. When they arrived, Brooke's flip-flops were found in the parking lot and her soap buckets were discovered next to one of the lampposts where she had been cleaning the light. At that point the police began a very thorough search of the apartment complex.

By 5:00 p.m. that afternoon, police were everywhere, flyers had been printed, television and radio stations contacted, a phone tree organized to ask help of LDS Church members while friends and Corvallis Search and Rescue were ready to begin. By 9:00 p.m. people began gathering in the Oregon State University Reser Stadium parking lot to help with the search. Students and friends poured in so quickly that the Search and Rescue leaders had a difficult time keeping all the teams organized. Greg, Jessica, our sons and sons-in-law joined with search teams, staying out all night until early the next morning, helping explore the park areas around the apartments. Nearly 300 people from all over the Willamette Valley participated in the initial search. Media congregated and began to spread the word of this beautiful, young, all-American girl named Brooke who had disappeared. Everyone's mantra became "Find Brooke." The community responded in a major way. The support was phenomenal, physical as well as emotional, and spiritual to such a degree that our morale was buoyed up and we were sure we would find her.

We often liken this experience to an iceberg. It quickly became very public and was reported by the media as "every parent's worst nightmare." What seemed so horrific was just a small glimpse of what we were actually experiencing. We told each other this was like living through a CSI episode; but it wasn't exciting, suspenseful or entertaining. The police were just as intent on finding Brooke as we were. They kept us informed constantly during those early hours and continued to question family members and other persons of interest. Brooke's siblings took the brunt of these sometimes grueling sessions, but we just kept telling each other that we would do whatever it took to get Brooke back. We vowed to cooperate, no matter how difficult it was.

I returned to our home with the police as they went through everything Brooke possessed. Her tubs of clothes and books from BYU were still stacked up, waiting for her to put them away! They searched through every notebook, drawer and computer-mail looking for any clue they might find; trying to "know" what kind of a girl Brooke was. They found notes like the one she had over her bed "Did you remember to pray?" They took any items that might yield DNA.

As a family, we were bewildered, confused, scared, exhausted and had only one goal—to find Brooke. We stayed with our daughter and son-in-law in their small apartment, rarely sleeping or eating. People were in and out constantly, so to keep police information private, they would give us updates in a small bedroom. During these updates, I would often become dizzy and nauseous. I would lay back on the bed while they talked because to stay sane I couldn't or wouldn't let myself think of what might have happened to her. I forced my mind to not wander down those paths.

We spent hours making flyers and fielding phone calls. We listened to everyone who called-in with a tip, hoping for that one golden piece of information. There were calls from all over the United States with tips and "sightings." The police had set up a hot line, but somehow people had gotten our phone number and called us directly. The search effort grew larger and the *Search Command Center* was moved to an LDS Church building. At times, so many volunteers showed up that they had to be turned away for lack of trained personnel. Those unable to search with a team made buttons, tied pink ribbons and distributed flyers. Large posters of Brooke were made and put around town, as well as the OSU campus. Billboards were created on the interstate freeway by anonymous individuals. One day, as I drove into Eugene, a city bus went by and as it pulled in front of me, I realized the whole back of the bus was a big picture of Brooke.

Searchers came from all over the state of Oregon and several came from out of state. They came from every walk of life and religious denomination. Many churches in Corvallis rallied to support the efforts by prayer and active searching. Several companies donated time for their employees to hunt. The search leaders continued to be overwhelmed by the number of volunteers who showed up. Massive amounts of food and water were donated by local businesses. The community responded in an amazing way. Thousands of volunteer hours were logged. Daily searches were conducted for about two weeks, after which searches were conducted in response to tips given to law enforcement. The love and generosity of people we had never met completely overwhelmed us. The case seemed to take on a life of its own.

By nature our family is private, but we realized to reach the maximum number people in the shortest amount of time, we needed to use the media. We consented to do many interviews with local and national television, pleading for anyone who knew anything to call the police. Brooke and her college roommate had made a video of themselves while on a trip to the coast just two weeks earlier. It was valuable in showing who she was to the public. We held press conferences to express our gratitude for all the support we received and continued to urge someone to come forward.

We all felt an unspoken urgency, knowing that in abduction cases, each day that passes reduces the chances of finding the missing person alive; yet our hope remained high that we would find Brooke. We still had a strong feeling something would surface. The faith, prayers, and love of so many kept us buoyed up. Our lives were shattered, but still we stayed focused on finding this daughter we loved so much. We had limited energy and it took all we had to keep moving forward. Time seemed to stand still, yet it was moving into weeks and months since her disappearance with no clues.

My constant prayer was that whoever had done this would make a mistake. Months later, that very prayer would be answered. Over that summer we had time to attempt making sense of the senseless. Staying positive was important; avoiding persons who were negative was a must.

Although Greg had continued to work, I questioned my ability to return to teaching, knowing how difficult it was to concentrate and perform. Demanding, higher-level tasks were challenging and I felt like I had been traumatized. Our family motto became "We Can Do Hard Things" and we pushed onward. Going back to school in September actually proved to be therapeutic because, when I walked through the school door each morning, it became a completely different world where I didn't think about my "other life."

Six months after Brooke's disappearance, a man with ties to Oregon was arrested in New Mexico after abducting a young woman at knife point. On a routine police call, similarities were noted and information exchanged. With this new information and evidence, police were able to put enough pieces of the puzzle together to give us an idea of what had happened on that fateful day. On May 24, 2005, exactly one year since Brooke's disappearance, the police received word that a DNA match had been made with evidence linking Brooke to Joel Patrick Courtney. We could not share this with anyone, and while many continued to be hopeful, we knew it would be a mission of recovery, not rescue, for Brooke. When the Grand Jury was convened in August, Mr. Courtney was charged with aggravated murder punishable by the death penalty. Hope was definitely gone at this point. The feeling of hope is difficult to define when you have it, but when it is gone, you realize its loss and the emptiness that is left. Many prayers had been answered to get to this point and, although we could never have imagined what a hill we still had to climb, we were so grateful.

On June 24, 2006 we held a memorial for Brooke. As I prepared the wall of pictures, I found myself joyfully reflecting on the wonderful life Brooke had lived. She had loving family, true friends and had made good choices which brought her success and great memories. Only when I stopped to think about why I was doing this, was I sad. It was a Brooke-kind-of-day; the sun was bright against the clean blue Oregon sky. It seemed as if her spirit were there, spreading her warmth and love.

Throughout the next five years after Brooke's disappearance, the authorities were constantly working on the case. Contact between our family and the legal team occurred several times a week, to several times a month, depending on what was happening. They kept us in the loop and we always felt we knew what was going on. We have the highest regard for the way our family was treated by the police and the District Attorney's office during the entire experience. Our lack of knowledge about how the legal system works was evident, yet they were patient and spent hours simply explaining procedures and what we could expect.

No matter what we did or how hard we tried to "get on with life," it was always there, looming just ahead. Each time we felt we had made progress moving forward, a legal issue or hearing would set us back and we would find ourselves slowly trying to locate our footing on life's path *AGAIN*. It took three long years of Mr. Courtney fighting the court system in New Mexico before he finally pled guilty and was transported to Oregon the spring of 2008. His trial for abducting and murdering Brooke was scheduled for February 2010.

After sitting through pretrial hearings held in early 2009, and listening to witnesses testify, we knew the trial was going to be an extremely difficult time for our family. In September, legal motions were filed which brought about an attempt to mediate an agreement with Mr. Courtney. For so many years he had not been willing to talk, but he finally began to show a willingness to negotiate. We endured three intensely anxious weeks of getting our hopes up one day, and hitting bottom the next, daily phone calls with the district attorney and waiting. At one point, I was asked to make a phone call to the New Mexico's governor's office, by way of the Oregon's governor's office, to share our desire that Mr. Courtney be able to serve out his sentence in New Mexico. Timing was never good—I ended up making that call as I drove home, having to pull into a service station parking lot. Unbelievably, agreements were made and on a Friday morning, while I was teaching school, the phone call came that he had agreed to tell what he did and where he hid Brooke's body.

Searchers were dispatched, but it was the next morning around ten o'clock—Saturday September 19, 2009—when the District Attorney called to say they had, with the aid of dogs, found human remains. Another two hours later he called and asked me to identify the watch Brooke was wearing when she disappeared. I remembered that watch well—it had been a Christmas gift she had really wanted. I sent the text message to him with the description, the silver band, the links, the Anne Klein brand. The text came back; it was Brooke's watch.

Even though Brooke had been gone over five years, and although we knew what the outcome would be, we felt numb once again as we cried. This time it was deeper, sadder, and more mournful. The long-sought-for sense of relief was not present, only silent pain mixed with gratitude as our family met together. Away from home, Brooke's youngest sister, now a freshman herself at BYU, found the news especially difficult to bear.

The case was always a part of her teenage life. It was thrust upon her and she overcame many challenges to emerge as her own person, while intensely missing the older sister she had always admired. We didn't choose to let it consume us; however, the public nature of the situation, the constant news reminders, and the lack of answers kept it constantly in front of us.

Early on Monday, September 21, 2009, our entire family attended the sentencing hearing in Salem, Oregon where Joel Patrick Courtney pled "no contest" to the kidnapping and murder of Brooke. In exchange for revealing the location of Brooke's body, he would serve life in prison without the possibility of parole. He would be able to serve his sentence in New Mexico as long as his behavior was acceptable. Joel Patrick escaped the death penalty and we escaped enduring a difficult trial. Our goal from the beginning was to find Brooke, and bring her home; and that was accomplished. We felt no anger, hatred, or revenge toward this person, who took so much from our lives. The hearing gave us the opportunity to look him in the eye and thank him for finding it within himself to tell where he had left Brooke.

From the courtroom we were taken to another room and the District Attorney shared the latest court documents, to be made public later that day. These contained the confession and gruesome details of the crime. We listened to the specifics of her last horrific hours, how she was taken at knifepoint, was kept bound in Courtney's van for several hours while he drove around and did drugs, and then was raped and trapped in the van overnight until Joel Courtney finally killed Brooke by bludgeoning her in the head. Courtney explained to his attorneys that "her reaction was so strong after he raped her, that he decided to end her life." Hearing these words brought every piece of the last five and one-half years avalanching upon us with increased force. Back in Corvallis, we were taken to the site where Brooke's remains had been recovered. Searchers, still sifting the area for traces of her, moved aside as we bowed in a time of silence. Incredibly, they were able to retrieve over 85% of her body. Regardless of how sensitively it is done, no parent should ever have to see how their child's body parts are gathered from the ground. Although I love the lush, green, wooded Douglas fir groves of Oregon, this was not a place I would return.

Then the news conference was held, making public the evidence we had received earlier. It is one thing to know what happened, but as it all became public knowledge, the little shell we formed around us cracked and our hearts were once again opened. Everyone has days which feel endless, and this was one of those!

But these days do end, and a new one comes forth. Changed it may be, but still rich with the promise that life can be more than the adversities which beset us all. We did not walk through the valley alone. Our gratitude has grown into deep love for those who have walked with us in whatever capacity. From those intensely involved on a daily basis to others who have kept Brooke in their thoughts and prayers; our family has felt the care given by each person. There is never "closure," nor should there be, when one experiences a trauma or untimely death of a child; but there can be peace. An adversity like this is never "over," but is always with you, just in a different dimension and from a different perspective.

Brooke Wilberger

That peace which is born of faith, gratitude and love can carry us forward with purpose. We are often asked how we "did it" and others have expressed that they couldn't have gotten through the long ordeal. To those comments we answer, "We didn't do anything. We definitely experienced the increased power that comes from the grace of our Savior and with that—we got up each morning and tried to keep moving." I often laughed with my fellow teachers that if I come to school in my bathrobe, they will know I'm having a bad day!

We have grown together as a family, letting each person grieve in their own way and time. We know that peace and comfort were given to us during this time; and are assured that Brooke received peace and comfort in a

She shoots, she scores!

greater measure. She was not left alone. We will always miss Brooke, but know that she is part of our eternal family. Brooke was a very loving young lady. Her last words in our home were to her sister the morning she disappeared. As she started to drive away she stopped, ran back into the house, and called out "I love you, Jess!" then was on her way. What a great legacy she has left for us—to love others. Even in her death, Brooke testified of all that is good.

At the time of this writing, the final service for Brooke has not been held. In a few weeks her sisters and I will lovingly wrap her remains in a soft pink blanket and place them in a small pink casket. In the presence of her family, and a few friends, they will be interned to rest peacefully in a grave over-looking the valley where she grew up.

Behind The Story

My home-town is Eugene, Oregon. While I didn't grow up knowing the Wilberger family, my parents were close to Brooke and her brother, Spencer, while serving as leaders of their youth group. When Brooke first disappeared, my mother called to share with me the sorrowful news.

Because of my parent's relationship with the Wilberger family, I was kept informed through the years of new details or progress in the search. The truth is, not much was said most of the time except how sad and tragic that there was still nothing to report! Months and years into the loss, it remained hard to believe Brooke was gone without a clue.

As I began collecting stories for *The Triumph Book*, I heard how inspiring the Wilberger family had become to the people in the Northwest. My mother told me how Cammy and Greg travel to churches and youth gatherings, speaking about their experience, talking specifically about FORGIVENESS! What a powerful message they give, considering the circumstances of the tragedy.

Thanks to my mother, I was able to reach Cammy to see if she would be interested in sharing their story in this book. Cammy was willing, but still deep in the midst of pretrial hearings at the time, which made focusing on writing a story (which was still unfolding) difficult. Despite the challenge, Cammy wrote a beautiful and hopeful message. It surprises me how a mother who is describing what is certainly a parent's worst nightmare can do so with hope and love from start to finish!

With the unexpected plea bargain by Brooke's killer, just two weeks before Cammy submitted her story to me, the narrative Cammy wrote is able to give a conclusion to the experience. I feel great joy to be able to share the FULL STORY of *Finding Brooke* in the pages of this book!

Five

Rolling Along the Path to Success
Author: Nick Wells

Thanks to a car accident, I now have a physical disability... I am a paraplegic. What might appear to be a great loss has become one of my life's greatest advantages. The challenges this disability brings have led to my successes. My name is Nick Wells and I am using my *abilities* to improve, impact and change the world we live in. This is my story:

Before the accident, my life was in total chaos. In spite of the fact that I was rebellious and drinking a lot, my wife Barbara still saw something good and married me anyway. My life gave true meaning to the phrase, *The Good, The Bad, and The Ugly.* In the beginning years of our marriage, my behaviors created a great deal of problems. We moved around a lot; always thinking a start somewhere new would allow us to escape the trouble. We lived in six different places during the first three years of our marriage.

I was working at an Army depot at the time of my injury. The construction company I worked for provided an apartment for their employees. Since I was working twelve hour shifts, I would stay there for a week at a time. My wife and I were fighting most of the time and we eventually separated. However, after a couple months of being apart, we started seeing one another again. We saw more of each other *after* I moved out than we did when we lived together!

After work, one Friday night, I was on my way to the apartment where my wife and children were waiting for me. While crossing a bridge, a tire went flat. Not having a lug wrench to change it, and being in the middle of nowhere, I wandered up to a nearby house. It sounded as if a party was going on inside when I knocked on the door…and that is the last thing I remember until I woke up in the hospital 72 hours later.

I knocked on that door around 7:00 p.m. It was around 2:00 a.m. that I was involved in a car accident four miles further up the road. I have no idea what happened. Clearly my tire had been changed. Perhaps I had gone into the house and partied. I just don't know. The police thought I may have fallen asleep, but I had never done that before. At a curve in the road, there were tracks on the ground as if I were trying to make the arc, but couldn't. The ground rose up in this place much like a ramp. With my vehicle traveling an estimated speed of 55 or 60 mph, I flew fifty feet in distance; and about ten feet off the ground.

The car landed on the passenger side and then lurched forward, causing me to fly through the windshield. A witness saw my headlights tossing around, and immediately came to the scene of the accident. Once there, this Good Samaritan rolled me onto my back to be sure I could breathe.

After I broke through the windshield, the car went end over end for a distance of more than 300 feet. A headlight was found near the place on the ground where the paramedics worked to save my life; so the car had literally nearly landed on top of me!

A Life-flight helicopter was called to the scene but was cancelled once the rescue team was certain I was gone. My entire rib cage was broken and there was no pressure to help me exhale. As one of the paramedics was packing to leave, she leaned against my side. This put enough pressure that it enabled me to breathe again on my own. A tracheotomy was quickly inserted and the paramedics resumed rescue efforts. A doctor later said my body was extremely twisted and sustained a compression fracture, all of which made breathing on my own nearly impossible.

Barb and the kids were waiting for me to come home and watch *The Little Mermaid* with them. As the evening wore on, the kids fell asleep and Barb began to worry. Eventually she was informed of the accident by our neighbors and she was told to contact the University of Utah Hospital.

Initially, Barb was told I was paralyzed. The doctors suggested that I *might* regain movement, once the swelling went down. The spinal cord had not been severed but I underwent a thirteen hour surgery to fuse my back.

When I woke up, I didn't even ask what happened. My wife and I both experienced a sense of "knowing" that this was a challenge we needed to go through. Even when my wife learned about my accident, she didn't panic. In fact, she felt extreme comfort and was consoling others who were distraught. Barb knew somehow everything was going to be okay. Her biggest relief was that I was still alive and no one else was involved.

At the time of the accident, I was driving a Honda CRX. Though the car had been full of beer cans, the medical personnel found none at the scene. Blood tests came back showing only a small amount of alcohol in my system. Initially we had been told there was no sign of alcohol—that I had just fallen asleep. Perhaps the police didn't charge me with drunk driving because they thought I didn't have a chance of living. My initial thought was, "See, I don't have a problem with alcohol!" However, when I later learned alcohol actually was involved, my attitude shifted completely. I recognized I did have a problem and that alcohol had been responsible for crippling me and nearly costing my wife her husband; my kids their father.

I needed to get my life back on track. During rehab I was told in life-changing traumas such as mine, it comes with a 97% marriage failure rate. My marriage was already on the rocks! Barb said, "We are separated and on our way to divorce, so I don't see how it can get any worse."

I was at the hospital for 17 days before being moved to another facility. During this time, I filed for Social Security, I found out it would take about six months for the checks to start arriving. The bills were already piling up! Barb and I wondered how we were going to get by during that time. The first thing I said was, "We need to start paying our tithe." It was shocking to Barb to hear me say this because it had never been important to me before. So we paid our tithe immediately. This truly marked a turning point. The contractor where I worked said he would continue to pay my salary for the six months until my benefits kicked in. He had also financed my car and forgave the loan. Two other loans were automatically paid off because I had disability protection. As it turned out, we had great insurance; we were better off financially *after* the accident than *before*!

A week or so after the trauma; and regularly in the weeks that followed, I was offered counseling. I turned it down each time. I was not in denial; I knew I would be a paraplegic. The professionals were concerned that I was handling it "too well." How do you handle something *too well*?! I had a great deal of support from friends and family. I said to Barb, "I didn't know I knew so many people!" Through this tragedy I saw how much of an impact I had made in other's lives as they came and impacted mine.

While I had my tracheotomy, phlegm needed to be routinely sucked out or I couldn't breathe. Before the "phlegm extraction" I felt like I was drowning. There were only two nurses on staff at night. One night my tracheotomy needed to be cleaned, and I couldn't do it myself. I repeatedly banged on the wall and pushed the nurses call button trying to get someone to help me. It felt like hours, though it was probably closer to fifteen minutes, before a nurse responded. This was the scariest part of my whole trauma experience!

Tilt tables are used for back injuries to keep pressure from being on one place for too long. Even though I was on morphine, every time the table tilted to the left side, I would scream in pain. Out of compassion, one of the nurses stopped the rotation. As a result, I ended up with a skin breakdown on my tail bone. So now I was dealing with physical therapy *and* a skin graft on my tailbone.

The nerves in my right shoulder were damaged in the accident. This caused me to have to struggle to even sit up in bed. Soon after my shoulder began to heal, I was taken to the weight room. Working alongside me were accident and stroke patients. One older gentleman in his 80's was lifting fifteen pounds; I couldn't even lift five. There was a smug look of confidence on his face when he realized he could lift more than me!

On the third floor of the hospital was a ramp I called, "Hell Hill." Patients are not allowed to go home until they can roll up that ramp. I truly thought I would never get up "Hell Hill." But eventually I did! It was a monumental day of achievement. I will never forget making the phone call to my wife that I had conquered "Hell Hill!" I was finally able to go home for an overnight stay.

My dad's cousins owned a construction company, so he and his crew made the necessary changes to our home to accommodate my disability. They built a deck the height of the house with a ramp up to the door which was widened. When Barb came to get me from the hospital, I had to use a sliding board to get into the car. Although I had beaten "Hell Hill," there was still a mountain of adjustment and learning to climb, or rather, learning to roll up. On my first visit home it took more than 15 minutes to slide across the tub bench when I bathed. The shower felt wonderful; what a relief to be independent! However, with the hour-and-a-half required to get my slippery body with powerless limbs back out of the shower, I needed to bathe worse after the shower than before.

Being allowed to go home for a visit is part of the learning process and one step closer to going home permanently. The experience allows you to see what it will be like once you are released; and the hospital staff discovers what more they still need to teach you. The accident happened in the month of August and I went home the day before Thanksgiving.

Being home for the holidays was wonderful! I had taken each difficulty in stride and was no worse for the experience. However, by January, six months after the accident, I had begun to feel lost and confused. I was beginning to question the uncertainty of my future. In fact, I was flat-out scared. There was a hole in my heart and life. I had felt bullet proof and happy. My disability was just another challenge in life I would have to roll with. But out of nowhere, I suddenly felt fear. My whole world was being rocked. Something was missing from my life. Why had things suddenly changed?

I prayed morning and night. Why was I feeling so dark? The anguish lasted for more than a week. Something was lost inside that used to be there. After a great deal of prayer, as I struggled to comprehend this profound change, I was quietly stopped by a voice inside. The voice was plain and clear. The voice said, "I've been carrying you all this time, now you have to make it on your own, otherwise you won't learn anything." After receiving this message, I envisioned the image in my mind of the foot prints in the sand. I saw a single set of footprints where God had carried me and then I saw His footprints next to wheelchair tracks. God was still with me, but He no longer carried me. I had to do this on my own now. I knew God would be there to help me, but He wouldn't do it all for me anymore.

There was a void now that I needed to learn to fill. The emptiness had been explained to me, so I battled it by studying scripture, praying and going to church. Before the void I felt untouchable; after the darkness came I was full of fear and worry for the future.

The first year after my accident, I didn't accomplish much. I had to regain my strength and learn how to live with new constraints and conditions. I began to read books, taking time to ponder the words and the story. I wanted to learn everything, and I wanted to think deeply. I started regularly attending church and putting my life in line spiritually. My accident turned me around. I was going south and now I was headed north. It was a 180 degree reversal which brought the greatest joy and happiness I have had in life. Without this adversity, I could have very easily been divorced, drunk, lost, or perhaps even dead.

I began to speak to youth groups about the highs and lows of life. It was wonderful to share ideas with others, and to see the impact it made in their lives. Because I had faced such intense challenges, I knew I had a message to share. I believe it was actually helping me as much or more than it was helping them. That is the great thing about serving others!

I have learned to *"never say never."* No one can say how they will react to a challenge until they experience it. What I do know is that all things happen in our lives as a positive learning experience. EVERYTHING! Sometimes you have to search for it; but, if you do, you will find something positive in exchange for what you have endured.

In the fall, one year after my accident, I registered at Weber State University to learn a new career. My construction career was over. The University was built on the side of a mountain which causes the campus to be on a gradual slope. I scheduled my classes so that I could work my way down-hill. I never had to worry about not being to class on time! At the end of the day it took a half hour to roll back up the hill to my car. This was good, strengthening exercise.

I majored in Technical Sales and minored in Computer-Aided Drafting (CAD). I started my own CAD design business doing blueprints for custom designed homes. After feeling that I was not contributing to society, I wanted to be working! I created home designs and became a general contractor. Making money with my mind instead of my body created a remarkable juxtaposition between the grunt construction labor from before to becoming the imagination behind the project.

I eventually started my own framing crew. Barb and I decided to build our own home as well. We found a lot to build on in a neighborhood that was perfect! Everything went smoothly, quickly and perfectly. My family and I literally built that house ourselves. I laid out the walls and my boys would carry in the wood. My wife and sons (who were six and eight at the time) nailed all the walls together and put up the plywood. Then my framing crew came to the house each morning before work to help put up the walls. Watching the house come together was immensely gratifying.

At the beginning of my construction business, a friend from Texas introduced me to a machine which turns the humidity in the air into pure drinking water. Over the next two years I built several custom homes while still being kept informed on the movement of this new idea.

In the summer of 1997, I was building a house for the *Parade of Homes* and was under a tight schedule to finish it at a certain time. In one of his updates my friend let me know he needed more capital for development of the water machine. I wrote a check and told him that I believed in his effort, but was too busy to be involved at that point. This same scenario played out several times over the next few months.

In October of 1997, things finally slowed down and I had time to look at my financial records. Realizing I had given my good friend a significant sum of money over the last few months, it was time to see what my investment had accomplished. I was living in the house I had built for the *Parade of Homes*. It had a three-car, heated garage with 1700 square feet. It was the perfect place for us to further develop our water machine; so the first manufacturing plant was established right there in my garage.

I was barely paying the bills for this huge home, but it was a tremendous benefit to have the manufacturing plant located there. There was every amenity needed and its size also brought us credibility. We appeared to have more money than we actually did, which inspired many to invest so we were able to grow the project. Meetings were scheduled with *Oasis*, a manufacturer of commercial water fountains, drink dispensers and dehumidifiers. This allowed us to purchase the parts we needed in bulk. Because of an immediate kinship with the general sales manager, we were allowed to buy products at truck load prices, even though we needed much less.

Though we rapidly made big strides, there was much more work to make this product available nationwide. After a year of functioning out of my garage, we expanded to a space double the size... then we doubled the space again. We met many people who supported our endeavor including a philanthropist who desired to provide 100 machines to the people on the isle of Nevis in the Caribbean. This person wrote a check to cover all the expenses and said, "I've never done this before, but I believe completely in you and your work."

My partner and I traveled to Nevis to present this life-sustaining gift to the island, where we attended a special ceremony with the Premier of Nevis. These machines went into schools, hospitals, clinics and other public places. The want for pure drinking water there is tremendous. We traveled through the island, witnessing first-hand the need. While witnessing these realities, we knew that not only did our nation need this, so did many third world countries. My business partner and I wanted to help meet this every-day, basic human need for millions across the world. We were inspired to work harder to make this available far and wide.

One morning in 1999, I woke to find my knee so hot I could barely touch it with my fingers. I found boils and blisters up and down my leg. I had a severe staph infection which I picked up on my trip to Nevis. It was literally boiling through my skin from the inside out. I was laid-up for the next two weeks spending most of my recovery watching predictions for what the new millennium would bring. My interest was captured by a program featuring interviews from the late 50's with some of the original industrialists of the U.S., such as Carnegie and Rockefeller. Three of the four persons interviewed agreed there would be a new product or concept called "Liquid Air" which would help to end world poverty and sickness. The words I heard caught my full attention. I sat up and thought, "That is what we should call our business!" So my company's name became "Liquid Air." However, there was a French company called "Air Liquide" which translates into "Liquid Air" in English, and because they were fielding phone calls for our product, we modified our name to "H20 Liquid Air."

We grew once again from our spacious facility in the U.S. to a mass production facility in China. This reduced our manufacturing costs by two-thirds, which resulted in cutting our retail price in half so it could be more affordable and available to far more people. We launched this product at the 2002 Houston, Texas Home and Garden Show. We sold many units at the show and were amazed by the global reach we had from this local event. Knowledge of our product spread to Africa, the Middle East, the Asian countries, Singapore, the Philippines, and Indonesia, just to name a few. Our plans went from small home and office units to the development of large commercial sized units which could feasibly create thousands of gallons of water a day. This dream was finally realized when we met with a local commercial dehumidification company in San Antonio which turned out to be the largest of its kind in the world. Our partnership has allowed us to develop products which produce as much as 3500 gallons of water a day.

These large commercial units provide clean water while at the same time generating free air conditioning as a by-product. We currently have a plan under development which has been presented to the government in the water-deficient country of Ghana, Africa. The plan is to construct a water-production facility which also serves as a large air-conditioned space for medical, educational and community services; all of which can be powered through wind and solar energy! The President, Vice President and Minister of Health in Ghana are anxious for many of these facilities to be established in their country. At a cost of at least $5 million per facility, we have been unable to proceed. I am currently working to seek funding for this cause.

Living with a disability is never easy, but it is *still worth it*. The challenges my disability brings have led to my successes. Knowledge gained through adversity is more valuable than what we obtain in ease and comfort. It's when we face extreme difficulty that we realize our true potential. Adversity provides the opportunity to achieve greatness. It is human nature to wish for the abilities of others: in the spinal cord injury world a quadriplegic usually will wish he or she were a paraplegic, a

Nick Wells

paraplegic wishes he or she could walk and those who walk wish to be like the fitness gurus on television. We often look outside ourselves at the gifts and talents of others, not realizing that we all have our own ability to achieve greatness. In comparing ourselves to others, we run the risk of abandoning our own destiny—the one which will ultimately bring us the greatest joy. If we can learn to look within ourselves for the abilities we possess, we can literally change the world. And that's just what I am working to do

---

Behind the Story

I first approached Nick's wife, Barbara, to see if she thought Nick might be interested in writing his story for *The Triumph Book*. I wanted an example to provide inspiration for those who have lost some form of physical ability to find purpose and meaning in their new, challenging condition. She brightened at the suggestion and told me that Nick is a motivational speaker and he would be perfect.

I then talked to Nick briefly on the phone about the idea and he was interested; so I set up an appointment to visit one morning. I figured I would spend about an hour explaining the project, but we had a discussion that morning which lasted four hours, and felt like a half hour. Though his height is shortened by sitting in a wheel chair, Nick is a giant of wisdom and inspiration. He gave me a powerful lesson that morning; a message about true wealth. He said that true wealth is good health.

He began by talking about tasks in life that people would rather not do... rolling the garbage can to the street, for example. He told me how much he would love to be able to do that, but he just can't in a wheel chair, with weakened arms. There are opportunities to provide service to others, such as helping someone move, that he is unable to give. Nick reminded me of all the things most people do every day, and don't think twice about... or even wish they didn't have to do... which would mean the world to someone who has lost that ability.

After sharing the development of his water purification business with me, Nick observed how those who are lacking safe drinking water are poor simply because they don't have good health as a result of the literally repulsive water.

"Think about how you feel when you are sick" Nick said, "You don't have the energy to do anything. When you are healthy, you are truly rich because you have the capability of accomplishing whatever you set out to do!"

It has been a pleasure to work closely with Nick. He has served both as an author of this book and a business coach offering me valuable advice.

Six

The Gift of Song

Author: Karyl Chase

I have never been inclined to turn down a challenge. I do not think myself great, but don't feel I should be judged by others who assume I cannot do something just because they say I can't. When I first joined the army, it was not only to get out of my small town; it was partly because everyone told me I could not do it. That one choice led me into a life of blessings and trials that have not stopped to this day. Upon completion of my military training, I was assigned to Ft. Hood, Texas. Of all the places I could end up, this was the last on my list. There are no mountains in Texas. All the things I had grown to love in my youth were missing and I was nervous to be out on my own for the first time in my life. Despite my reluctance, Heavenly Father had a plan for me. Within a month of moving to Ft. Hood, I met a wonderful young man, Allen, who soon became my husband.

I must tell you, I had developed a habit of protesting the events in my life. Before I joined the army, I swore I would never have anything to do with the military, but the moment I talked to the recruiter, I felt that it was exactly what I should do! I swore I would never move to Texas; then the Army stationed me in Ft. Hood. I also swore I would never date the man I would later marry. Now 15 years have passed and I am still married to him, grateful I did not heed my own ridiculous notion in the first place. I have been humbled and I have been taught by experiences over the years. I have found myself resisting change, but changing anyway. Life has a way of giving you what you never expect, and sometimes what you think you don't want.

The first time my husband, Allen, told me he was going to deploy to Iraq, I remember offering a prayer to my Father in Heaven. I stated that I expected He would never do this to me because He loved me too much. The answer I received to this supplication was that, "Yes, I love you, but I also love my other children." The words hung in my mind with so much power; I could only begin to understand that there was a greater purpose to the coming events. It was two years later when I said goodbye to my husband and sent him on his way; and it has been three years since then, but I still remember every touch and whisper we exchanged on the day he left. We were sitting on the bleachers in a gym that normally holds basketball games and other carefree events. It was a stark difference to our assembly: children clinging onto their parents and holding tight to the neck of the deploying member of their family; solitary soldiers sitting at the top of the bleachers, having already said goodbye to their loved ones; looking sad and torn.

This was not how I had seen it in film. Movies show families waving hankies, throwing confetti and kisses as the band plays in the background. Crowds are pushing forward to hail the soldiers onward. No, this was not anything like the movies. This was difficult. I wanted to make time stand still so I could hold onto my husband a little longer. Our children crowded around him and took turns telling Daddy about everything they were going to do when he was gone. They asked questions about where he was going, what he would see. They talked about how they would miss him.

Then there were moments when we could not think of anything more to say. In those moments, we sat close together and watched everyone else sharing the exact same goodbyes. I held back my tears as long as I could. I did not want mascara running down my cheeks and red-rimmed eyes to be the last memory my husband had of me. "Just breathe…" I whispered to myself. It worked for a good long time. My tears stayed tucked deeply behind my eyelids.

The final moment arrived, though, and the soldiers were told to line up in formation. Time had not stood still and now it was flying quickly past us. My husband gathered each of our children, one by one, into his arms. One by one he gave them a crushing bear hug and told them how much he loved them as he kissed them goodbye. Then he turned to me, grabbed me around the waist and kissed me. Finally, at that moment, time stood still. Every tender thought, hope and dream he had for me, for us, was expressed in that single instant. He loved me and I knew he was telling me goodbye for what he knew could be the last time.

As we took a step back from each other, he quickly rushed down the bleachers to the gym floor and lined up with the rest of his group. The Chaplain offered a prayer for our soldiers before they marched out the doors and began loading onto the gleaming white buses, with their engines humming loudly in the parking lot.

As the last soldier left the building, the families and friends pushed their way outside to catch a glimpse, one more time. It was difficult to see through the darkened windows, but every now and then a soldier would press their face up against the glass and we would be able to identify who it was. Suddenly, all those little gestures meant the world to us and I would have given anything to have one more goodbye.

Before the buses began to move out of the parking lot, I learned that no matter how alone I felt, I was not really by myself. Our three year old daughter, who was especially attached to Daddy, threw herself onto the ground crying for him. I tried to pick her up, but struggled to do so with our baby tucked in my other arm. My older boys tried to carry her, but they found it difficult to help a distraught little girl who suddenly realized her Daddy was not going to be coming home for a very long time. That is when a complete stranger came to us, picked up my daughter, and held her until she stopped crying. The kind woman helped us across the street and to our car before letting go. Yes, I still felt very alone, but I suddenly sensed hope and comfort. There would always be someone who would offer a hand, a shoulder or an ear when it was needed most. I would soon find myself indebted to friends and strangers alike, and would learn that the only way to repay their kindness was to do for others what was done for me.

That night we headed home and crawled into bed. I forced myself to bolt the door behind me, feeling guilty that I had locked my husband out. Most of the children climbed in bed with me and snuggled around Daddy's pillows. They had raided his shirt drawer and sprayed on his cologne so they could smell him all night. They were endearing, to say the least. I almost wished I was small enough to wrap his shirt all the way around me and cuddle up with his pillow like my six children were trying to do that night.

During the first month, we did not have the opportunity to hear from the soldiers. They were in transition and until they were at their final destination, we would have been lucky to hear from them at all. By Thanksgiving, though, we had fairly decent contact with them and it helped us get into the holiday season a little better. We spent the day with my in-laws and kept tradition by building graham cracker houses. I am certain we ate more candy than what ended up on our house, but it was wonderful not to be alone.

It never fails that when I get to this part of the story, I am at a loss to go further. There are so many things I would tell someone who is listening. I would tell them of the friends that give you strength or of the funny things that kids do. I would be willing to share how lucky I was to see my husband on webcam nearly every day at this point. Or I could tell you how, despite all the blessings you receive during deployment, there is nothing that prepares you for the loss of a loved one in combat.

I had always known my husband would come home safe. The feeling was strong and the Spirit had confirmed it to me. So, on a Sunday shortly after the New Year, I was counting my blessings that we had arrived at church on time, with all the children dressed and getting along. I sat in church thinking how nice it was to finally have everything fall into place. The house was in a rhythm, my children had fallen into regularity and I felt I might possibly make it through deployment without falling apart after all. However, about thirty minutes after the meeting started, I felt the deepest grief wash over me. Tears began to trace their way down my cheeks while my mind raced to find the cause of this feeling. The talks were all touching, but not so sentimental that I would feel this sad. My mind did not match the feeling in my heart at all. I felt as if I were in two different realities. My mind was in church thinking about the talks and the children; but my heart was in a world filled with a sorrow I had not felt since my Grandfather had passed away years before.

I began to weep openly and excused myself from any further meetings as I found a quiet corner to sit. Many of my friends tried to help by asking what was wrong. But what do you tell them, when you don't know yourself? I ached from the deepest part of my heart and though I was surrounded by dear friends, I felt completely alone.

I returned home from church to see a short message from my husband in Iraq. He said, "I need to talk. I lost my friend today."

When a soldier dies, everyone is put on blackout. It was more than three days later that I would be able to talk to him. In the meantime, I was feeling this intense grief that had started long before I read the message. It hit me while I was sitting in church. I could not place the feeling, and so I asked for a blessing. In the blessing it was stated that this was a manifestation of the Spirit to let me know what my husband was feeling,

68

and that it would not be the last time I would experience it. I was told that I would need to share this with others. I had no idea how. We all have stories that tear at our souls at times and mine was no different. It was just very personal.

After a few weeks had passed, my husband was finally able to share with me the circumstances of the death. He and his close friend Eric had been riding in an armored Humvee together when a sniper shot rang out and hit his friend, who was a gunner, straight in the head. He instantly slumped forward and Allen knew something was wrong. He pulled Eric into his arms after slicing through the straps that held him in place. As Eric lay in my husband's arms, he exhaled one last time. My husband leaned forward and kissed him on his forehead and said, "I love you brother." Then he treated his wounds as though he were alive, held him and prayed over him until they returned to the FOB (Forward Operating Base). He carried him from the vehicle and placed Eric in the hands of others who took his lifeless body away.

The two things that have stuck with me ever since include the whispered message "I love you brother," and how my husband prayed over Eric as he returned to the FOB. It was a witness to me of the terrific love that has developed between men who were once perfect strangers, who in almost any other circumstance would not qualify for the depth of love they have for each other. It struck me powerfully how, during the darkest time in someone's life and the ugliest times upon this earth, something as glorious as love can grow.

I do not think that anyone really knows their potential and the gifts that lie in store for them. I had no idea. Out of adversity come some of life's greatest gifts. As we were enduring so many emotions which could not be expressed in words, I felt strongly that I needed to find a way to deal with them. I discovered a powerful healing channel which I had never used before. Out of our grief I developed a deep interest in and talent for writing music.

Two weeks before I began to write my first song, I was visited by my sister and her family. Her husband sat down at my piano and shared a song that he had written. Song writing to me was always so amazing and serious that I was blown away when he played the funniest little song I had ever heard. It was complete *fun*. He taught me a great lesson in that moment, which is that I need not take myself so seriously when creating music; I should just let things happen.

The first day of writing songs started as my husband was slipping deeper into the grasp of PTSD (Post Traumatic Stress Disorder) and everyone was feeling the ill effects of it in our family. I sat myself down at the piano and began plunking out one note after another until I found a pattern of notes that reflected the feelings in our home. They were not dark, but more of a calming pattern which fit in, the way the right words can when comforting someone you love. I played them over and over again. The next day I repeated those notes, but found another tune emerging that matched well with that day's feelings. I began to write them down on paper and after two weeks, new melodies emerged and began to blend with each other until all those weeks of detached melodies became a song.

I was so excited to have written a song! I was so grateful for the gift that my Father in Heaven had given to me at such a critical time in my life. I expressed gratitude in prayer and before my prayer was finished, it was

Karyl Chase and her family

impressed upon my mind that I needed to write more music in relation to the first and create an album; and that I had not written my most difficult song yet. Throughout the next eight months I wrote one song after another, wondering if this was the most difficult or the next. Some songs were easy to play through. Most were about how others felt. Some were about the loss of dear friends and some were about the loss of memories that could never come to pass: like that dance with daddy or the walk down the road holding hands with the one you love; the chance for the boys to learn how to ride a bike or play baseball with their dad. I wrote about things so simple, yet important, which were being lost by the separation of deployment and loss of life.

It has been a year and a half since I was blessed with my first song and I am still grateful for every song that comes my way. Each one brings a new element to my life and thoughts that are unique to each person listening. I am often reminded of a scripture..."Let your light so shine before men that they may see your good works, and glorify your Father which is in Heaven." Matt. 5:16. What great direction that is, as we all have so much to share with others; some in deed, some in word, some in art and some through other acts of kindness and talents. From all of this, not only has sharing helped those I've reached, but it has strengthened me daily. I still have moments that bring me to my knees. I still have days when I wish for simpler times and for my family to be together again and complete. I guess that is why charity never fails. It is an act of love that lifts you as well as all those you serve.

Behind the Story

The trail of bread crumbs which led me to find Karyl and her beautiful music is a story in itself! In the fall of 2007, I was attending a conference called *Time Out for Women*. This is where I met a music composer named Kathaleen May. I carried Brynn's storybook with me to the conference that day and had an opportunity during a break to share it with Kathaleen, who cheerfully told me she had seen it before. I had given Brynn's book to someone she knew... small world! Then Kathaleen told me of her most current composition. She had recently recorded a song she wrote called "Edward's Lullaby." I was thrilled to learn about her talent because I had a desire to create a short video featuring Brynn's storybook, sharing the message that our stories bring healing and preserve the memory of our loved ones; so I asked Kathaleen if she might be willing to compose a song to go along with Brynn's video. She said she would be honored to create music so special for me and then handed me a demo copy of "Edward's Lullaby" as she had one with her.

I listened to her music on my drive home from the conference and was soon sobbing. *This was the song!* "Edward's Lullaby" was written as a ballad the character Edward, from the *Twilight Book Series*, could be singing to his love, Bella, as she slept. In the story, Edward secretly watches Bella sleeping, being careful not to touch or wake her. In many ways, the words and tempo of the song fit the feelings and message of Brynn's story perfectly. I can no longer touch her. When I arrived home, I immediately called Kathaleen and told her how perfectly the song fit the message of my video, and that it needed only a few revisions to the words. I asked her if she would be willing to write the small changes for me and if I could use this exact song for my project. Without a moment of hesitation, Kathaleen agreed to make the changes. This was on a Saturday evening. The very next Tuesday evening she was able to re-record the song, with Pat Autry's beautiful tenor voice singing the emotional and melodic verses. On Wednesday I sent Brynn's storybook overnight to a friend and expert videographer, Kris Malandruccolo, to have them combined into a video (*www.elegantvideosbykris.com*). By the very next Saturday, the video was finished.

From start to completion, from the moment I met Kathaleen to the creation of the video, was exactly one week! To me this was divine evidence that what I am striving to share with others is important. You can see Brynn's video, with "Brynn's Lullaby," on the Publish Your Story page of *www.TheTriumphBook.com*.

This narrative is the prelude to how I met Karyl Chase, but there is a little more story to be told. As I was fully immersed in developing the bereavement writing program, I was flying home to Eugene, Oregon, listening to an iPod (borrowed from my husband) for the first time. I was in awe of having my entire CD collection at my fingertips. As I was listening to the wide range of music I have collected over the years, I heard a song which carried such profound emotional ties that I began crying right there on the airplane, for no apparent reason other than the song, and my memories, struck me with great sentiment. In that same moment I had a realization: *music is an important a part of the writing and healing process in the program*!

I had begun recognizing that people frequently write music as a form of storytelling and healing from grief; and so I thought a CD of custom songs, designed as a companion to the writing program which helps evoke the emotions of the subject matter, would be a perfect addition. I called Kathaleen to see if she had additional songs which would be fitting for this need. She said she had a few and that a friend of hers, Karyl Chase, has been writing incredible songs as a form of therapy and a way of coping with her husband's Iraq war experiences.

And so the trail, approximately ten months after meeting Kathaleen, led me to Karyl Chase. What was most remarkable about meeting Karyl, and hearing her music, is that she was writing the *exact songs* I was looking for! She had songs entitled "Sorrow," "The Tears That Fall," "Hope" and "Joy." The titles of her songs were *key words* in the program I was creating! Equally amazing was that Karyl had never written music until a year previous to our meeting. Since my introduction to Karyl's music, she and Kathaleen have created a companion CD to *The Triumph Program*. The CD is entitled *One Journey,* as we all travel the same path of mortality together, and is available at *www.TheTriumphBook.com*. Most of the music is instrumental and a perfect tempo for writing and thinking. I couldn't have commissioned the songs more exactly for this program than they already were written.

Karyl continues to write and submit songs to me for sharing. I often ask her if she has written the hardest one yet. Karyl says she isn't sure, because each one is full of emotion and many are difficult to write, but she thinks it has not come to her thus far. She will be sure to let us know when it does!

Seven

Ryan's Song

Author: Jeff Salisbury

On the afternoon of June 4, 2005, my wife, Denise, and I noticed our son Ryan sitting and staring at his computer for a long time. This was not unusual, as he enjoyed playing internet games with his friends. This afternoon, however, was different. It was June 4, 2005. Ryan was struggling to finish the last paper required to graduate in just a few days from Churchill High School in Eugene, Oregon. It was complete, except for the final few summary sentences. Ryan just could not do it. The minutes turned into hours as he sat frozen, staring motionless at the monitor. Finally, Ryan acknowledged that he couldn't finish. I sat down and typed in the last three sentences for him so that he could graduate.

Ryan was a good student and had written many excellent papers in the past. Why couldn't he finish the last sentences of this final, important project? Why had he sat virtually motionless in front of his computer for so long? Something was very wrong! We later learned that Ryan had bipolar disorder. Over the next, and final, year and a half of Ryan's life, this anxiety repeated many times over. We watched as his life spiraled out of control, ultimately ending in a tragic and violent death. His death devastated our family for a very long time. This is Ryan's story—his legacy, his *song* and how our family has worked through the grief and pain. It is our hope that others experiencing similar losses will be encouraged and can realize that they deserve to gain a measure of peace and happiness despite the sadness and emptiness left behind by departed loved ones.

The Good Years

Up until that dreaded afternoon in June, Ryan's life had been filled with boyhood discovery, growth and happiness:

Animals & Nature

Ryan loved animals and nature. He found them kind, interesting and loving. As a five-year-old goalie for his soccer team, Ryan was more interested in the beautiful spotted leopard banner draped around the goal than the soccer game. He frequently stared at it—with his back to the players. When the crowd cheered because someone had scored a goal he was supposed to stop, he was startled back into reality! He didn't care because that leopard was *cool*.

When Ryan got a little older, Denise and I got him a pet rat, which he adored for the year he had it. When the rat died, Ryan cried, and when he looked up, we were crying too. Ryan felt sorry for its suffering; he knew he would miss his friend. Placing the rat in a Kleenex box coffin lined with tissues, we made our way to a grave we dug behind our house. Ryan cried, we prayed, and then he felt better.

As Ryan grew older, it came time to do his Eagle Scout project. Choosing the project was easy—he knew it would be at the Greenhill Humane Society. Ryan led a group that leveled ground and built a nice chain link dumpster surround; then we cleaned and striped the parking lot. It took eight to ten of us five Saturdays to finish. It made this special place nicer for people who love animals.

Toward the end of his life, when things got bad, Denise bought Ryan a pug puppy. That was a dream-come-true for Ryan. He called him Plugs. Boy was he a funny looking dog! I guess that's why Ryan loved him so much. Whenever Ryan came home, he hugged and kissed and chased him around the house on all fours. When they slept, Plugs was on Ryan's chest, snoring like a chain saw.

During high school, Ryan enrolled in the school's environmental program. They taught him to respect nature and keep the environment clean. They created a nature preserve and studied its growth.

Ryan enjoyed making movies with his friends. Austin, Chris and his other friends would go into the woods and film funny, scary movies. They called one of them *The Blair Scare Crow Project*. It made absolutely no sense, but they had a blast running around, screaming and spooking each other on film. Today that film is a precious family memento.

Scouting

Scouting has always been big in our family. When Ryan was a young boy, he, his brother Sean and I were *Native American Guides.* We went to pow-wows, and he'd sit between my legs. He was "Flaming Arrow" and I was "Flaming Tomahawk." Native Americans are spiritual people. We learned to dance and sing their lore and to appreciate their closeness to the earth and God.

In Cub Scouts, Denise was Ryan's den and pack leader. She taught him much, but he taught her more about boys, their energy and love of life. She feared he was hyperactive, but soon learned he just loved life, as did the other eight-year olds in her den. They had many good times together. Ryan's grandfather, Bob Thompson, was an engineer so Ryan did well in all the Pinewood Derby miniature car races. Ryan loved Grandpa Thompson for that. Ryan's smashing success bugged some of the other kids a bit, but everyone had a good time.

I was Ryan's Boy Scoutmaster. He loved the hikes and campouts. One time we did a long backpacking trip down the California Redwood Trail. Together, with his good friend Musashi who was from Japan, Ryan found a beautiful pool of deep clear water with high sand dunes around it. The whole troop swam for two solid hours. Later we hiked along the beach and camped by the ocean. The Redwoods were one of Ryan's favorite places on Earth. Musashi and Ryan were soul mates. They understood each other and laughed together constantly. Ryan called him "Sushi" and he called Ryan "Raman." Ryan always loved laughter. Two days before Ryan turned 18, he received his Eagle award, just like his older brother Sean, my father and I. It is a family tradition.

Sports and Friends

All three of Ryan's brothers, Sean, Ian and Kyle, played soccer, so Ryan did too. Playing the game was okay, but he liked it mostly because he could be with his friends, Austin, Chris, Paul, Marco and the others. His favorite play of all time was when Austin centered a shot to him from deep in the left corner. Ryan headed the ball hard into the left side of the net. Boy did he have a headache that night! The best part of the game was celebrating that play afterwards with his teammates. Friends and fun were what was important! He played high school soccer as a freshman, but his heart wasn't really into it. When it became highly competitive, it was no longer fun for Ryan. He sometimes just jogged up and down the field in games instead of running hard. He yearned to do something *different* from his brothers.

When Ryan's friend, Trevor, who is from Hong Kong, told him about a rugby team that was forming, Ryan's heart jumped. He wanted to be part of building this new team in a novel sport to our community. Austin, Trevor, and Ryan started playing at lunch, getting together with some kids from South Eugene High, forming a team. This team changed Ryan's life. They practiced in the mud and played on crummy fields with makeshift goal posts made of sticks, but they became a family. They would live and die for each other because they loved one another with all their heart. That's all that counted. The girls formed their own team and became their *sisters*. The boys were always there for them, and the girls always cheered for the boys, even when they drove farther distances, to Medford or Portland, for the games.

The first year the boys lost almost all of their games. But each year got better, and by the time Ryan was a senior, they came in second place in their region, missing first place by just one score. That didn't bother Ryan because he played rugby for the sheer joy of the sport. He especially enjoyed teaching newcomers how to play the game. The fact that Ryan was captain, team MVP and chosen for the Oregon All-State Team three years in a row was nice, but not as important as being with his friends.

Ryan's friends meant a great deal to him; he held his friendships sacred. Loyalty and trust were everything to his little band of brothers. They understood each other implicitly, and as boys will, they did some crazy things together. Such as the time Ryan put on snow skis and was towed behind a car for two blocks near the University of Oregon campus at midnight; or the time he climbed 30 feet to the top of the cliff at Triangle Lake and did a belly flop—on purpose. Or the time they went bush diving, and Ryan jumped into a big one, only to discover (and almost land on) a woman going potty on the other side. He told us he'd never forget the look on her face!

Family

Ryan's mother was his guardian angel. She saved his life numerous times during his last year and a half of life. She woke up once every night, often twice, to check on him. She tried to stop him from drinking or doing marijuana, which he did occasionally to self-medicate away his terrible, very real, mental pain. Her efforts bothered him some, but he grew to understand that she was trying to stop him from crashing the car or making his depression worse. Denise never gave up on Ryan and I believe loved him more than life itself, as she does all of our children. She took him to psychiatrists and counselors every week. At times Ryan's pain was so intense that he would cut his arms to try to divert his agony. It is hard to imagine how much pain he was in, but the fact that he would cut himself for relief is a clue to answering that question. Denise would hold him tightly in her arms after his more excruciating episodes. Ryan knew of her great love for him. I am so thankful for all of Denise's work, tears and love for our son.

As for myself, well, let's just say Ryan wore an old suit coat of mine around for the last two years of his life, rain or shine, almost every day. During the two years I served as his Scoutmaster, I had the joy of camping with him 20 times and of taking two 50 mile hikes together; one down the Rogue River in Southern Oregon and the other down the Redwood Trail at the California-Oregon border, and all the time with Ryan as my tent-mate.

Ryan and his brother Sean were intertwined like a pretzel. They did everything together when they were young, including sharing a room for the first nine years of Ryan's life. They created their own rope swing with their bedroom sheets tied together to swing from the upstairs to the downstairs like Tarzan. They had a lot of fun, until Ry told Mom about the swing!

Sean, Ryan and I built a big fort with a roof and secret passageways. It took us all summer to create. Ryan's younger brother, Ian, is something special too. One night in family prayer, when Ian was just a baby, I asked the Lord to help us all be obedient. Mixing-up the word "obedient," Ryan jumped up and yelled, "Please don't *beat Ian*! I won't beat Ian!"

Ryan always watched out for his little brother. To Ian's surprise, and laughter, Ryan would sneak attack him with bananas and other fruit. Ryan often used Ian to practice his rugby tackles. Ian knew of Ryan's strength and was nervous at times, but he trusted his brother and knew he'd never hurt him. The fact was Ryan loved to wrestle with his big and little brothers, to the detriment of the house at times.

Ryan's little brother, Kyle, was the apple of his eye. He looked out for Kyle, loved him so much, and would have done anything for him. There is not one family picture where Ryan isn't smiling big with his arm around one of his brothers. Ryan also loved and respected his Aunt Kim, who fights the same bipolar battle that Ryan fought and who understood him well. Ryan's other relatives were dear to him, especially his grandparents. He wore my father's (his "Papa's") red scotch plaid tam cap until the day he died because it made him feel close to him. Ryan knew Papa loved him because Papa squeezed so hard when he hugged him that he would almost suffocate. Our family calls that a "Papa Hug" to this day. Both of Ryan's grandmothers had a big soft spot in their heart for him as well.

Church

Ryan was a faithful churchgoer. His church is where he came to know his Savior, Jesus Christ. When he was 13, I took him alone to Utah for a couple of days. We saw a film about Christ's life and teachings. When Ryan watched Christ bless and minister to the people, he said he felt the Holy Spirit so strong he cried like a baby. I could tell right then that Ryan knew that God lived and loved him.

I think that's why Ryan went to a church class for four years during high school at 6:30 each morning. During his senior year, Ryan started not being able to fall asleep until the wee hours of the morning, even with getting up at 6:00 a.m. every morning. We took him to a sleep specialist, who wasn't able to help, but not because he didn't try. Ryan didn't want to stop his early morning scripture study but he was starting to fall asleep in school. That's when I agreed to study scriptures with Ryan at night, so he could get some much-needed sleep in the morning. We now know this inability to fall asleep was one of the first signs of bipolar, but along with the doctor, we didn't want to jump to, or even think about, that diagnosis because of the reality of what it would mean. So every other possible reason was explored.

Ryan's Final Days

After more than 17 good years, things started to go bad at the end of Ryan's senior year at Churchill High. This brings us back to the beginning of my story, and the end of Ryan's life. As noted, we finished Ryan's paper for him, and he did indeed graduate a few days later. This was not the happy ending we would have wanted or expected. Ryan began to have increasing anxiety and fears. Things he was able to do with ease before became daunting tasks; simple endeavors such as getting a haircut or talking on the phone. Ryan was barely able to leave the house without great anxiety. Even the most ordinary tasks would take great courage for him to attempt.

His good friend, Mushashi, had moved to Hong Kong a year earlier, but they made plans for him to come back at graduation and go hiking in Yosemite with Ryan's scout troop. They had planned all year. Even as Mushashi flew to Eugene and Ryan's backpack was ready, Ryan was too riddled with anxiety to come with Ian, the troop and me to this long-planned dream trip. He didn't know why and, as everyone left without him, he broke down in tears and knew he needed help. Miraculously, he got in to see a psychiatrist within the next few days. Usually this would take weeks, if the psychiatrists were even taking new patients at all. Ryan was diagnosed with severe anxiety disorder and depression, a condition caused by chemical imbalances in the brain. Doctors believe this is genetic, and Ryan's family did have a history of depression, anxiety and bipolar disorder.

Ryan responded well to medication and was finally falling asleep at night with little effort. His psychiatrist thought he was doing well enough on his new medication that he could go to college, as he had previously planned. He started his first year at Utah Valley State College (UVSC) in Orem, Utah, August 2005. This school has one of the best four-year paramedic degrees around, as well as a top-notch rugby team. Ryan did alright for a while. I'll never forget attending the BYU versus UVSC rugby game. Ryan not only made the varsity team, he was their starting scrum half (i.e., quarterback). BYU ranked second in the nation at the time, and they shellacked UVSC. Ryan played flawlessly and fearlessly that night. He loved every minute of the game, despite the lopsided final score. Denise and I watched proudly from the sidelines, our hearts brimming with happiness for our strong, handsome son emerging into manhood before our eyes.

Sadly, Ryan's medication levels were difficult to maintain correctly, so he started feeling bad later in September. Things got worse. He was sad, lonely, couldn't sleep and felt like a failure because he couldn't bring himself to go to all his classes, even though he made a sincere effort. Late one Sunday night, he wrote me an e-mail. I received it Monday morning. At first I was ecstatic to open it and hear from Ryan, but my happiness turned to horror when I read the e-mail he had written at 3:05 AM:

"When we talk on the phone, I lie. I am not okay. I don't like it here. I can't get sleep and I miss most of my classes. I feel un-motivated. I haven't made any friends. I've never felt this depressed in my whole life. I can't explain it, I feel like swallowing all of my pills and killing myself. This place is not for me. I need to get out of here."

81

Denise flew-in on the first plane she could catch. Ryan had an emergency doctor's appointment scheduled for early the next morning. After Denise arrived in Utah, she had dinner with Ryan, and he seemed a bit calmer. When she went to pick him up the next morning, Ryan didn't answer the door. As Denise walked into the apartment she noticed blood throughout the bathroom and Ryan passed out on his bed. He had taken a bottle of sleeping pills, another bottle of anti-anxiety medication and, for the first time, had cut his arms terribly with a razor blade that night. Denise took Ryan to the local hospital immediately, where they pumped his stomach. He spent the next week in the psychiatric ward where he received treatment from a psychiatrist who used to play rugby and took a genuine liking for Ryan.

After being sedated for a day, the doctor told Denise that they were amazed at how Ryan had been actively helping the other patients by talking with and showing great compassion for them. Ryan told Denise he did this because he could see they were having a harder time than he was, suffering from such difficult mental illnesses. A nurse asked Ryan why he wanted to become a paramedic and his response was that he wanted to help people in trouble. A few days later, the doctor diagnosed Ryan with major depression and anxiety. Then he was released to return home to Oregon with Denise. On the way, Ryan told her how sorry he was about everything and promised to try to do better. Ryan confided that what he feared most was setting a bad example for his two younger brothers. Denise pulled the car off the road at that moment; they held each other and wept openly together.

At home, a week later, Ryan went into a manic rage. He cut his arms with a kitchen knife and repeatedly banged his head hard against his bedroom wall and the garage door. Denise and I called 911. A remarkable firefighter came and calmed Ryan down, then took him to the emergency room. Ryan spent the next week in the psychiatric unit in lock-down. He didn't like it there because of all of the sad people who had such serious problems. There again, after a few days, Ryan found peace by playing his guitar for the other patients and helping them in any way he could. The psychiatrist diagnosed Ryan with severe Bipolar Disorder. They had seen the depression and anxiety, but now they saw the manic side—the last piece of the puzzle needed to diagnose him.

Over the next several months, Ryan had good and bad times. The good times were hanging out with his friends, strumming his guitar and playing computer games. He liked the guitar and computer games because he could do them without failing, so they were safe. The bad times were late at night when he was unable to sleep, being alone and sad about life. The Bipolar Disorder made Ryan feel actual pain throughout his body. It was very real. That's one of the reasons he would cut himself, drink alcohol and take marijuana on occasion. One night he was down and hurting so horribly that he went to the garage at 2:00 a.m. and ran his car with the doors shut to suffocate himself. When Denise went to check on him that night, she found him pale and dazed in the car. Panicked, she and I raced Ryan to the emergency room. To our surprise, the nurse thought what Ryan had done was actually funny because, as he told us, exhaust from cars made after 1995 can't hurt you because they don't give off much carbon monoxide. Looking back, I guess all of our panic and commotion might have looked comical. I think even Ryan felt it was amusing!

Constant doctor visits and counseling sessions with people who wanted to help never did much good for Ryan. The hope he had gained several months before was fading, although he continued to fight courageously for his life. He felt increasingly trapped in a state of nothingness, sadness and failure. During his last month of life, beginning mid October 2006, Ryan lost the 20 pounds he'd gained as a side effect from taking the various medicines prescribed him. I remember looking at his bottles of medication, seeing that there were six of them to be taken daily and he was barely 19 years of age. It made me cry like a baby. It wasn't fair, and we all knew it; but Denise and I were at a pitiful loss as to what to do for this son that we loved so much. Ryan eventually stopped spending time with his pug dog, Plugs, and even with his friends. His girlfriend couldn't help what was attacking him, although their love and our family's love helped, and we did have some good times together. The more Denise and I tried to help, the worse he felt, because he comprehended that we couldn't, which brought a sense of dejection, believing he was constantly letting us down.

Ryan's psychiatrist told us during this time that he needed a second opinion because Ryan should be responding better to his medications. Ryan had fallen into a state of deep depression and anxiety. Ryan agreed, and a week before his death, as we sat in the new doctor's office, Ryan told him that he wanted to live but he was afraid and needed help. The doctor said he wanted to increase his medications, but that doing so would create a risk of sending him into a dangerous manic state.

With Bipolar Disorder, it is always hard to reach the delicate balance between manic and depressed states, as medications can tilt victims dangerously to one side or the other. All of us knew that Ryan needed to take this risk. We were all-but-certain to lose him if we didn't get him out of his deeply depressed, suicidal condition. Things were so bleak during this period that every time I opened a door within our home, I feared seeing Ryan behind it, lying dead.

After a week of the new medication, and some very hard and frightening times for Ryan, he woke up at about 10:30 p.m. on November 13, 2006. He said he felt better than he had in a long time. He felt the new medicine had finally kicked in. He had been asleep for the last 24 hours and wanted to work off some energy, so he informed us he'd be gone for a couple of hours to play video games with his friends. We were relieved to hear he was feeling better.

A few hours later, Denise realized that Ryan had taken his night-time medicine, which included anti-anxiety medicine, and that he shouldn't be driving. When Denise called him on his cell phone in the wee hours of the night, his speech was slurred, and we knew his high doses and mixes of prescription medications had altered him. To make matters worse, he was driving his car with two close friends riding along. Denise and I had previously vowed we would not allow Ryan to drive under the influence of alcohol or drugs, legal or not. We decided to meet Ryan and bring him home, dropping his friends off along the way. What we didn't know at the time was that Ryan's good mood upon waking earlier that evening was merely the start of him spiking into the dangerous manic condition that we knew was a possible risk of the medication change.

When Ryan arrived home, he was overcome by a raging power and force the likes of which I've never seen. Upon leaving the car in the garage, he smashed a window with his fist. A few minutes later, inside the house, he took his electric guitar and smashed his bedroom window. Then a moment or two after that we began to hear Ryan smash many of the other windows and walls in our home, along with other objects. There was a tremendous amount of noise. As Denise and I look back on it all, we're convinced the reason Ryan did this was to help him get ready to die. The explosion gave him courage and a bigger reason to succeed in finishing what he had not been able to do before. He did not smash our family pictures, any pictures of Jesus Christ, my father's retirement clock, or the hutch filled with family mementos that had belonged to Denise's mother. Ryan still loved and regarded our family, and the Lord, even though life had been unfair to him and he did not understand how that could be.

During the chaos, I heard Ryan downstairs and went to calm him. I was scared for him, afraid for my family and even for myself. Ryan brandished a kitchen knife and told me to back off or he'd use it on himself right then and there. Not knowing what Ryan was capable of in his hyper-manic state, Denise and I gathered Ian and Kyle, along with our nephew who was visiting, into our walk-in closet in the master bedroom area. I had just undergone shoulder surgery and lacked muscle strength, so I grabbed a telescoping Billy-club. Then Ian and I moved a couch in front of the inside of the bedroom door to barricade Ryan out. We huddled together as a family as the banging and crashing resumed, afraid, traumatized, and listening to our beloved boy, trapped in the throes of a titanic psychotic break, destroy our home and himself in the process.

We had called 911 not long after the episode began but we hung-up the phone before the call went through. We were afraid that the police might come and only make matters worse. We held out hope for a few minutes that Ryan might calm down. We were most afraid that any of our actions might cause Ryan to stab himself. When it became apparent that this was not going to happen, we called again, and the police were dispatched. We were always told by the doctors that if we ever needed help getting Ryan to the hospital, we should call the police as they were trained to handle volatile situations better than we could. This was the case a year earlier, when the well-trained firefighter calmed Ryan and helped bring him to the hospital for desperately needed medical help. We begged the 911 operator to prevent Ryan from being hurt. He was experiencing a Bipolar psychotic break and needed hospitalization for help. We asked her to have the police arrive silently, without any lights glaring, as we feared that might only agitate Ryan more. She asked us to stay in the room, on the phone with her. Almost fifteen long minutes after our call, the police finally arrived, unbeknownst to Ryan. In the meantime, he had gone down to the crawl space beneath our house and swallowed a box of rat poison. He was suffering unspeakably.

After that, Ryan stormed up the stairs to our bedroom. Despite our couch barricade, and notwithstanding Ian and my best efforts to hold the couch against the door to keep it closed, Ryan smashed himself into it with incredible force. He burst through to our room, with the kitchen knife at his side in one hand and the box of rat poison in the other. Denise and I looked at each other, dreading whatever would happen next. I was acutely aware of Ryan's superhuman strength and my utterly weakened surgery condition. One of the hardest things I've ever had to do was ask my son Ian to stand by me, ready to defend Denise and Kyle to the end if necessary, against my own son; a son that I loved dearly.

Leaning through the doorway, Ryan surprised all of us by merely throwing the rat poison box in, telling us he had swallowed its contents, and then saying, "See, this is what I've done." Never intending to harm us, he tossed the box toward us, did an immediate about-face and left the room—and the house. I felt ashamed and guilt-ridden for ever doubting Ryan's love for us and for thinking that he might try to hurt us, or worse. That was never his intention, and I will always regret those feelings and the fact that I doubted him.

From there, Ryan left the house to go to the park across the street to die alone. I know in my heart that he took the knife to use on himself in case the poison didn't work or, alternatively, to use as he had in the past to cut his arms and redirect his intense pain. Denise and I went to the bedroom window, which overlooks the driveway leading to the sidewalk and street below. We still had hope that the police would know what to do and help us get Ryan to the hospital for the medical help he desperately needed.

The police, much to our chagrin, had their lights swirling and flashing. There were four of them, and each had assumed military sharpshooter positions with high-powered rifles trained on Ryan. That was a sight we would have given anything to avoid. The street was empty, as it was 3:00 a.m. The police had barricaded themselves behind our neighbor's large SUV. Once again we told the 911 operator that Ryan didn't hurt us, so please tell the police not to hurt him, and that what he needed was to go the hospital. The momentum toward a tragic conclusion was becoming unstoppable. I held on to Denise at the window, watching in disbelief at what was happening just 50 feet away, on our driveway under the nightlights of our garage.

Ryan headed down the driveway to cross the street toward the park. He was surprised to see the officers at the bottom of the driveway with guns trained on him. One officer shouted at Ryan at the top of his lungs to "Drop the weapon!" Ryan was walking toward the park with the knife at his side, never raised. The officer nevertheless sounded like an army drill sergeant, barking out a command. Ryan decided not to drop the knife, because he wanted to die, not live-on only to suffer more. The police then shot Ryan with beanbags, which we later learned were like being hit with a 90 mph fastball. Just one is supposed to stop a man. Ryan was hit four times, but kept walking right through them, which is not uncommon for someone in a mental health crisis, as we learned later.

Within seconds, the officer shouted one last time, "Drop the weapon!" Ryan couldn't. He had poisoned himself and wanted to die. He just kept walking down the driveway and told them "Shoot me, man, shoot me!" At about 20 feet from the riflemen, Ryan crossed within a few steps of the police union's magic-line of self-defense, authorizing the use of deadly force. One of the officers decided to shoot our boy, five times with his rifle, and he did it in less than two seconds in rapid, metered precision, striking his torso.

I turned away just as the shots were fired, not able to bear the sight. My dear, sweet wife, however, looked on steadfastly as Ryan crumpled to the ground onto his back. I smashed my fist through our bedroom wall near the bathroom. We rushed downstairs and headed out of the door, only to be stopped by one of the officers. He told us we could not go to our son because "it was a crime scene"... acid in our wounds. We were scared of this man and his gun, after what we had just seen. We just wanted to hold our Ryan to tell him we loved him before he died. We weren't allowed that small comfort. We ran back upstairs and wept bitterly with our young sons. We knew we couldn't help Ryan, but tried to at least be there for our other sons.

The Aftermath

Immediately after losing Ryan, in the midst of the agony, the miracles began, though we did not see or even want to acknowledge them at that moment. Denise and I knew this would be a heavily publicized tragedy, which the media could hardly ignore. That meant our family's most private moments would be tossed to the wind for the entire world to know. We also perceived that this event would change our lives forever, and there could be no turning back. Right at that exact moment, we resolved to forgive the officers. They were just doing their job; they were not heroes, but neither were they villains.

They acted out of fear, as would most of us. We forgave them not because we were good people, but for the simple reason that we did not want to live out the remainder of our lives as bitter people, and I personally did not want to rob my beautiful wife and children of their right to seek joy in life. Thus, Denise and I resolved two other commitments in that hour—to always tell the plain and simple truth about Ryan and to honor his good name faithfully. Our unwavering decision to forgive the police and truthfully honor Ryan through the remainder of our days has been the key, allowing us to move forward with our lives with a measure of peace.

In the midst of the tears that early morning, I gathered our family and read them two scriptures. The words sunk in deep, and we clung to them tightly. After the trauma, noise and chaos of the tragedy subsided, we traipsed our family across the street to the home of our good friends,

Rodger and Cindy Shaver. We spent most of the day crying in one another's arms and calling family members to share the devastating news. I can vividly remember calling, first my mother and then my two sisters, each one responding the same—shrieks, whimpers and tears. I hated having to make those calls, as I knew the news would only break their hearts as our family's had been broken. Denise made similar calls to her family, with identical results. The hardest call of all was to our oldest son, Sean, who was in Utah at the time attending school. Upon hearing of the loss of his beloved little brother, he cried out in anguish and threw his cell phone down to the pavement where he stood.

Later that day, a large group of friends and community members came by our home and worked all day to clean-up the broken glass and board-up the windows. That evening our son Ian was scheduled to play soccer with his high school team in the Oregon State Semi-final championship. He couldn't play; he just did not have the heart for it. We attended the game as a family, in support of Ian, who sat on the bench with his teammates. His teammates all wore blue arm bands in honor of Ryan and dedicated the game to his memory, playing like angry dragons, but losing a heart-breaking game in double overtime, 1-0. Determined not to allow the loss of Ryan to claim our home, we drove there quietly and spent a grief-stricken night together inside our boarded-up house.

Carrying On

The next day the prediction that our grief would not be private came true. A large picture of our smashed-up home was on the front page of the local paper, distributed throughout our county of over 300,000 people. The coverage continued similarly with front-page stories and pictures of Ryan over the next three days. Then the TV media began calling.

Denise and I talked and agreed that we had to go public with Ryan's story because the truth of that night was not being told. The world had to know that he never threatened to hurt us during his last moments, and equally important, we wanted everyone to know that he was a good... a great... courageous person who had succumbed to a terrible mental illness. Later we came to realize that we had been given an important opportunity to speak out about Bipolar Disorder. We needed to teach the public that its victims are not crazy, but need medical and psychiatric help, just as anyone suffering from any other disease needs professional help. We began to give interview after tearful interview to the press and the local TV stations. As we did, the truth about Ryan and about Bipolar Disorder began to emerge.

At the same time, our family started receiving an outpouring of love and compassion from family, friends, and community members, many of whom we had never met. They were moved by our sad drama, often because they too had loved ones suffering from various mental illnesses. First, there was a trickle of gestures, then a torrent. The boost we received from each card, bouquet, visit, meal and phone call was enormous. We remember thinking how each gesture sustained us for an hour or so until the next one arrived.

Denise and I began each day, over the next week, by waking-up and crying like babies in each other's arms, usually for about an hour. We would then shower, crying ourselves out in the warm flowing water. I can remember thinking how convenient it was to have the tears washed away down the drain without having to soak tissues or handkerchiefs. Sean and his beautiful fiancée, Amy, flew home from Utah to be with us, and other family members soon joined us from Arizona, California and Colorado. One of the tenderest moments Denise and I witnessed was Amy sitting on the couch with her arm around our youngest son, Kyle, quietly snuggling close, sharing their grief and the early kernels of healing.

The second day after the loss, we received word from Ryan's rugby friends that there was going to be a vigil, an outdoor candlelight observance, held the next night in the park across the street from our home. That evening the vigil began as scheduled. At first, we could see a few teenagers gathering in the park, their candles flickering in the cold breeze. Then it started to rain, and the candles went out. We couldn't have that, so we invited them into our home, an invitation they gladly accepted. An amazing thing happened that evening as more and more youth showed-up at our house. They came from our local Churchill High School as well as our cross-town rival, South Eugene High School. They came together that evening to share their pain and to strengthen one another, as they were members either of Ryan's rugby team, the girl's rugby team, or just friends of Ryan or friends of friends of Ryan. It was a gathering of the two highly competitive schools in the community. A gathering of love and closeness between these two groups had never before occurred and may never again.

When all was said and done, there was a throng of 60 or 70 kids in our house. They spread-out through the halls, in Ryan's room, in the entryway, and across every nook and corner they could find. They would gather in large group-hugs on the floor, crying, then laughing, crying and laughing again, as they remembered Ryan. We prayed together on our knees through the choked-up emotions, and the youth spoke softly to

Denise and me of Ryan and his impact on their lives. As the evening concluded, the youth filed out of the house reverently, one by one. Every single one of them told us, as they left, how special Ryan had made them feel. Every one of them gave us a big hug as they left through the door. We knew the hugs were for Ryan, but we appreciated them nonetheless. We were drained and filled at the same time. We were especially humbled and in awe at the greatness of our son as witnessed to us by his many loving and loyal friends.

This feeling of awe continued two days later on November 18, 2006, when funeral services were held for Ryan Stewart Salisbury. About 400 people came to pay their last respects for this young teenage boy. We sat together as a family, but when Denise saw Ryan's best friend, Austin, quietly weeping alone, she gathered him into our family's midst, and he sat the rest of the evening shoulder to shoulder with us.

Our family's hearts were full that evening, full of love, of grief and of gratitude, full of so many different emotions swirling within us. Two of Ryan's friends, Sarah and Austin, through strength and tears, spoke of their memories of Ryan. Denise and I were stirred and so proud when our oldest son, Sean, gave a talk about Ryan and how the grace of the Lord Jesus Christ would bless him. I then gave Ryan's eulogy, which was the hardest thing I have ever done, other than closing Ryan's casket after the viewing had taken place just before the service. Then there was a beautiful rendition of "Going Home" sung by a friend with a superb base-voice, which penetrated deep inside all who were present. The service concluded with the powerful call of bagpipes, a hail that pierced us to the deepest core.

The generous gestures we were receiving were all loving and supportive—everyone wanted to do something but were unsure how to express their sentiments. We quickly learned that how they expressed themselves really didn't matter; what counted was what was in their hearts. Thus, every communication from someone's heart touched us deeply, regardless of the form it took. Each communication helped us along our way until the next bouquet was delivered, the next meal was dropped-off, or the next visit from well-wishers occurred. These expressions were like stepping stones on which we depended to get us across dark, murky waters toward a distant light, which grew a tiny bit brighter each day.

A few days after the funeral, we received a phone call from Robert Lehner, the Eugene Chief of Police. He wanted to visit us with Alex

Gardner, the Lane County Assistant District Attorney. We agreed to meet with them and were anxious to hear what they had to say. As a practicing attorney, I surmised they wanted to dissuade us from bringing a wrongful death civil lawsuit against the city. Looking back, that in fact probably was their aim. However, as Denise and I told them at the beginning of the meeting, we did not intend to file suit, though we had discussed that possibility. There were two reasons for this decision: first, we would not drag the memory of our sweet son through the public mud of litigation... and we would most certainly not do it for money; second, we knew that a lawsuit might only canker us and turn a tragic loss into a bitter war of words and emotions.

I believe that expressing no desire to sue changed the course of our meeting. Shortly after indicating our intentions, Chief Lehner revealed two things to us which I doubt he would have ever shared otherwise. First, an immediate member of his family suffered from a serious mental illness. He made it clear, in very personal terms, that he understood much of what we had experienced. He then changed directions, looked us in the eye and told us that, had his officers been armed with taser stun guns, there was a good chance that Ryan would have survived that fateful night. That revelation struck Denise and I with force, and it started us thinking, not about vengeance, but about the good that might come out of our heartache. We wondered how many other victims of mental illness the police might have shot as a means of subduing them, rather than using other, non-deadly forms of force.

Honoring Ryan's Legacy

While we pondered this epiphany, we took note that some of the cards we had been receiving included money donations. At first, we had no idea what to do with these gifts. We thought about passing the funds along to Greenhill Humane Society, our local animal shelter, because Ryan had loved animals so much and had performed his Eagle service project there. One day we read a letter to the editor in our newspaper. A woman named Sue Archibald wrote it. She suggested in the letter that a fund be collected in Ryan's honor to establish a police awareness-training program on how to deal with people in mental health crisis like Ryan had been. She called the program Crisis Intervention Team Training, or "CIT."

Crisis Intervention Training[1]

When Denise and I read that letter, we began to think long and hard about whether we should devote ourselves to a cause in Ryan's name. On the one hand, we were already busy people with work, family, church and other obligations. On the other hand, the memory of Ryan worked deep within us, and it did so in a way we could not fully understand. We simply knew we needed to do something with this loss, partly because of our love for Ryan, partly because of the very public nature of his death, and partly because we wanted Ryan to have a legacy, a legacy that would both honor him and benefit our community. Mostly it was because we didn't want any other family to go through the pain, heartache and loss we were enduring.

We resolved then and there to spend the time and emotional energy necessary to contribute to the City of Eugene, not a contribution of money, but of time, labor and tears. We knew the task would be neither pleasant nor convenient, but that didn't matter. Something had to be done. Our son was a wonderful young man; he deserved to leave a legacy despite his short life. Thus, our goal became to benefit Eugene, Ryan's memory and, frankly, ourselves. We realized that by channeling our grief into something positive, we could find a way to let go of some of the pain and emptiness. We hoped that by staying busily engaged in doing something for others, others who faced challenges similar to ours, we could one day look back and see goodness come from the loss of our son.

After reading Sue's letter, Denise and I called and arranged a visit together. She told us during the visit of an organization she was forming called Approved Steps to Supplement Emergency Responder Training (ASSERT) intended to develop CIT in Eugene and Lane County, the county where Eugene is located. ASSERT operated under the guidance of the National Alliance on Mental Illness (NAMI). We gave Sue the funds we had already received from our friends and concerned citizens. We then let the newspaper and other friends and neighbors know about our association with Sue and ASSERT and that we would gladly accept donations for this worthy cause. I sent out e-mails to my professional contacts, many of whom responded generously. Our neighbors, the Shavers, made a generous contribution. On and on went the outpouring of generosity. Within two months, approximately $8,000 had been

---

[1] To learn more about Crisis Intervention Training you can visit these websites: _www.nami.org/cit_ or _www.cit.memphis.edu_.

contributed, mostly in $25 and $50 increments, showing that people of limited means made many of the donations.

Denise, Sue and I began to read more and more about CIT. The essence of such a program is to teach police officers how to de-escalate traumatic situations involving mentally ill or emotionally disturbed individuals. The objective is to calm the situation down, leading to a peaceful, rather than a tragic, ending.

Sue told us that CIT began in Memphis, Tennessee, through the leadership of a visionary police chief. Memphis found that the death and injury rate in such situations declined markedly. Not only were the mentally ill safer, the officers also fared better when properly trained in CIT techniques. Denise and I learned the reason is simple: *mentally ill people are not criminals; they are just like you and me*, except they have a chemical imbalance within them that skews their thoughts and actions. That slant need not be dangerous however, especially when those suffering with a disorder are treated with knowledge, understanding and respect.

Over the next two years, Denise and I attended numerous meetings of the City's Police Commission Mental Health Subcommittee. We shared our story of Ryan several times, usually through a hail of tears. We emphasized how the police shouting at Ryan to "Drop the weapon!" only heightened his disoriented state, and how a trained, calming influence may have saved his life. The members of the Subcommittee listened keenly. They were always courteous and frequently emotional. After each appearance, there were the inevitable television and newspaper interviews, which we routinely obliged in order to spread our message and galvanize public opinion in favor of CIT.

Over time, it became apparent that CIT would be approved by the City for implementation by the police department. I'll never forget the joy and happiness of learning from our friend, Sue, that the City had formally approved its first week long CIT of approximately 20 officers. We were humbled when asked, as a family, to be guests of honor at the small "graduation" ceremony conducted at the end of each of the police CIT training sessions.

Since then, additional CIT have been scheduled in Eugene and we have learned that CIT has been funded at Lane County for their sheriffs. At the state level, CIT is being included at officer training school, though not at the full 40 hour level. CIT is gaining momentum. Quietly, in our hearts, Denise and I are pleased and even fulfilled by our conviction that, thanks to Ryan's "song," played and heard around our hometown and county, the sanctity of life will be better honored. More people will be saved as our police force gains and uses its valuable new CIT techniques for many years to come.

Taser

The other branch of the Police Commission, the *Use of Force Sub-committee*, had also been stirred by Ryan's violent and tragic death. I was reminded of Chief Lehner's acknowledgement to me that the use of a taser might have saved Ryan's life. Here again, Denise and I saw an opportunity to give our city something it had avoided for years—the use of an alternative to lethal force. Our hearts swelled with hope as we thought about the powerful combination of life-saving tools our police would have if both CIT and tasers were provided in tandem. During Ryan's tragic incident of November 14, 2006, the police could have first, tried CIT de-escalation techniques on him and then, if that didn't work, a taser stun force could be applied. Either of these would have brought the situation to a point where the police could simply take Ryan to the hospital for treatment.

Historically, Eugene had resisted taser usage adamantly. Chief Lehner made that clear to Denise and me when, during his visit, he told us that he and previous chiefs had been trying to get taser usage approved in Eugene for years. The City has a powerful and effective segment that made clear its view that taser usage was painful and cruel. While I have never denied the real and painful five-second 50,000-volt electric shock administered by a taser, I am convinced that such a shock is a more humane method of dealing with a deeply agitated person than shooting them. What we would give to have our Ryan back alive with us, even with a nasty taser experience in his past and a couple of tiny burn marks on his body! We have no doubt that all family members of every police-killing victim would feel the same way, as would the police shooters themselves.

Denise and I were committed, and we were not about to let go, or to let down the potential, future victims of police lethal force. So it went, hearing after hearing, month after month, testimony, media interviews, tears, and anguish. Then there were the drafting sessions where the language eventually settled upon allowing for taser usage in limited circumstances, i.e., when necessary to protect against imminent bodily harm and as an alternative to the use of lethal force.

A consensus was eventually reached, after more than a year of struggle. Once a detailed directive had been created, it was forwarded to Chief Lehner in whom the final decision rested. We had no doubt he would sign the proposed policy and implement the directive, which he did—promptly. There are now forty taser guns assigned to Eugene duty police officers and we expect the rest of the force to have them soon.

Since the distribution of tasers over just the past year or two, there have been at least six major incidents involving the use of tasers documented in our local paper. We have read them with great interest. In each instance, tasers were used as an alternative to lethal force. Some members of the community predictably voiced their opposition based on the pain inflicted on the suspects targeted by the police. Upon hearing that opposition, Denise and I recalled the pain and anguish inflicted on Ryan and on us, his family. We quickly re-confirmed in our mind the saving virtue of the taser shocks which in all likelihood saved most or all of those six lives.

Ryan's Song

In addition to our faith in Christ, what kept us going through all of this was our love for Ryan, our family and our desire for his life to take on added meaning. He'd already provided, during his life, great meaning to us as a family. He had been our sparkplug, the one that got us excited and jazzed about everything. He brought passion and zeal to our table every day. He had been similarly meaningful and loved by his friends. Using his life and memory to shake up Eugene was a natural extension of Ryan's own way of life, something he'd always done.

More than three years have now passed since Ryan was taken from us. We continue to miss him dearly, at times bitterly. We don't expect that those emotions will ever completely go away. He was too much a part of our life. We poured too much of ourselves into raising him. He was a great soul. We would be untruthful if we pretended these deep and tender feelings didn't exist. Denise and I vowed we would never be dishonest about anything relating to Ryan, because that, in and of itself, would be a form of dishonoring his memory.

At first, after losing Ryan, I felt a heavy sense of guilt, not for thinking I could have been a better father to him, which I'm sure I could have, but for fearing that someday I would be healed from his loss. That was something I dreaded because to be healed would only cement his death and loss in the book of history. Early on, I didn't want to lose any part of my connection to Ryan, even one tenuously grief-ridden. Now, however,

Denise and I are beginning to understand the circle of life in a way that we could never understand before Ryan's death. It is an understanding of our own mortality, one that we must face regardless of whether it arrives sooner or later. Humility and peace comes from this understanding. The humility follows from comprehending our human limitations, limitations of all varieties, limitations we used to brush aside. Peace comes from knowing that it's normal to have limitations, and from knowing that we need not impose expectations on ourselves—or anyone else for that matter—that are arbitrary or unrealistic. There is a meaningful acceptance of self, friends, family and life itself, which has evolved from this experience. There is a warming fire inside that burns brighter than before, which makes us want to do whatever we can to help those around us, just as Ryan devoted his life to being there for his family and friends.

Ryan Salisbury

Despite these hard realities, each member of our family has been given great gifts because of our season with Ryan. As time has passed, we have experienced what I could only describe as the slow but certain miracle of *healing*. Drop by drop, as we have continued to love one another, to care about each other on a daily basis, we feel stronger and better able, not only to hang-on, but to strive for happiness. This was another issue we faced after losing Ryan—were we worthy to be happy individuals? How could we be content ever again after losing a beloved child, a child whose life was cut short, while we plodded on with our own? Was that fair to Ryan? We eventually concluded that not only are we entitled to happiness, but we also must seek and experience it in order to be good parents to our family and loving spouses to one another. My wife and children are beautiful people who deserve a joyful life; we need each other emotionally, physically and spiritually. Ryan would have wanted that; it was the way he lived his life.

Ryan's Song plays on, gently in the back of my mind, as I know it does within Denise and our children, every day of our lives. Even though he is gone from us now, we sense his spirit close by and we live a fuller and richer life because of him. We made a choice early on to honor him by the way we conduct ourselves. That is a powerful motivation to press forward, enjoying the blessings of life that we have been given. The fact that, thanks to Ryan's memory and legacy, we have been able to give a little something back to our community has been a meaningful tribute to Ryan and a healing salve to us. We trust that with God's good grace, we will

Ryan tackling an opponent in Rugby

be able to continue onward and accept, as would a little child, the hand that fate has dealt us, while still counting and being grateful for the many blessings we perpetually enjoy in life. Our choice is for gratitude and for happiness, and what a worthwhile choice that is proving to be!

Behind the Story

I met the Salisbury family many years ago when I moved into an apartment complex which they owned in Eugene, Oregon. The apartment sits across the street from Churchill High School, where Ryan would eventually graduate and which had been my high school. The Salisbury family lived just a few doors down from my apartment, while their home was under construction.

At the time I had one child, Danny, who was barely a year old. All of the Salisbury children, including Ryan, would play with Danny in the little playground in front of our apartments. They were wonderfully sweet and kind to him.

Jeff Salisbury went out of his way, just before my little family moved in, to make our apartment comfortable and attractive. There was new carpet and linoleum on the floor and fresh paint everywhere. Though the apartment was older, it felt brand new. A storage closet belonging to the complex was located next to my unit. Jeff cleaned it out and offered me a key to use as I needed. I was able to store boxes inside, but there was also water and electricity available which Jeff encouraged me to hook up a washer and dryer to, saving me from walking the distance to the coin operated laundry with my toddler; the expenses of these utilities being the apartment complexes and not mine.

Soon after signing our second year lease on the apartment, and being pregnant with our second baby, my husband found a large duplex with a fenced back yard where our children could play. I have lived in many nice homes since this time, but I never wanted to live in a place more than I did that cozy and perfect-for-our-needs duplex. I was nervous to tell Jeff that we wanted to move, both because he had gone to great lengths to make us comfortable, and because we had just signed another year lease which would have a fee to break. We didn't have much money at the time, so this concerned me greatly. When we told them, not only were Jeff and Denise completely supportive, but they never mentioned anything about the contract or a fee. Jeff even assisted in the moving process. For these reasons, I have *always* loved the Salisbury family. They are Salt-of-the-Earth!

When I heard about Ryan, through my parents who are equally close to the Salisbury family (as I had since moved to Texas), I was devastated for them. Such a tragedy couldn't have happened to kinder, more charitable people. I remembered the sweet little honey-haired boy playing with Danny years before and it was nearly impossible to believe this was to be Ryan's fate. As shocked as I was by the news of Ryan's violent death, I wasn't surprised at all to learn that the Salisburys would not be suing or seeking redress. That is the kind of people they always were; they stayed true to their way of living and serving no matter the circumstances.

While staying with my family in Eugene recently, I was able to visit with Denise, share my project with her and ask if they would be willing to include Ryan's story in *The Triumph Book*. Though extremely busy with their community involvement, family, church, school and work, they carved out time to write; which required a great deal of emotion and grief to revisit this experience in so much detail. I am thankful to the Salisburys for providing us with *Ryan's Song.*

Eight

Learning How to See in the Dark

Author: Becky Greer

I can't believe I am still here. No one could have told me it was possible that I would be alive and functioning fifteen years after the death of all four of my children. Nobody, not my parents, not my friends, not my pastor, not the president nor the pope could have convinced me I would live through this nightmare. I also believed that no one could know the deep, dark depths of despair in which I found myself. Therefore, I knew no one who could help me find my way out. I did not believe it was possible. Yet here I am. How can that be? How is it feasible that I am still here living and breathing in a world where my precious children are no longer present?

People will still say, "How do you do it?" I don't really know how any of us accomplish what seems to be impossible. We just do. What I know for certain is that it is a choice, or a series of choices, that we must make; and somewhere along the way, much to my own surprise, I made a choice to live. I made a choice to live... not just exist.

I have learned that there are many levels of darkness and I found myself in the deepest, blackest pit that you can allow yourself to imagine. In a word, it was hell. I have tried many times to describe the despair. The best explanation I can come up with is that it was like the darkness you find inside a cave in which no outside light can filter through.

I was born and raised in Kentucky where the world's largest known cave system, Mammoth Cave National Park, is located. My family loved to visit there and take a tour that descends into the caves. Once inside, the ranger would turn out the lights so that we could experience total darkness... pitch black, abysmal darkness. They say you can go crazy in that condition if you stay there too long. I believe it. In this kind of isolation you cannot see in front of or behind you. There is no sense of direction. You are stuck; it is so black you can't see the way out.

This is the gloom I lived in while moving and breathing in the light of day. My heart was beating, my lungs were taking in air, but my spirit was dead. I was here, but I was not here. I certainly did not want to be present. So what can you do when you find yourself in a deep, dark pit of emptiness; when it is so bleak you see nothing and feel overwhelming pain, grief and suffering? You just be. You be still and remain in the blackness until your inner eyes begin to adjust. You hang on until Hope breaks through. After a short time, the ranger in Mammoth Cave lit one match which illuminated the cavern just enough to see a few feet in front of you. One tiny match in a very big cave, this single match in a fathomless hallow pit can "show hope." A tiny "pinhole of light" is what saved me.

I share my story, a very personal story, which is sacred to me, because it is my desire to "show hope" to others who might find themselves in this kind of darkness. I share it because it has been helpful for me to hear the stories of other people and how they have found their way through the trials of life. I share it because I do not want my children to be forgotten. I share it because it is a way of bringing meaning and purpose to my own life. This is not the life I dreamed for myself, yet here I am. This is the life I have been given. Will I live it? Will I not live it? Will I just exist? Will I go forward? Will I give up? Will I live for my children? Will I find meaning and purpose again? What am I to do with all the love I had for my children? I must share it!

We all need each other, whether we are aware of it or not. There have been many who have helped me along the way. Other bereaved parents continued to reach out to me even when I rejected their efforts. They were persistent. They did not give up. They finally convinced me to attend a conference for parents who have lost children where I met Elaine. She was the keynote speaker at the gathering. Elaine lost a son and a daughter in a car accident nine years previously. It took every ounce of energy my husband and I had to be there that day. I remember I was in absolute awe that Elaine could be standing in front of a group of grieving parents, sharing her story. I was amazed that she could laugh, joke and relate the happy, wonderful memories she had of her children; as well as how she was making it through her struggle with grief.

In telling her story, Elaine was helping us; but I realize now that she was also helping herself. As she was speaking I remember thinking, "What a wonderful thing she is doing by sharing what she has learned about grief and how to survive it. She is helping me just by being willing to share her story!" I remember thinking, "I would love to be able to help other people someday, but I can't even help myself, so how in the world could I help somebody else?" Elaine told me she was thinking about writing a book called "*10 Reasons to Get Up in the Morning after Losing a Child.*" I thought, "Ha! She has come up with 10 reasons to help *HER* get up in the morning, but that doesn't mean her reasons will work for me!" So I said, "Name for me just one reason, because I am struggling to find a reason to live, let alone get out of bed in the morning." She immediately responded, "I get up in the morning so that my children's lives won't be erased." She said "If I stay in bed all day with the covers over my head, people will soon forget about me and they will certainly forget about my children."

It was as if a light had been turned on! I was in such a dark place in my grief that I truly believed no one would ever be able to give me a good reason to continue to live in a world where my children were not. But Elaine gave me one good reason to go on. It was enough. When Stephen died at age two, my son Buzzy, who was seven at the time, became my reason to go on. However, sixteen years later when Buzzy, at age 23 died, his brother Todd at age 14 died and his sister Kami at age 10 died, I COULD FIND NO REASON TO CONTINUE TO LIVE. But here it was; it made perfect sense! It was a wonderful reason! It was reason enough! Of course, I do not want my children's lives to be erased. No mother wants her child to be forgotten. So I get out of bed.

I have to admit many times I go out when I would rather not. It would be so much easier to stay in bed. I still have many "not so good days" when I don't want to see or talk with anyone. But, I have learned that it is a choice. I can choose to be miserable and wallow in my pain, or I can choose to be thankful for the time I had with my precious children. To have never known them and loved them would have been a much bigger loss. So even though it is a great burden to bear, I would never trade the short time I had with them for a life with no sorrow.

People feel sad for me when they hear I have lost all four of my children, and it is a heartbreaking story. But don't forget to be happy for me too. Be happy that I was blessed with giving birth to them, nurturing them, knowing them, loving them, and receiving their love. I am truly grateful for the time I had with them. Fifteen years later, I still have bad days, but I also have good ones. I even have days with laughter and joy. JOY!

I hope finding this purpose and fighting the desire to give up makes my children proud. I know that if it they had been left behind instead of me, I would certainly want them to have happy, full, meaningful lives. I have wished many times that Gam and I could have died with them. It would have been so much easier. But, I have had to face the reality that my children are gone and I am still here. I am trying to live my life in a way that will honor my children and my God. Since hearing Elaine's story and many others, I have gradually made my way back into life and returned to the world. It is not the same life, but it is a life, not just an existence. There came a time when I had to decide if I was going to stay in this world. If the answer was "yes," then I was going to live, not just exist. I know that when people see me, they wonder how I am able to survive. It is my prayer they will recognize that I survive by God's strength and not my own. I share my story with a hope that you will read something in it which may help you along your journey.

We all have dreams. The life that I have now is not the life I dreamed for myself. As a little girl, my dream was to become a mother. I knew from a very early age that, plain and simple, I wanted to become a mother. I did not want to be a teacher or a nurse, as my mother suggested. I desired no career except that of a mother, grandmother, and then great-grand-mother. I married at a young age and started my family. Allow me to introduce my family to you. This is me and my husband, Gam, on our wedding day and on our 33rd anniversary.

Becky Greer with husband, Gam

You decide which is which!

Our oldest child is John Michael. He was nicknamed Buzzy before he ever left the hospital. Buzzy was a very sensitive and loving child who always wanted to please. He dreamed of being a guitar player in a rock band but also loved classical guitar. Buzzy lived his whole life in 23 years and two days.

Buzzy

Stephen

Stephen joined his brother Buzzy and our family five years later. Stephen was a precious, sweet, loving, innocent baby who did not live long enough to dream of a future. Stephen lived his whole life in two years, seven months and 20 days.

One year after Stephen died, Todd was born. Todd was very self-motivated and goal-oriented. He had big dreams and was already pursuing them with passion. Todd dreamed of becoming a basketball player for the University of Kentucky Wildcats. Todd lived his whole life in 14 years, one month and seventeen days.

Todd

After three boys, we were finally blessed to welcome a beautiful little girl to our family. Kami was very much a girl, but she was also somewhat of a tomboy. She loved animals and playing softball. She dreamed of becoming a veterinarian and a writer. Kami lived her whole life in 10 years, five months and nine days.

Kami

We never know what any given day will bring. However, some days are etched in our memories forever. I remember it was a Wednesday and there was a slight drizzle of rain as we drove Stephen to the doctor for a routine physical on October 17, 1979. It began as a regular morning and ended with a diagnosis of leukemia. He was immediately admitted to the hospital and chemotherapy began that very day. Gam and I were only 27 years old and had no tools or life experience to help us deal with anything like this. Exactly one month later on November 17, little Stephen died in my arms. I remember asking Gam, "What are we going to do?" Of course, he had no answer.

Our world was shattered. I did not think I could survive such pain, but I knew I had to find a way to go on for Buzzy, who was only seven years old at the time. I felt that losing Stephen was the worst thing that could ever happen to me and I trusted God to get me through that terrible, terrible time. I was able to survive this loss because I knew that Buzzy needed me. He became my reason for living. We made it through that horrific event and later Todd and Kami joined the family.

Our lives would never be the same without Stephen, but we were able to pick up the shattered pieces and try to live a life that we hoped was pleasing to God. Buzzy, of course, always knew and remembered his brother, Stephen, and even though Todd and Kami never got to meet him, they always knew that they had a big brother who was in Heaven. As most mothers do, I loved my children and did everything I knew to make their lives happy, healthy and safe. However, life continues to teach me how powerless we really are.

When Buzzy went away to school he was drawn into something he couldn't seem to escape, no matter how hard he tried. He became involved with drugs and the dark world of that culture. As so often happens, Buzzy became a prisoner of the drugs and evil people who take advantage of misguided youth by selling drugs and using them to further their selfish purposes. It is very important to me that others know that Buzzy was a very sensitive, loving and good person who made some very wrong choices which led to not only his destruction, but the destruction of our entire family.

January 16, 1995 began quite ordinary. It was Martin Luther King Day, so there was no school. After having a big breakfast together, we all went our separate ways. I took Kami to ballet and tap class. She was so happy that she literally sang the whole way home. Gam took Todd to basketball practice and he was also happy and excited because he had had his best practice ever. To hear him tell it, just about every shot he put up that day went in. Nobody could stop him. Buzzy went to visit a friend.

That evening, when we all came together again for dinner and were sharing what a good day we had, there was a phone call. It was for Buzzy. When he hung up the phone, Buzzy pulled out a gun that was hidden in his pocket and started shooting. When the gun was finally empty, Todd, Kami and Buzzy were all dead. Gam had been critically shot three times.

It was not that Buzzy was trying to spare me; it was just that no bullet struck me. When Gam came out of surgery, I asked him, just as I had when Stephen died in my arms, "What are we going to do?" Once again, he had no answer. Once again, our world was shattered...

We later learned that the phone call was from Buzzy's girlfriend who had called to tell him she was seeing someone else. I believe that he just "snapped" after hearing this and started shooting. We also later found out that the so-called "friend" Buzzy had gone to see that afternoon had sold him a gun.

I was in a fog for weeks and months afterwards. I stayed busy taking care of Gam's injuries and worked very hard trying to put out of my mind what had happened. As time passed, Gam's injuries got better and he didn't seem to need all my nurturing. But nurturing was my job! I am a mother! My children were gone, Gam was well; now what was I supposed to do? I had too much time to deal with what had happened... and I didn't want to deal with it. The reality was just too painful. Many times we tried to run from the pain of reality, but I could find no place to run, no place to hide; darkness set in.

I began to question God. How could you let this happen? Are you not the same God who comforted me and helped me make it through the pain of losing Stephen? Are you not the same God I trusted to get me through that terrible time? WHERE ARE YOU GOD? HOW COULD YOU LET THIS HAPPEN? This is not fair! What about all the evil people in the world? What about all the drug dealers? What about all the people who don't even care about their children? They still have their children! WHY GOD WHY? Questions, endless questions... Questions with no answers. But, still we ask.

I became very angry with God... I got so angry that I even questioned His existence. I call this time of questions, anger, loss, and loneliness my "dark time." I was in a deep, black hole and could not find my way out. I could not even discover a reason to come out. I wanted to die. I wanted to be with my children. I believed no one could help me; no one knew my pain. I was lost, sinking and it didn't matter. Nothing mattered... nothing.

I did not want to see or talk with anyone during this time, partly because I knew there were no answers to my questions and partly because I didn't want anyone to know I was having such terrible dark thoughts. I wanted to end my life. My children were my reason for living and they were gone. My identity was wrapped up in being a mother. Who was I if I was no longer a mother?

What kept me hanging on was that I had one last thing to do for my children; it was to see they had a proper monument to honor their lives and remind people that yes, Buzzy, Stephen, Todd, and Kami did live and walk among us and influence our lives. It ended up taking over a year for the monument to be built and erected in our local cemetery. During this time of waiting, I began to see what I call a tiny "pinhole of light." That tiny pinhole of light continues to grow bigger and bigger even today. By the time the monument was erected, I was no longer in the dark place and I had found reasons to live.

It was through the love and persistence of fellow strugglers that I was able to find light in my darkness. My friends, as well as God, were always there for me; it was me who would not let them in. It is important that we reach out to others, but it is equally important to be willing to allow others to extend their support to us. Once that tiny pinhole of light broke through my darkness, I began to see hope again. I saw hope only slowly at first, but as I let the Light (which is God/Love) in, the pinhole got bigger and bigger each day. I found God again. The truth is God never left me; it was me who left God.

Though life is still a struggle and dark times can creep in, I have found meaning and purpose in my life again. My identity was wrapped up in being a mother and I believed that being a mother was my reason for existing. I have learned that my true purpose is to honor God no matter what circumstances this life may bring. I can honor my children by living life in a way that would make them proud.

Here are a few things I learned in the dark:

- I am not alone.

- Each one of us has to make our own personal journey, yet we can learn so much from each other.

- Everybody grieves differently. Gam and I both lost the same children, but he did not lose what I lost, and I did not lose what he lost. We each make our own way in our own time, and that's OK.

- It is not true that nothing matters, as I believed in my dark time. LOVE MATTERS... the love that we have for our children and the love that they had for us MATTERS.

- Death ends a life, but it does not end a relationship.

- I have a choice. I can choose Love and Life or I can choose death and darkness.

Be still. In the stillness I found the place that Love lives. It is the place where Peace lives... that Peace we all long for.

I'd like to close my message by sharing a very special Mother's Day story:

"When the blooms die, plant it outside Mom! That's what the lady at the florist said to do and it will come back next year!" exclaimed my nine year old daughter, Kami, as she proudly presented me with a beautiful potted stargazer lily on what would be the last Mother's day we had together. I told Kami I didn't believe the lily would come back.

"But Mom, the lady said it would!" When the blooms faded and died Kami kept reminding me to plant the lily outside and I kept putting her off by saying that I just didn't believe the lily would come back. Kami remained insistent until I finally relented and together we went outside to plant the lily in the backyard. Winter came and the lily died. Kami and her brothers, Todd and Buzzy, also died that winter. My world became totally dark.

The following spring, when the lily sprouted and grew to produce 27 beautiful fragrant pink blooms, I became filled with inexpressible joy. Joy in my darkness! How could that be? Without my children I believed I could never feel joy or happiness again. What a beautiful gift! Kami, an innocent child, had no trouble believing that the lily would live again. Jesus said we are to have the faith of a child. God can resurrect even those things which we believe can't be resurrected. I did not believe the lily could survive the darkness of winter and I did not believe I could survive the darkness of my grief and suffering after losing all four of my precious children.

God was working on the lily in the darkness of the Earth and He was working on me in the darkness of my grief. I just didn't know it. Just because we don't experience God's presence, doesn't mean He isn't there. God has not promised that bad things will not happen to us, but God has promised that He will never leave us. God has kept His promise to me and I am thankful.

Even though I can no longer hold my children, or look into their eyes, or hear their sweet voices, or see them smile at me, they are still very much a part of my life. It is the Love we share that lives on...

Behind the Story

Searching the internet for stories which might be similar to the ones I was seeking for **The Triumph Book**, I came across a story randomly posted on-line about a mother who lost all of her children: *Becky Greer*. The story I found was not part of a website, article or any other traceable source… it was simply a narrative with the name of the author included.

I searched the name, *Becky Greer*, for anyone who might fit the description as the writer of this story. In the process I stumbled across a bereavement conference being held in New York one month from that time, where a Becky Greer was presenting. I figured this was likely the same mother, and so I emailed the organizer of the conference with a message. I asked if she would pass along my email to Becky Greer which detailed the purpose of **The Triumph Book** and asked if she would be willing to contribute her story.

It took nearly a month before I heard back, but Becky finally received my message and responded positively. It was a miraculous "find" because the story I discovered on-line was a speech she had given at a picnic years before and Becky wasn't even aware it had been shared on the internet. Not only that, but speaking at this conference was Becky's *first public appearance*, outside of the picnic, talking about her children.

As part of Becky's reply to my email, she shared the following message:

I have an interesting story to tell you. When I was in New York to speak at the BP/USA (Bereaved Parents/United States of America) Gathering I realized that the other speakers were professionals, authors, Ph.D.'s, etc. There was a speaker after each meal, beginning on Thursday night. I spoke on Saturday morning and by then I had heard four very polished presenters. The speaker on Friday night was Ann Kaiser Stern who was a psychologist and author of several books. My husband told me after her speech that I sure was in a high class of speakers.

Well, I had been doing pretty well keeping myself calm up until that point and then my stomach started to churn. I began to ask myself "What in the world am I doing here? These people are going to be disappointed. I'm just a housewife, mother, bereaved mother, with no letters attached to the end of my name." Ms. Stern's talk was about how she had interviewed around 40 people who had significant tragedy in their lives and how they had risen above their tragedy and loss and went on to become what she called "Triumphant Survivors." I realized, as she was speaking, that that is exactly what I am... a Triumphant Survivor!

When I introduced myself to the group the next morning, I told them that I was a housewife, a mother, a bereaved mother, and that I had discovered the night before that I was a "Triumphant Survivor." Then the entire room rose to their feet and gave an ovation. I share this story with you because I believe it is no coincidence that our paths have crossed at this particular time. Therefore, I want you to know that I will be honored to include my story in your book. It is a wonderful thing you are doing in order to help others.—Becky Greer

Nine

Robert's Story

Author: Autumn Ater

My name is Autumn Ater and I am Robert's mother. Robert was a very unique and special little boy, even before he was born. My husband, Scott, and I prayed for a child together... a son. Scott was father to three daughters from a previous marriage and I had a daughter as well, so we desperately wanted a child together. I longed for my husband to have the son he yearned for so deeply and I uttered a prayer that I will never forget... I pled with God, "If you will please bless us with a son, I promise I will suffer or endure anything." I didn't realize that what I was asking for, I would fully receive. However, it would turn out to be the greatest blessing of our lives.

We tried for over two years to conceive and eventually enlisted the help of a fertility specialist. The insemination procedure normally takes several attempts, but we were elated to learn that I was pregnant with the first procedure. I knew at that moment I was going to have a son. There was never any doubt. My faith was strong and I trusted that God would honor my request. I never gave thought to the other part of my prayer; you know, the "I will suffer anything" part, but God did not forget. He had a plan in mind, a purpose and He was going to reveal all through His divine love. The trials we were about to face were not a punishment for my request, but a preparation for a great work God had in store for me.

The pregnancy was not an easy one. I had many problems from the beginning and by five months of pregnancy, there were so many issues, I lost my job. As a result, my obstetrician bailed on me due to the loss of my insurance. I thought perhaps this was the suffering I told God I would endure. But God did not forget me and good prenatal care was provided. At 38 weeks my water broke and little Robert was born. We happily gave him the name Robert Scott Ater. It sounded like a movie star's name; and to us, he was a star, that's for sure!

He entered this world rapidly on August 12, 1991. A 7 lb. 11oz. blue-eyed baby boy, 20" long with a head full of hair! He was a quiet baby, adorable and loved instantly. The family gathered around and we all welcomed our newest member to the family with great joy. But the delight would not last for long. By two-and-a-half months old, Robert had his first, of what would become many, seizures. We rushed him to the hospital not knowing it was a seizure, or what a seizure was for that matter. After a CT scan and MRI, a very concerned doctor entered our little ER room with news that would change all of our lives forever, especially mine; not that it did not affect my husband, because it did, but I was his mother and had carried him. I wondered, "Was it something I caused?"

This young neurologist told us that Robert's brain had not completely formed in uteri. He had a condition called a congenital brain malformation, known as a Migrational Cell Defect, and his seizures were a result of this abnormality. They would keep him a few days and medicate him to see if the seizures could be controlled, but their prognosis was not hopeful. By this time, Robert had endured over 15 seizures and it seemed they were never going to stop.

A drug called Phenobarbital gave Robert some relief, and so he was sent home... and we waited. It was only a short time before a new symptom developed. Robert was jerking very hard to the left and it was different from the other seizure we observed. I immediately called the neurologist's office and was told to bring him in. It was quite clear to his doctor that Robert had begun to develop one of the worst types of seizures a child could have; they were called Infantile Spasms. The prognosis became worse and worse, leaving us a mess. I was horrified and could not believe that this was real.

Robert was not developing mentally as he should and by his first birthday, he had been suffering over 100 seizures a day with the developmental progress of an infant. He was worn out. We had tried every seizure medication available, even experimental ones, and nothing was working. His neurologist then recommended we see a Neurosurgeon at Dallas Children's Medical Center to discuss Robert's candidacy for a Hemispherectomy. This is a procedure where one of the lobes (or hemispheres) of the brain is removed. They would evaluate Robert and, if he were a candidate, we would begin a series of tests and pre-surgeries to prepare him for this operation.

Robert met the criteria. Without the surgery, he would most likely die very soon. His seizures were now affecting other areas of his organs. He could not eat by mouth any longer and needed a gastro-intestinal tube, or G-Tube, to feed him. Because of his neurological deficiencies, he had lung and eye problems, as well as a multitude of other issues.

I was exhausted. I had lived in hospitals on and off for over a year and a half and I missed being home; having a normal life. I would not leave Robert. I stayed weeks at a time, 24 hours a day, sleeping in a cot beside his crib. My nerves were shot. I didn't know what to do, so I prayed and prayed and prayed! Then God gently reminded me how He was always close.

At eighteen months old, I handed my son over to a nurse in the operating waiting area and told Robert that I loved him with all my heart. He underwent a long eight-hour surgery, which was a great success; at least at first. When I saw him after the surgery, I wasn't mentally prepared for the view. There were so many tubes and monitors; there was not a place on him that wasn't covered by or hooked up to something. His little head was all bandaged. Robert was swollen and had a tube down his throat into his lungs, breathing for him. I remember just crying and thinking to myself, "What have we (I) done to you?" I truly felt that this was entirely my fault. Even though I had taken excellent care of myself while pregnant, I did not drink or smoke, no drugs. I just couldn't figure it out. I still blamed myself for everything.

Slowly, over the next few days, Robert began to awaken and I will never forget the smile on his face when he saw me. He could not talk, sit, crawl, or walk, but he could smile. Robert recognized me and that melted my heart. I had a peace then that was not there before. I finally quit blaming myself and saw hope for the first time in a long while.

Over the next few months Robert recovered wonderfully, holding his head up for the first time, reaching after objects and looking from side to side (even though the surgery left him partially blind and deaf in his left ear). Watching him for the first time rocking back and forth on his knees was all very exciting and hopeful... and then it happened.

Prior to Robert's surgery, we purchased our first home and moved to the country for a rural life with cows, chickens and all the pleasures of a country life-style. One cool June evening, our small baby chicks needed warmth or they would die, so we put them in a cardboard box and brought them into the laundry room. We placed a lamp in the box, thinking this would be just for the night. Regrettably, the chicks had airborne salmonella. One by one that evening they began to die and we couldn't figure out what was wrong. Then I became very sick. It was contagious and turned out to be the worst 24-hour intestinal virus I ever had.

Four days later, Robert got sick too. I had vomited so badly I thought I was dying. Robert had a feeding-tube as he also had a procedure called a Nissan or Fundoplication which did not allow him to vomit due to excessive reflux destroying his diaphragm. He was rendered helpless and within a few short hours was so lethargic that he was rushed to Cook Children's Medical Center for evaluation. It had only been four months since his brain surgery, so it was not clear what might be going on. Cooks Medical Center did not do Hemispherectomy surgeries at that time, so they were unaware of his condition, history, or even how to treat him. They simply admitted and treated Robert for gastritis.

Within a few short hours I noticed a bulge on the site where the surgeons had entered his skull via a port hole or burr hole, as it is referred to, but I was assured by the nurse that it was a blood vessel which had probably broken due to Robert's heaving. The doctors had given Robert Phenergan medication to stop the nausea, and he passed out. But, something dreadful was lurking and about to reveal itself.

I gently picked Robert up and noticed that he had no head control, it just flopped from side to side and his pupils were extremely dilated. He was breathing strange and his nostrils were flared. About that time Robert's Pediatrician came in, took one look and listen to Robert, and then hysteria took over.

Robert was barely breathing and needed to go to ICU to have a breathing tube placed immediately. He was in critical condition. After sitting in an ICU waiting area while they stabilized him, our pediatrician informed me that Robert had what appeared to be meningitis, probably a result of his recent brain surgery. I was told that he was very sick and the doctor did not think Robert was going to make it. They were sending him to Dallas immediately to the original surgeon who worked on Robert. For the moment, he was barely stable, and very critical, but he was alive; and there was hope!

I was in shock. I cried hard and could not believe that my little boy might die. All I could do was say, "NO!" over and over again. I went with the ambulance to Dallas and Robert was taken directly to ICU. No one was allowed in and once again, we found ourselves sitting in a little room, with a chaplain this time... not a good sign. The neurosurgeon stated that Robert was very ill, that his ICP (intra-cranial pressure) was higher than he had ever seen in all his years of practice and that we should not expect him to make it through the night. I fell apart and wanted to be with him. They finally allowed me to see Robert and I never once accepted the fact that he might die.

Each day this miracle child proved he was stronger than anyone could ever have imagined. We finally learned Robert had a potentially fatal illness called Salmonella Meningitis and had likely contracted it the same way I did, through the air. Those little sick birds were the culprit. Who would have ever thought that something like this could happen?

Specialists from Infectious Disease were called in next. At the time, Robert was the 10th person to have contracted this illness, and there was only one that had survived. Well, Robert would make two! He became a medical miracle after all was said and done.

We spent six weeks at the hospital, had five more complicated neuro-surgeries to clear out the salmonella cysts, had a VP Shunt placed and finally went home. None of this was without its toll on Robert's body. The seizures were back with a vengeance and he lost all milestones. However, I kept on and together, with his neurologist, we found a way to better control his seizures and give him a chance, at least.

Though Robert's seizures never completely went away, and he never regained much developmentally, he was smarter than you might expect. Robert knew Mama. He could even say it. And he smiled; oh how he smiled!

Robert had many series of illnesses and surgeries, one after another, treating this and correcting that throughout his years, totaling 11 brain surgeries and 32 body surgeries. All these were in an attempt to give him what we believed in our hearts was a better chance for survival. Regrettably, by the time he was nearly 10 years old, Robert's lungs were becoming weaker and weaker.

He had chronic lung infections and pneumonia on a regular basis. Robert was on oxygen, breathing machines, suction machines and more medications than the sickest of persons I ever knew. We spent his lifetime in hospitals and emergency rooms. He tried hard; he was such a fighter! Each time Robert recovered from one thing, another devastating illness struck. No matter what I did to protect him, he was just always sick. Robert's own body was at war with him and by the time he was 14 years old, his weakened body had taken its final toll on his health and his organs began to fail.

He now had contracted RSV (a fatal lung infection that generally affects infants), his kidneys were shutting down and his organs were going into failure. We could put him on an IV for fluids, but that was only prolonging the inevitable, so we went home with him, cried, prayed and made the decision to let him go. Robert was not tolerating his feedings at all anymore, gagging and excreting high doses of bile, therefore not receiving proper nutrition or medications, and he was clearly suffering. He coughed and choked all day and night. Robert's lungs were filled with fluids and we were suctioning him 60 plus times over a 24-hour period. Robert was lethargic and weak; and the look in his eyes told me *"Please let me go home Mama."*

We held an Ethics Committee Meeting at Cook Children's with his pulmonologist, pediatrician, other physicians and professionals who are on the board and citizens who are dedicated to serve this committee and its families, to determine Robert's quality of life (his condition) and discuss end of life issues. Immediately after Dr. Sami Hadeed, MD, (his Pulmonologist and Director of the Ethics Committee) introduced Robert's history and then us as his parents, and the trials we had been through, everyone in attendance gave us a standing ovation; and we cried. They had acknowledged that we had been excellent parents, and had gone beyond our calling to care for him. We were told Robert was a lucky little boy to have us, but we saw it the other way around. We were the blessed ones. They agreed that there was nothing left to do medically for Robert. It was the hardest, yet most merciful decision we could make to let Robert go.

The dreadful time had come. We were to make a decision that we couldn't bear to live with, but Robert was willing to endure. He was ready to go on, and we had to let him. On April 15, 2006, after much prayer and many tears, we made the difficult and sad decision and agreed to let him pass. We knew in our hearts that his suffering here would end and Robert would truly live for the first time, in a new and healed body with the Lord. On April 22, 2006, just seven days later, he peacefully passed away in his own bed, in his own room. The entire family was in the home to surround Robert with love.

I write this with tears streaming down my face as Robert was my life. I was consumed with his care. What I thought was going to be a lifetime commitment, being caregiver to a special needs child, would prove otherwise. Yes, it was a calling for me, but one that was preparing me for another calling by God to continue serving others. Robert was so special and taught me so much. Although I have tried to think of ways, I can never repay God for the great gift He gave me in Robert. He touched every life he encountered, and is my everyday reminder that God is always with me, and for that, I am forever thankful.

We had four of the best nurses in the world who, over his lifetime, became his second mothers and permanent members of our family. Robert loved them and they sure loved him! We had a wonderful group of physicians who were very fond of Robert and I was touched to see them at his viewing and funeral. It was also the multitude of people that I didn't realize he had touched that were at his viewing and funeral that blessed me so deeply. Many loved Robert and for that, I will be eternally grateful.

Over the "better years" of his life, Robert received a wish from the Make-A-Wish Foundation of North Texas. He was given a rainforest room and the vibrant colors intrigued him. Later, another organization learned of Robert and, through the generosity of the community and commercial businesses, a special handicapped bathroom was added to his room with plenty of storage and space. We had been greatly blessed over the years. Robert always had a smile for the workers as they came in and out of his room or assisted in whatever way they could. He was adored by so many! Though he could not have a conversation verbally with you, his eyes said it all!

I was inspired by Robert and went on to college just two years before he died. I was an honors student and threw myself into all the university had to offer. I graduated just two weeks after his death... knowing he was proud of me. What was to come would shock me and open my heart and eyes to a completely new world.

Just one year after his death, God spoke to me, a mother who plead for His help. As I lay there in my tears God gently and specifically told me, *"Serve others."* I was not sure what I was hearing and asked, "How?" That's when He reaffirmed it with this message, *"By continuing the ministry you have already begun in obedience to My will."* I was immediately reminded of all the other bereaved moms that I had been involved with and it was then that a seed was planted and a ministry born: *A Hole in My Heart.*

I founded a faith-based support group for bereaved moms, and it has been the most humbling and healing experience of my life. God used my own loss and pain to reach out to other mothers by giving them a safe place to come and share their loss. We cry, laugh, pray and comfort each other as only another grieving mom can do.

Autumn and Robert

In the *A Hole in My Heart* program, I encourage any bereaved mother to visit *www.aholeinmyheart.com* to find hope and inspiration from the words and pages created just for her special situation. We are all vessels, and God has a plan for you, just as He did for me. He is not ready to receive us home until we have fulfilled all of His purposes and promises for our lives.

In the meantime, He provides others who will stand right there beside us. He places those amongst us who walk in those same grief shoes, so we may share with each other, comfort each other and love each other through the unspeakable pain of our losses. As my friend and author Susan Duke says in her book entitled *Earth Angels*, *"These are the ones who have graced our hearts with more love than we could ever be worthy of"* (v). Oh how true that statement is and oh how thankful we are as well!

Although Robert regrettably lost his battle on this earth and went home to Heaven due to complications related to his many disabilities, he has proved a vital part of my existence (and this ministry). I now understand I was not just called to be a caregiver, though that was part of my duties and description. Robert showed me, through my faith in God, that he was called and purposed here to teach me to be a servant. Not just to attend to his needs, but to others as well. Even though he is deeply missed, there is

Autumn's Special Little Angel

something quite humbling about the knowledge that he existed as a vessel, himself, in serving others.

I very often tell people that I feel I can relate to Joseph from the book of Genesis in the Bible. God has rescued me from a deep pit of grief to one of joy in serving others.

Letting your grief identify who you are is not what God intends for us. There is hope and healing in our Lord Jesus Christ. Just trust in Him.

I leave with you a beautiful scripture; one that reminds me of the trials Robert and I faced. It is my greatest hope that you know the peace of God and the healing that only He can give to the hole in our hearts.

"The LORD himself goes before you and will be with you; he will never leave you nor forsake you. Do not be afraid; do not be discouraged." (Deuteronomy 31:8)

Behind the Story

I met Autumn through a radio show host who had interviewed Autumn and gave me her email. I sent a message to Autumn and invited her to write a story for this book. It was clear that Autumn would be a perfect contributor because of all the work she has done to comfort and support so many out of the compassion she gained through her own adversity.

Recently I had a friend whose child needed an extended stay at the hospital and whenever I visited them, as I walked the halls, I thought of Autumn and all the time she "lived" at the hospital with Robert. I could feel how powerful her love and endurance was to spend so much time in an environment that could never take the place of home. After reading this story, thoughts of her love and sacrifice stayed with me for a prolonged time and I found myself frequently pondering the events of Autumn's and Robert's lives together. I have been truly affected by this powerful and enduring love story between a mother and her son!

Autumn's website and ministry *A Hole in My Heart* provides many services and opportunities, and is one of the few faith-based support groups centered exclusively on Bereaved Mothers to give hope and understanding. Autumn encourages the group to find comfort, understanding and healing by sharing with those who walk this same grief journey. You can learn more about Autumn's endeavor by visiting the website: *www.aholeinmyheart.com.*

Autumn has also been involved with *The Make A Wish Foundation* of North Texas as a wish granter. Together with her husband, the Aters are a secondary sponsor family for *The Pythian Home* of Weatherford, Texas, which provides housing for orphaned children. She is also currently in the process of writing a book about grief and its journey entitled, *"In God's Special Place"* which will be available at *www.InGodsSpecialPlace.com.*

Chapter Ten

The Faces of Grief

Aftermath of a Tsunami

Author: Keith Arden Colley

Horrific Discovery

Driving back into Dallas from my parent's home after celebrating Christmas with the family, I was listening to what was left of my Holiday CD, attempting to hang on to one last moment of the season. As I drove into the parking lot of my apartment, the familiar creak of the gate woke my dogs and the calm was broken with them bouncing all over me and the inside of my truck.

While unloading the truck, I flipped on the TV to watch the news. I stopped in utter disbelief as I witnessed a wall of water rolling over a concrete barrier dividing ocean and land. My first thought was "Where is this happening?" as scene after scene of devastation flashed across the screen. The destruction was unfathomable—water was literally swallowing villages whole.

Most of the buildings were still standing, but almost everything else— including the unfortunate inhabitants of the town—was being swept by the raging water as it surged through what was left of the streets. Buses weighing tons washed away like twigs in a river. The most shocking images were of people clinging to the buses, trying to save themselves while at the same time attempting to help those caught up in the river of pandemonium, grasping at anything they could find. Most of the people prostrated on the buses were knocked away by the debris and pulled under, never to be seen again. I witnessed the fear on their faces just before their sudden disappearance. I watched this carnage, alone, completely speechless.

I was able to discover the locations of this devastation in the scrolling words across the bottom of the screen; it was literally happening on the other side of the planet! I felt so removed from this part of the world; it just didn't seem real. Watching these scenes of tragedy was akin to a movie unfolding with growing suspense: who of these anonymous characters would survive, and who would disappear in an instant? It was macabre and surreal... I could not stop watching.

If there was one word which described my mounting emotions, it would have to be *Grief:* that feeling which pricks the darkest corners of your soul, the kind no one wants to talk about. Strangely, this cataclysm wasn't happening to me; not directly, nor personally, not in any way... yet my emotions were absolutely raw.

I am not sure I slept at all that night. If I did, it was a restless slumber choked with nightmares from the calamity I had witnessed on the news. The faces of those people would not leave me. With so much devastation and death, I wondered how they would ever see beyond this tragedy to begin any kind of recovery, physically or mentally. I tossed and turned; and wondered, "What is this nagging ache inside of me?"

I woke with a peace that comes from conviction. I had made a decision somewhere in the night that would change me forever. I had to go! I had to do my part, no matter how insignificant it might be in the big picture. I knew how to swing a hammer and I was not afraid of work. It would take an army to rebuild their world; I could at least be a foot soldier.

At church the next day I shared my intentions to go to Indonesia. My friend Jane joined in my commitment, and the plans began in earnest. After writing a list of the important necessities clearly lacking in this upheaval, we divvied up the items and got busy.

I called my college and asked if they knew of anyone in the tsunami ravaged regions to whom I could offer my support. "Yes, Sri Lanka! Steve Bycroft and his wife Shanthi are there, and they have been hit hard." was the response. I got the number of their U.S. contact and thus began one of the most challenging and rewarding adventures of my life.

I spoke with Steve's sister, already busy organizing items to be sent to the Bycroft's. As we talked, she related stories of the losses in their village of

Koddai Kallar, Sri Lanka. I was speechless. Her narrative confirmed that Koddai Kallar was exactly where I needed to be. Reality was settling in; this was actual, not just a news flash on the television. There were names, real people, a destination and no turning back.

The first and most pressing concern was how to get to Sri Lanka. I had worked at a travel agency in the past and the owner of the business was lovingly dubbed *The Iron Marshmallow*, hard on the outside, but soft in the middle. I called and asked if I could meet to discuss something important with him. I felt this was not a request to be conveyed over the phone. When I arrived at the office, he called me right in and closed the door.

I began to share the stories from Sri Lanka and my compulsion to somehow make a difference. While I spoke, he began typing on his computer. Mid-presentation he booked me two tickets into Colombo, Sri Lanka in a week. I cried and he cried with me.

Gathering Up

We've all used the cliché, *Domino Effect*, but I have never seen it happen as fast as it did that particular week. Once everyone knew the departure date, all else fell perfectly into place. My parents, who lived a state away, spread the word to my family. My aunt Daisy, who worked at a hospital in Oklahoma City, took it to the "powers that be" and was able to gather cases of medical supplies. My parent's church oversaw a gathering of equipment and funds to help with the trip.

My church served as a drop-off point for all the donations. Our Sunday school classroom began to look like a warehouse. Bottles of water and baby formula were stacked everywhere with cases of bandages and medications filling the tables. There was still a load being prepared in Oklahoma that had not even arrived yet! I was seeing true love in action.

I had concerns about our upcoming trip. Just the night before, my neighbor, who has traveled all over the world as a bodyguard for the upper officers of our military, was home for a break from Iraq. He told me he needed a moment to give me an important warning. He did not mince words. He began by telling me about the civil war going on between the government and a group called the *Tamil Tigers*. He also said that if the Tamil Tigers were to turn on us, as U.S. citizens, we would not survive. This did not sit well with me, but of greater concern were the images of the victims in the television reports and the stories from Steve and Shanti's village. That's what kept me focused.

Departure

On departure day I woke after only a couple hours of restless sleep, to finish what little packing I had left. After checking in all the cases at the airport, it was time to go through security and say goodbye to my send off party. No one said it aloud, but the thought that this might be the last time we would be together was ever present. I walked away with a simple "see you later."

While in the Hong Kong airport waiting for our flight to Colombo, Sri Lanka, Jane and I met a group who were headed back to the States after working in Indonesia. Their stories were astonishing and their exhaustion was palpable. As they spoke of the people, the so-called survivors, they did so softly. There was a quiet respect, even though they were now miles from the tragedy. I would soon come to understand first-hand the reason for their reverence.

Arrival

We landed in Colombo and made our way to customs, seeking the cases of supplies which hopefully made it all the way. This is where the troubles began. We were held up in customs for hours because of men's razors... yep, men's razors! For some reason this sent up a red flag. From what we could determine, the authorities thought we were planning to sell them. Cases and cases of medical supplies and they were hung up on a few razors! Based on the inquisition we endured, selling razors appeared to be as criminal as smuggling guns or drugs. Our heavy load of medical supplies were ready to meet the urgent needs of their citizens and these men were deliberating over a few sharp objects which posed no great threat, especially compared to all the country had just endured.

Steve Bycroft hands off plastic water containers to Keith Colley and many of the local children that resemble the ones from ancient times when they would draw water from a well. These were some of the supplies that were distributed throughout the region following the tsunami.

Steve, waiting outside customs to meet us, was growing anxious not knowing what the holdup was. The airport was now empty and the lights were shutting off, yet we still could not settle this dilemma. Finally Steve was allowed in to explain the purpose of all these supplies.

With the senseless deadlock finally resolved, we hurried to load Steve's van with the cases of supplies. After official introductions were made, it was past time to find a place to rest. Steve leaned over and said that he had forgotten that, "Jane was a Jane, not a John" and sleeping arrangements were not going to work. We were so exhausted; I told Steve a hotel would be preferable anyway. We needed all the rest we could get. Tomorrow we would make the 185 mile journey to Koddai Kollar, a village on the opposite side of the country and one of the regions severely damaged by the tsunami.

A City of 1,000,000 People

When we woke the next morning, I truly felt in *the midst of it all*. We had stayed in the city of Colombo with more than 1,000,000 people who seemed to all be filling the streets at once. It looked as if the tsunami had hit here, though we were not yet in the actual destruction zones. I remember saying to myself, "It is hard to see where the city stops and the tsunami begins."

I waited for the shop across the street to open so I could order a much needed cup of coffee. When it did, I was the first one through the door. I was treated like royalty. Before I could even order my coffee, they brought it to me as if I were a regular. I brought the cup to my lips, anticipating my first sip. Talk about disappointment! This concoction was mostly sugar and NO coffee. It was tea. But I drank it anyway. As they say, "when in Rome..."

I was handed a Sri Lankan newspaper which I expected to be in the native language, but no, it was in English. Pictured on the front page was a passenger train washed away by the tsunami. Fifteen-thousand people saw the wave coming and clambered aboard, hoping for refuge. Instead, everyone was killed. The paper was filled with personal stories and pictures of the devastation. I was amazed at the advertisements for loans already being marketed to help people rebuild.

Once outside, signs of poverty were everywhere. We needed to pick up more supplies to be distributed to the people who now had nothing. All I could think about was reaching the community we were there to serve. I was ready to go, becoming frustrated that many days had already passed and still we had not accomplished much.

Crossing the Country

All ten in our party squeezed into a van. Space was tight because of the mounds of supplies we were bringing with us. Finally, at long last, we were on our way to the other side of the island! What we had envisioned as a quick and simple trip was proving to be complicated and lengthy.

There was a check point every few miles for repeated inspections. Our sardine-like traveling arrangements made this more than an inconvenience. At times we were bribed to be allowed to continue. We actually had to *pay* gun yielding men with faces showing the hate embedded in them in order to proceed on our errand of mercy. There were military posts nearly every five miles and caution was required at each turn in the road. As we drove, Steve shared with me how his life had been threatened more than once and that he had actually been stoned!

As the LONG drive across the island was coming to a close, we rolled into a town called Batticaloa. This was a city of around 100,000 people. Steve said the death toll was already at 10,000 plus. As we journeyed through the town, there were sticks with white flags scattered everywhere, each one marking where a body was found and either buried or burned on the spot. We were now at ground zero. I was trying to comprehend how, not long before, there were thousands killed instantly in the very place I was traveling through.

Keith with Priyanthan (Jr.) in Koddai Kollar after arriving back from a nearby village passing out supplies at a tent village

We then headed south to reach the village of Koddai Kollar, where Steve and Shanthi lived, and thousands more victims were killed or homeless. Everywhere we looked, there was nothing but destruction.

Within our rescue party was a twelve year old boy, Steve and Shanthi's nephew, named Priyanthan. I enjoyed his company and teased him like a kid brother. Since Priyan-than's name was too hard to pronounce, I told him I would have to call him Jr. until I could say it correctly. Well it stuck, and he was Jr. the whole trip. Priyanthan became a key member in our endeavor, fulfilling the role of interpreter, quite an important service for one his age.

We arrived on the outskirts of the village of Koddai Kollar in the late afternoon. As we drove through, Steve and Shanthi began explaining what "used to be." The beautiful lagoon that Shanthi described in such great detail was gone; only a lone palm tree remained. It was the first thing you saw when arriving. Steve explained that Koddai Kollar was a small island off the island of Sri Lanka and the causeway needed to reach the island had been washed almost completely away with the tsunami. They had managed to shore up only enough dirt for people to escape the tiny island without using a boat. As we rolled into the village, we could see many damaged structures now being called home. As we drove further inland, towards their house, the structures seemed less damaged and Steve told us the wave stopped just short of their road.

As we turned onto their street (which is nothing like what the average person would think of as a street, it is really a path with ruts, barely wide enough for one vehicle), we were greeted by many who followed alongside the van until we arrived at the house. Everyone was anxious to see Steve and Shanthi; it had been a week since they left and clearly this couple had been a solitary strength in the midst of chaos. When we pulled up to the house, five adorable children came bustling out followed by many more people. With kids scrambling all around him, Steve mentioned that these were all part of his household now. The company of survivors numbered seventeen.

After the cramped travel space, followed by a pressing crowd, I needed to stretch my legs and be alone. I informed Shanthi that I was headed out for a walk and she suggested I take Priyanthan (Jr.) with me until the people got to know me better. As we were leaving, Jane decided she would come along as well.

During our walk, we stumbled upon a huge black plastic tank sitting on a corner. Jr. informed us that it was one of the units brought in for drinking water, but it emptied the first day and was never refilled. Just then the villagers spotted us by the tank and ran up, animated with optimism and hope that strangers had come to their rescue with water for the tank. The look on their faces, at the realization of their mistake, was complete anguish. What were we to do? There were no phones, no electricity, no food and no water! Jane and I peered up at each other in helpless desperation, propelled by the desire to fulfill a need we were unable to meet. We hurried back to the house; afraid to build up any more false hope among the villagers who might be thinking that because "the foreigners" were here, all their problems would be solved.

As bed time approached, the original seventeen house dwellers, Jane, myself, Jr. and his dad, stayed under one roof. Let's just say, it was cozy! We were scattered everywhere and silence fell.

After about an hour, I was still awake and decided to write in my journal when I heard someone crying. There were so many people in the house I couldn't tell where it was coming from. It was a quiet cry that went on for a while before it slowly faded into the night. It was a doleful way for someone to fall asleep.

The next morning, I woke to the most unusual sound. It was a scraping noise. Curious, I rose to discover what it might be. I went outside to find one of the resident ladies raking the sand in the yard. There was no grass, just dirt, and she was combing it as if she were trying to make it look nice

for the day. I asked Shanthi about that activity later and she told me this woman had lost everything in the tsunami. Her raking was a defiant act, confronting the loss not only of tangible things, but control over life it-self and all that surrounded her. In this small effort, an

Jane is in the back row holding a child.

otherwise helpless woman was still taking charge. She was doing her part, no matter how unnecessary.

It was still dark when Steve came out and joined me for some introspective moments before the start of another eventful day. We were presented with our morning tea by the same lady I had seen earlier, mothering the yard. I felt I should be serving her after all that she had been through.

New Plan

Steve and I talked for a long time, discussing the "new" plan for being here, recognizing there was nothing to rebuild at this point. He suggested I meet with families, offering them grief counseling. Steve felt rebuilding the broken hearts was the greatest and most immediate need at that time. I readily agreed and he began scheduling the sessions.

Jane was now awake and told me about a girl who had cried in her room through the night. I responded that I could hear her sorrow from where I was sleeping. When Shanthi joined us, she said that it was Nona, who is a seventeen year old young woman that had lost her entire family in the tsunami. Shanthi told us Nona has been crying herself to sleep ever since the tragedy. I cannot imagine what must go through her mind when she closes her eyes at night!

Steve came to tell me that the first couple I was to counsel, Vijay and Ananthy, had arrived and were waiting in the living room for an introduction. As I came around the corner, all I could think was that this was the first time I could honestly say I have seen *The Face of Grief!* There is no way to describe the look on their faces; they were so void of life. After an initial greeting, there was silence. It was an appropriate quiet, we did not need to speak for the moment. After a while, Vijay started crying. He pulled a picture out of his Bible and handed it to me saying, "This was our daughter." Ananthy then began to cry while Vijay related their somber tragedy.

We were in church that morning and I was preaching in our new building. We were so proud and excited because we were going to have the dedication in a few weeks; and it was Christmas. Everyone was dressed for the holiday, settling in for a special time of fellowship and celebration. As I spoke, two young girls came up to one of the openings in the wall and hollered through the crack, "The ocean is coming, the ocean is coming!" I thought nothing of it; assuming they were kids, just playing.

As quick as the girls came, they were gone. Seconds passed and "it" hit. The building filled with water and everyone was trapped inside. Being solid concrete, the walls held tight and acted as a prison while everyone went straight up."

Ananthy interjected that as she was pushed upward by the rushing water, she grabbed their daughter Ausher (not sure of the spelling) and they rose up together, only to be slammed against the ceiling and then dropped back down again, just as fast as they went up. She continued the story saying that without any thought, everyone ran out the entrance of the building which faced the ocean. The wave had gone and they continued to run around the building to check on the village, only to discover that it too was gone! Nothing; there was nothing left!

Ananthy was still sobbing while trying to paint a picture of the scene for me. She said that the sand looked like boiling oats as the water was still sinking back into the sand.

Vijay said he looked back at his congregation and could see the distress on everyone's faces. In the maelstrom of crying and yelling, he felt they should pull everyone together for prayer. He expressed there was nothing else he could offer at that point and the people were looking to him for comfort. They gathered in a circle and he began to pray for those who might be missing, and for understanding of what had just happened. No one had any idea, at this point, what had leveled their village; all they knew was that it was gone and they alone had been spared!

Shanthi, shielding her face from the heat as she passes by the tree where Ananthy was hanging upside after the second wave which rolled her around through the barbed wire and where the realization, that their baby was now gone, first struck.

As Vijay began his supplication "it" hit again. The second wave drove up the land with a vengeance and the people, who now had no protection, were rolled up with the wave and torn apart from each other in mere seconds. Vijay said that as he was being thrashed around by the water, he grabbed onto the first thing he could reach. He had no idea where he was; just that he was not rolling around anymore. When the wave crashed back into the ocean, it was then he realized he was in the top of a palm tree, many feet up in the air; everyone and everything else gone. EVERYONE! He could see no one. He yelled for Ananthy and Ausher... nothing. There was no sound. For a brief moment, he didn't see any point in living; he was alone!

Finally he heard a voice breaking the silence of the air. Vijay managed to move around enough to see Ananthy's brother in the top of another palm tree pointing down towards a short tree with wire-like limbs. Then he saw it... Ananthy was caught in this trap, hanging from her leg with her clothes completely torn from her body.

Vijay had no idea how he got out of the tree that day, but he did, and ran across the slippery, water-soaked sand like it was solid, dry ground. He said when he got to his wife, he could not help but notice that their precious little girl was no longer with her. He could not bring himself to ask what happened. He didn't have to. As he carefully lowered Ananthy out of the tree, despite her injury, she began frantically begging to look for their daughter. Vijay told her there was nothing left. Everything, including their new church building and their entire congregation, was gone. Everyone was missing except for them and her brother, who was still up in the palm tree behind them. Ananthy, now with a sense of relief, told Vijay it was alright. She had given Ausher to her brother. Somewhere in the midst of everything, she remembered handing their little girl off to him in the middle of the wave...

Then "it" happened again; the third wave hit! This time they were washed away together. While tossed about through the waves, Vijay remembered that they were drug out to sea more than once. The thought passed through his mind that it would all be over soon, and then the wave flipped so they were washed back inland where they were ultimately pulled out of the water by two military personnel.

Ananthy, now weakened by her injury, was begging to look for their baby. She beseeched the men to help find her brother, who she thought still had their daughter, Ausher, with him. Vijay did not want to tell Ananthy that he had not seen their daughter when he was talking to her brother in the tree. Vijay, now lost in his anguish, thought, "What if there is a chance that she just wasn't in her brother's arms?" They began to run in a frantic search effort!

A photograph of Vijay and Ananthy, who lost their entire church and many family members including their daughter.

When they were able to get close enough to the trees where Vijay and his brother had been, they realized that neither he nor their precious baby were to be found. The third wave must have taken them. It was at that critical moment when the full magnitude of the event became real. They not only lost their whole church and village, but also their child, Vijay's sister who was pregnant, (the only one found after the tsunami was over); Ananthy's two brothers and what appeared to be, for the moment, their lives. After recounting this story for me to this point, there was nothing more to say. Tears replaced words.

I continued to meet with grieving people for days. The unimaginable stories of human loss replayed in my head so much that at night I could not sleep.

One day we went inland to meet with a family that was affected from a distance. When we arrived at their home, we were greeted by a rather large family who, because of the tragedy, now had to live together in the small space.

As was the tradition at each home we visited, we were greeted with tea and some sort of snack. In the midst of all their losses, these people were still generous with what little they had. I was seated with those who brought me when out of the house came a couple with the same look of grief that I had seen on Vijay and Ananthy's face. They began telling their story with intense passion. They had sent their daughter to the coast with

a family member to spend the day at the beach, not considering that they would never see her again. As the couple went into detail of how they tried to find their daughter, I learned a great deal about how the families went looking for their lost loved ones.

The father explained that at birth, in their culture, a bracelet is given which is unique to the baby. No one else has one like theirs. When they began looking for their little one, they searched for her unique bracelet. There were so many bodies following the

Here is the picture which the family wanted shared. You can see the bracelet on the arm.

tsunami that the only thing that could be done by the authorities was to take a picture of the deceased and then bury them. The pictures were then placed in public places such as the so-called post office.

He could hardly talk through the tears as he began to describe what it was like searching through hundreds of photos for their little girl. As he spoke, he handed me a piece of folded notebook paper and asked me to open it. I held the paper for a few moments and then, almost reluctantly for fear of

132

what further sorrow it might contain, I opened it to find a picture of a tiny, unrecognizable, child. The effect that water has on the human body is shocking. Now I was seeing it first-hand in the picture of a small child, whose precious body was swollen and broken. As I looked closer, there was in the image, a bracelet. The interpreter shared that the family felt blessed because the picture was taken with the bracelet visible and it belonged to their daughter.

This is just about the most tragic thing I have ever seen. Just when I thought there was not much more that could get to me, my interpreter said that the family wanted me to take a picture of the picture and bring it back to the U.S. to give proof of how bad things are for them. I told the interpreter I did not feel right taking a picture of this, and so the little girl's grandmother came up and placed her hands around mine with the picture in the middle and in English she said *"Please!"* With that imploring look, I left with the picture and a promise.

Six Years Later

It is hard to believe that six years have passed since that devastating morning which took the lives of over 295,000 people, 30,957 being from Sri Lanka. Overcoming a catastrophe of this magnitude could not take place over night, but life has continued and some version of normalcy has been restored. Sadly, the massive loss of life was not the only loss experienced. The survivors have memories that haunt them every night as they close their eyes, only to awaken and go out where they are once again reminded of the tragedy because much of the rubble has not been removed. With that said, the Sri Lankan's are a very resilient people. They have chosen to move forward and not dwell on the actual event, but to continue with their lives as proactively as they can. The rebuilding, not only of the structures, but of their lives, continues to this day.

Steve and Shanthi have continued their roles as leaders in their community, meeting the needs both physically and spiritually of those in the village. They are legal guardians of five of the children orphaned by the tsunami. They are working on a remodel of their home to accommodate their growing *family*. In addition, they have opened a clinic with the supplies we hurriedly gathered and brought with us. The supplies were of great value to the medical personnel who came to help following the tsunami.

Nona, still with Steve and Shanthi, has stepped into adulthood as a gifted leader. She has faced her loss and uses the strength she has gained to help other young people who have experienced losses similar to hers. It is her purpose to show them, through teaching and example, how to find peace as they overcome their personal tragedy. Her tears are still there, but don't come as often as she continues growing through her grief.

Jr. is all grown up now and is studying Science in Batticaloa, preparing for exams. With modern technology everywhere, we are able to stay in touch via text messaging. He still wears the yellow band that I gave him while I was there. He says it reminds him to always walk with faith and stay strong.

Vijay and Ananthy... the depth of their grief is unfathomable! After the loss of Ananthy's two brothers, Vijay's sister who was about to give birth, their whole congregation, the entire village outside the walls of their church building, and most of all, their precious daughter, one would wonder how they could move beyond this.

They have quietly begun a new life as they continue to put the pieces back together. They have been blessed with a new child and are presently ministering to another congregation. The beautiful location where their building once stood overlooking the ocean is now a protected zone. There can be no structures near the water to avoid the same catastrophe, if there were to be another tsunami. Vijay and Ananthy's grief was, and continues to be, felt deeply in their souls.

As time has gone by, and they continued to help those around them, Vijay and Anathy's grief is being replaced with peace; the kind of peace that comes from tragedy which bestows a gift on those who endure with certain knowledge that life is fragile, but still worth living.

I guess that just leaves me! When I arrived back in the states, I was different. There is no other way to state it. I experienced my own kind of grief that I am not sure I can put into words. I am so grateful to my mom for encouraging me to journal while I was in Sri Lanka. I had never kept a journal, but I can honestly say it got me through on a daily basis. When the day was done, and it was quiet, I lay on the concrete floor listening to the sounds of everyone sleeping and began to shed what I could from my experience into that journal so I could sleep. The words flowed without effort. There was not time to mourn while I was there. I guess I knew that one day I would read the words I had written and then my grieving would begin, as that was not the time.

I took the picture of that small child home and kept my promise! Everywhere I went to speak about the tsunami, I shared their story and showed her picture. As I prepared everyone for the picture in the PowerPoint presentation, I was taken back to that moment when it was actually given to me. Each time I shared, my voice would break. When the picture popped up on the screen, without fail, there was always a collective gasp. It was at that very moment in the presentation that I knew the audience grasped the full magnitude of what the people of Sri Lanka had experienced.

I work in Bereavement now with Hospice and know that my experiences in Sri Lanka have laid the foundation for some of the most rewarding times of my life. I did not know it at the time, but I wrote what was to be my first poem while in Sri Lanka. I couldn't get the image of that precious little girl out of my mind, as she left the arms of her mother to be lost in the waves on that dreadful morning. I now write poetry for all the families I am blessed to care for.

Behind The Story

I first met Keith when he phoned me, after hearing about the grief recovery program I was pilot testing in the Dallas area. As a bereavement coordinator seeking innovation for his company, he was interested in learning more about the work I was doing. We decided to meet for breakfast and discuss our common vision for helping people to overcome grief and be whole again. At our meeting we talked for three hours and left the restaurant not having ordered or eaten a bite!

In the course of our conversation, I told Keith about *The Triumph Book* and the role it plays in my bereavement program as a tool to show that *it is possible* to overcome grief. Often we can find hope simply by seeing the example of others who have healed. I told him that *The Triumph Book* can be an opportunity to reach farther than just the bereavement industry, as the message itself is dealing with all varieties of adversity. Then Keith shared with me that his fiancé passed away just before they were married. I was intrigued, thinking this may be a great story for *The Triumph Book,* as he is now a bereavement coordinator helping others through similar losses.

So we discussed the possibility of including his story in the book, but then Keith told me how he had another story, which he would like to share even more, about the time he spent in Indonesia helping survivors during the aftermath of the tsunami. As he told me about his experience there, I thought this would be a powerful and unique story to include. A first-hand look at what such a calamity is like, and how people overcome utter devastation, would be phenomenal!

Since first meeting Keith and gathering his story, he has become a true hero to me and a great champion of our common purpose. The work I have watched him do in the bereavement field is innovative and truly effective. He is changing the way his hospice looks at bereavement; making it a service and support which is offered before death, as well as reaching out to many other organizations in the community to provide bereavement support outside of the halls of his office and location.

There is a ripple effect beginning to happen as other organizations take notice of all he is doing, and it is the catalyst for a much needed change! Because of Keith's powerful work, he is quickly becoming recognized as a leading expert in his field.

Eleven

Cancer x 3

Embracing the Healing Journey as Supporter, Survivor and Mom

Author: Nancy Hopps

All things happen in their own perfect timing, in their own perfect way. It took me ten years (after my own cancer experience) to begin writing a book about my healing journey. Much of my richest learning has occurred during this last decade, as my journey has interwoven with others'. The experiences I've shared—especially, with my daughter Annamieka—have in a very real sense become a part of my own healing journey—which I've come to learn has no finite ending.

Although centered around my cancer-related experiences, the insights and truths shared in these pages are universal. Whether your life has been touched by "the C-word" or not, I trust your heart will resonate with the stories and insights presented. *Our dramas may differ; the truth remains the same.*

My intention is to share my experiences in a way that makes your heart beat with a joyful recognition of shared humanity. My story is simply one version of an individual's journey into the depths, in order to find the light. Yes, there were moments of fear, doubt and deep despair, but mostly, this is a tale of joy, awe and gratitude. Embracing the depths of one's being, choosing to welcome the full experience of *what is*, holds astounding rewards.

*****

"You must go to Iowa."

This inner directive was just one of many synchronistic occurrences that helped guide me through my cancer healing journey. Sometimes the guidance was perfectly clear; sometimes—as in this case—it was still a bit obtuse!

Where, when and how did my cancer healing journey actually begin? When does *any* chapter of life begin, and another end? It seems they all overlap and merge with one another in a divinely-orchestrated dance. That's certainly how *my* life feels. For now, let's start with what seems to be the preamble to my own healing chapters. Let's start with Elina's story...

*****

My son, Aaron, eighteen at the time, was deeply in love with Sarah Elina, a nymph-like, sparkly little being who was his first serious romantic relationship. It was an absolute joy watching the two of them together. By the time she left for college in the fall of 1997, Elina, as she preferred to be called, had become a part of our family, actually living with us much of the time. Aaron, still in his senior year of high school, remained home in Eugene, Oregon, as she headed for college out of state.

In November, Elina came home for Thanksgiving break. Complaining of fatigue and chest pain, she went into the emergency room the evening before Thanksgiving. She came out with a diagnosis of multiple tumors in her lungs, which were later confirmed as an advanced stage of metastasized Wilms' Tumor, a rare form of kidney cancer she'd had as an infant. We were all in shock. How could this *be*?

For Elina, the following months brought a barrage of treatments, family reconciliations, and profound emotional and spiritual healing. She began healing a strained relationship with her mother, and deepening her bond with her largely absentee father.

An amazing maturation process occurred as Elina dealt with issues far beyond her years. Over the course of the next year or so, she and Aaron developed the strength it took to face what life was presenting to them—a seemingly tragic ending to this otherwise storybook romance. The tale had gone from dreams of living "happily ever after" to coming to terms with some of the most profound life lessons any of us ever face: learning to let go, finding peace in the midst of seemingly unbearable circumstances, having the courage to keep the heart open when it wants to close in pain and self-protection and endlessly grappling with the unanswerable question, "Why??!"

As Elina's body gradually wasted away, her spirit continued to shine brightly. Her sense of self expanded to include more than just her fragile physical form. As it became clear that her time on earth was nearing an end, her bravery and spunk remained an inspiration to us all.

*****

By October of 1998, nearly a year after Elina's diagnosis, no known healing options remained. Elina's mom, desperately pursuing any possibilities, attended a lecture by a respected healing practitioner who "happened" to be passing through town. He suggested she bring Elina to his treatment center in Fairfield, Iowa. He thought he might be able to help. So the decision was made: Elina's mom and dad would rent a Winnebago, and drive her to Fairfield the following week.

At this point, after nearly a year of caring for Elina, while also caring for my own family, teaching, seeing clients, and managing my rapidly-growing CD business, as well as rehearsing and performing in various musical and theatrical productions, my own reservoirs were running a bit low... to say the least. Humbling as it is to admit, here I was, a "relaxation/wellness expert", totally exhausted and in deep denial of many of my own basic needs.

In my experience, when there is a spiritual lesson to be learned, we are first given a gentle little nudge. If we don't respond to that, we get a heftier tap on the shoulder. Ignore that, and it might be Cosmic Sledge Hammer time.

It was that time for me. I'd ignored the gentler warnings. Now, my body was trying desperately to get my attention. My menstrual cycle was really not much of a *cycle* at all anymore—I was bleeding profusely. Hence, I was severely anemic, and ridiculously fatigued. I'd become so used to running on adrenaline, because I felt I had to "just keep going," that I was truly unaware of how dangerously burned out I was. But I knew I couldn't go on like this much longer. Little did I know, a rather big change was just around the corner.

*****

I was lying in bed at 2 am that week in mid-October of '98, so overtired I was unable to sleep, reading a chapter of Elizabeth Kübler-Ross' autobiography. Suddenly, out of the blue, I heard the very clear words: "You must go to Iowa."

First of all, I'm not the sort that hears voices on a regular basis. I can count on both hands the clear, "Thou shalt do this" sort of verbal messages I've received in my life. This was not my normal modus operandi. But this one was undeniable.

Yet, my rational mind immediately tried its best to refute it.

"*What!??* I can't go to Iowa!! I'm sick, I'm exhausted, I have classes to teach, a huge project to complete, kids to consider, etc."

Resist as I might, I knew, for whatever reason, I *had* to go to Iowa. Selfishly, I also didn't relish the thought of being cooped up in a rolling metal box for four days with Elina's divorced parents who had difficulty being in the same room together! But sometimes we're called to serve in ways beyond our understanding... *and/or* our comfort level!

So two days later, with Elina snuggled in bed in the back of the Winnebago, attached to the oxygen tank which was now her near-constant companion, Elina, her folks and I set off for Iowa.

Although I have many bittersweet memories from that trip, I remember one moment most clearly. It was about 10 p.m... I was driving on one of the interminably long stretches of open highway in Montana. Elina was seated next to me, her mom beside her. Dad was asleep in the back. The three of us were giddy with exhaustion, but true to form were attempting to sing. We'd spent many joyful hours singing together over the past year. It always felt healing.

This night, however, Elina could barely squeak out the notes, because her breathing was so restricted, and I, too, found I could hardly sustain a sound. I just felt completely drained of energy.

It was at that point that Elina's mom, a hospice nurse, said, "Nancy—you have *got* to go get checked out." She gave me a stern lecture about ignoring my own needs, and made me promise to first look into getting health insurance, then make a doctor's appointment immediately after returning home. I promised.

*****

We arrived in Fairfield after four very long days of driving. Due to Elina's severely compromised lung capacity, we'd had to take the longer northern route from Eugene, Oregon, to avoid the highest Rocky Mountain elevations. As the sun was setting over the corn fields, we settled into a Norman Rockwell-type farmhouse B&B on the outskirts of town, and prepared for our next morning's appointment.

At 10 a.m., when we walked into the sunlit office, I immediately understood why I had been compelled to come to Iowa. As Tom, the practitioner, entered the room to greet us, he and I both did a double-take. I knew this man. I'd never met him before, but I *knew* this man. He literally stopped in his tracks, too, staring at me, and asked, "Have we... we haven't met before... have we?" It bordered on spooky.

Tom and I arranged to have dinner together, given that I was to fly home the following morning. Dinner extended late into the evening. We talked for hours, experiencing an undeniable "resonance" with one another. Our meeting was certainly not an accident. We agreed the connection was not romantic, but it remained mysterious to both of us what this deep connection was all about. We vowed to keep in touch. Perhaps professional liaisons were to develop?

*****

Back home, I immediately launched back into a busy work and performance schedule, plagued by uncontrollable menstrual flow and accompanying fatigue. Two days before opening night of our professional chamber ensemble's annual Madrigal Dinner, Dr. Jan (pronounced, "Yahn") Stafl, my ob/gyn, suggested a D&C procedure, which removes the lining of the uterus. It is a fairly simple in-office procedure that often remedies this sort of situation.

Not being a big fan of any kind of invasive procedure, I reluctantly agreed. Grateful for my hypnotherapy training, I underwent the procedure without the usual anesthesia. I wanted to avoid their side-affects, and be fully alert for our final dress rehearsal that evening. All went well, and as I was leaving, Dr. Stafl said, in passing, "Of course we'll send samples to the lab, just as a matter of course, but I'm sure everything's fine."

*****

A week or so later, having the Madrigal Dinner performances under my belt, and the bleeding fairly well under control, I continued with stepped-up rehearsals for *The Descent of Inanna*, a very physically and emotionally demanding theatrical production in which I played the title role. According to ancient Sumerian myth, Inanna is a goddess who descends into the underworld to save the Sumerian culture from self-destruction. It was not a light, fluffy role to play!

I'd also just recently been offered the role of "Kate" in Shakespeare's *Taming of the Shrew*, another very physically demanding role, and one I'd wanted to play for years. At 44, playing the young, feisty "shrew" was probably a last-in-a-lifetime opportunity, so I'd eagerly accepted the role. Rehearsals would begin soon.

On December 15th, we were exactly a month away from opening night of our fourth production's run of *Inanna*. At 5:30 pm, as I was on my way out the door to rehearsal, the phone rang. It was Jan Stafl, who said, "I got your test results back. Can you come down to my office and talk?" Needless to say, my heart skipped a beat and I drove immediately to his office.

I sat across from Dr. Stafl, as he gently told me of his utter surprise at the lab results. Upon hearing the diagnosis of grade two uterine cancer, I had two simultaneous thoughts: "*How* am I gonna tell the kids?" (...that while Elina is dying of cancer, now their *mom* has cancer!) and "Oh, okay—it's time to play out this chapter, and get on with what it is I'm *really* here to do!"

Thank God, the latter thought, and accompanying feeling of peace, was so strong, that I absolutely *knew* everything was going to be okay. I was going to live. The cancer would be healed, and I was going to come out stronger for it.

*****

Spiritual knowing notwithstanding, a cancer diagnosis is a life-changing event. My world turned upside down in an instant.

Those first few days after my diagnosis were an emotional blur of oncologist appointments, phone calls and to-do lists, discussions with my partner Thom about how to tell the kids, who else to tell, and not tell. It just seemed so unreal. I remember feeling wave after wave of "Wow, this is really happening! I can't rewind and play this out differently... this is what *is*, and I have to deal with it!" I found I needed a lot of quiet, alone time to digest this bizarre left turn in my life.

And yet, as overwhelming as it all was, there was an underlying sense of rightness... even, dare I say, excitement? I knew on some level, this was indeed a part of my life path, and I was in an odd sort of way *excited* to see what growth and learning this chapter would bring. This was a Big One!

*****

A few key decisions needed to be made quickly: Contrary to the oncologist's advice, NO, I would not have an immediate full hysterectomy, and contrary to many others' advice, YES, I would continue with both theatrical commitments. I listened to many points of view. Ultimately, I listened to my own inner voice.

Learning to listen to, and *trust* my own inner knowing, to sort out what was true for *me* from amongst all the inner and outer cacophony of voices and opinions that were presented along the way, proved to be one of the most important aspects of my healing journey. The surgery decision is just one example.

*****

Given that, as an adult, my orientation has primarily been toward more holistic, natural healing methods, I was not ready to say, "Sure, go ahead and make a large vertical incision down the middle of my stomach and abdomen, and remove my uterus, ovaries and surrounding lymph nodes... just in case."

Please understand: for some, this would have been a perfectly sound and "right" choice. It just wasn't for *me*.

Instead, I began researching many different "complimentary" or "alternative" healing modalities. Fortunately, with the type of cancer I had, I felt I had time to research and reflect, rather than having to make choices immediately, while still in the post-diagnosis state of shock.

One realization that came almost immediately after hearing the diagnosis was "Oh! Now I know why I had to go to Iowa!" I called Tom and told him the news. His reply was, in essence, "Come... stay with me. I have an extra room in my home, you can use my car, and I will treat you for free for as long as it takes." We both now knew at least *one* reason why we'd met!

We arranged for my first trip to Mexico, where his practice was now based. He, like many "alternative" practitioners, had moved his practice south of the border to escape FDA regulations. I would go for initial testing and treatment immediately after *Inanna* closed.

*****

By mid-January 1999, between the D&C, the iron supplements, and the new regimen of other nutritional supplements I began after my diagnosis, I'd actually begun to feel better than I'd felt in many months. I now had considerably more energy, and was able to meet the demanding rehearsal and performance schedules.

I also let go of a number of other obligations—things I felt I "should" or "had to" do, but really didn't *want to* do. It's amazing the amount of stress I released just by letting go of a few of the "should" activities in my life. And funny thing, the world somehow continued to turn! It was humbling to admit how well I fit the "over-giver" profile often typical of a cancer patient. Now it was time to learn to give to myself.

I began working with a friend and colleague who helped me heal the vestiges of some long-standing emotional/psychological issues. At that point in my life, I found it very humbling and healing to admit that, a) I still *had* issues, and b) I could accept help dealing with them. One of the most important lessons of my healing journey was that none of us can do it all alone, nor should we try. Asking for help does not equate with being weak or incapable. In fact, sometimes it takes great strength to admit, "I don't have all the answers."

The next months were full of much life-changing inner and outer activity. I explored difficult emotional territory, releasing long-held guilt and blame primarily regarding prior miscarriages. I strengthened my already very strong spiritual foundation. I honed my already very healthy diet, and added many nutritional supplements. I continued with regular exercise. I took a number of sojourns to Mexico and to Germany for further diagnosis and treatment. I underwent a series of treatments in an alternative/complimentary form of energy healing. I did some very deep soul searching, and made a few important lifestyle changes that helped reduce the stress of a chronically over-busy schedule.

*****

In addition to the benefits of the treatment I was receiving, my time south of the border afforded me lots of time to myself. On days I wasn't receiving treatment I swam, continued my self-study Spanish lessons, cooked macrobiotic meals, and looked through old journals and photos. I meditated, chanted and prayed. I took stock of my life and I learned to slow down.

This learning was not always painless, however. One of the most powerful memories of this period was one particular morning, when I had absolutely nothing I "had" to do that day. And yet, as I sat alone, eating my breakfast, my inner "should" voices were spinning out of control.

Here I was, in Mexico with absolutely no obligations, other than occasional treatment sessions, and yet my mind was relentlessly spinning with "shoulds." I still felt the same kind of pressure, the not-enough-time-to-do-it-all feeling that plagued me in my normally overloaded schedule.

"I should be doing more." This was the recurring theme. Whatever I was doing, it wasn't quite enough... or *good* enough. The theme had a number of subtle variations, to fit nearly all occasions!

After breakfast, as I sat on my bed, still trying to decide what to do with the day, it became painfully clear that the pressure was totally self-induced. So, having changed plans numerous times already at the whim of the moment's most dominant "should," I said aloud, *"This is ridiculous!!!"*

I decided the most beneficial thing I could do that day was... *nothing*. I would simply sit there and witness this inner tyrant. I'd experience whatever emotions came up, without distracting myself with any outer activity. It was one of the most challenging afternoons I've ever spent.

Nothing was happening "out there" that was affecting my peace of mind. My peace of mind was being obliterated by this cacophony of inner voices. All chattering away in response to... nothing! *Nothing* was happening. And therein lay the challenge.

I could not attribute this feeling of upset or dis-ease to some*thing* or some*one* outside myself. There was no outer *cause* of my stress. I knew I had the inherent power to respond to *anything* by maintaining a deep sense of underlying peace. This is always the wiser choice—one of those simple, but not always *easy* choices!

So here I was, choosing to open my Pandora's Box of emotions, long ignored in my over-busyness, and simply *be* with its contents. I'd made it through the initial "crisis" part of my healing journey: diagnosis, logistics, travel, emotional and physical exhaustion. I knew I was good at holding it together in crisis mode. I'd proven that many times in my life. I'd already done lots of deep emotional healing. So why was this mundane stuff of life so surprisingly difficult to deal with? I had a deep, unrelenting feeling of discontent, a feeling that despite the *many* blessings in my life, it... or perhaps *I*... was "not enough."

It's funny—when I received my cancer diagnosis, my predominant response had been a deep sense of calm acceptance, a feeling of "rightness." Yet here I was, on this beautiful sunny day in Mexico, feeling physically fine, free of outer responsibilities, and I was driving myself crazy with self-induced stress!

Enough was enough. That afternoon, I drew the line in the sand.

As I sat on the bed simply observing, feeling, allowing, it was like turning to face the monster in a dream, one who's been chasing you and causing all sorts of fear and uproar. When directly confronted, most often the beast loses its power, and is able to be seen for what it is: an illusion.

This was my experience as I confronted my inner "should" monster. It roared and kicked and screamed for a while, but eventually—actually, amazingly quickly—it just ran out of juice, when I stopped "feeding it" with resistance.

By taking that little step back and not engaging, I was able to actually *appreciate* what it was trying to do. According to *its* programming, in order to be loved, I had to be "good enough," which meant always doing "more," always doing something to *earn* that love. Always *doing*. Just *being* was not enough. As I was able to compassionately observe and allow myself to fully *feel* the effects of such an idea, I experienced the utter fallacy of that programming.

It was wrong. I *was* enough, just being who I AM!

These were words I'd read, heard and spoken for years. But on this Tuesday afternoon, I really *got* it. I've found that often the most profound breakthroughs occur in the most unlikely settings, with little pomp and circumstance, just deep desire and readiness. This was one of those important moments.

Would I be forever changed and never be bothered by "shoulds" and "not-enoughness" again? I'd sure like to say yes, I've lived in blissful present moment awareness ever-after. Truth is, although this experience was a major turning point on my path to "Nirvana", I'm not a full-time resident quite yet.

*****

146

While my learning and healing continued, the endless cycle of life... and death... carried on around me. On Wednesday, March 3rd, at 9:15 pm, Elina "began the next part of her journey," as her dad put it. She died peacefully in her little cottage home, surrounded by immense Love, near and far. There was sadness, of course, but at the same time there was a great Lightness, unlike anything I'd experienced before.

We spent that day lovingly creating a photo wall of compiled memories, bathing Elina's body and clothing it, as requested, in her blue satin prom dress. Adorned with her favorite scarves and accompanied by her two favorite stuffed animals, she lay at rest in her own living room for the remainder of the day, in a simple but beautiful pine box that family members had made for her. The coffin was lined with the handmade quilt that had comforted her through her entire ordeal. Now her lifeless body was nestled within its familiar folds, ready for the journey Home.

Located in a small, historic cemetery on a wooded hillside in south Eugene, the final resting place of Elina Windsong has come to be the most unique and inspiring gravesite I have ever seen, a place where loved ones and strangers alike are drawn to commune quietly in this place of beauty, grace and wonder. The site conveys the never-ending, joyous flow of life that Elina so exquisitely embodied during her brief time on earth.

*****

By June of 1999, after many inner and outer journeys in search of *my* truth, I made the decision to have surgery. Jan Stafl, my ob/gyn had said he was willing to "stick my professional neck way out" and disagree with the oncologist. Based on test results showing that the cancer cells seemed to be minimal and fully contained within the uterus, he offered to do a partial vaginal hysterectomy. Though there had been apparent improvement from the alternative therapies I'd been undergoing, now, for various reasons, I felt it was time to incorporate the western medical approach into my healing protocol. Given it had been five months since Jan had made this initial offer, he (and many family members and friends), were greatly relieved at my decision!

As much as I knew I had to find *my* Truth, what felt right for me, I naturally was influenced by the thoughts and feelings of those around me. I knew the adjunctive approaches I'd utilized up to now had been essential elements of the over-all healing process; I knew I would continue this healing work, whether I'd opted for surgery or not. I also realized I could let go of the self-imposed pressure I'd been feeling to heal myself without any western medical intervention. That was a big one for me.

In the course of my healing journey, I came to understand that w*hat to the ego may look like failure or tragedy, may on the soul level be revealed as Divine Perfection. An important part of my learning was that I had not "failed" because I didn't cure my cancer "naturally".*

Throughout and since my *own* cancer experience, I've learned a great deal about the value of *integrative* medical approaches—utilizing the best of *all* healing modalities—and about the distinction between *healing* and *curing*. *"To heal" has been defined as "to set right, to make whole;" "to cure," as "to recover from a disease."* In my personal journey, I feel deeply grateful to have utilized an integrative approach that resulted in both tremendous healing *and* a complete cure.

Once I made the decision to have the surgery, I felt at complete peace with it. Trained in hypnotherapy, I chose to have no general anesthesia, oral or intravenous narcotic pain meds. I received only a spinal block, so I could be fully awake and alert during the surgery. Not everyone's cup of tea, I realize, but for me it was perfect. I'm very grateful my doctor and anesthesiologist were willing to work with me in this way. I was in a heightened spiritual state during the entire procedure. I felt as if I was symbolically offering my earthly womb, which had given birth to my two incredible children, in exchange for the Divine womb of my own spiritual rebirth. Highly aware of the Presence of Spirit, I felt this prayer form in my heart: "How can I best serve? Use me, God. I'm ready." It was one of the most profound moments of my life.

*****

A couple weeks after the surgery, now completely cancer-free, I resumed my Mexico treatments to further heal and fortify my immune system. In hindsight, I think at least as important as the treatments themselves, was the time those next six months afforded me to continue to reflect, feel, integrate and take stock of my life.

So many "miracles" occurred during this journey. One that comes to mind is an "angel" benefactor who appeared out of the blue one evening. It was the evening before I was to fly down to Mexico. Thom and I were sitting at the dining room table, going over finances and feeling more than a bit of stress as we tried to figure out how to cover all the mounting expenses. And then the phone rang. In that *exact moment*, the phone rang. It was Gordon Tripp on the other end of the line. Gordon was an enigmatic acquaintance, in his eighties at the time, and to have him call at this very moment was, to say the least, surprising! The gist of the phone call was that Gordon insisted on covering all expenditures for my remaining Mexico jaunts. A simple service I rendered years earlier came back to me more than tenfold.

But the blessing didn't stop there. A few months later, when my "official" healing journey was over, all my treatments were completed, and test results were all giving me a squeaky clean bill of health, I found myself poised at an important juncture. My prayer of that time period was basically, "Okay, God, I'm still here, in this body. What do you want me to do?" The answer came quickly.

*****

Soon after my final return from Mexico, Gordon called and invited me to lunch. On April 5th, I arrived at his home at noon. He'd prepared a delicious soup and salad, which we enjoyed while catching up on each others' lives. Then, after listening to me ponder what was next for me (more audio recordings, private practice, theatrical pursuits, writing, or...), he leaned forward and said, "Young lady, I believe in you. I believe in your work. You decide what it is you want to do, and I'll give you money to do it."

Again, I was left speechless. But this time we were face to face, and I became aware that my jaw had literally fallen open. I'd always thought that was just a figure of speech, but mine literally fell open in utter speechlessness.

When I finally could respond, I said, "Gordon, do you realize you've just taken away my last excuse for why I'm not doing what I *know* I'm really here to do?!" I promised to think about it. He gave me strict instructions not to limit myself, and not to think too long.

Two days later, another truly "miraculous" opportunity presented itself. Bottom line was: as a result of an unexpected opportunity to spend a week in internship (and contemplation) in the mountains outside Guadalajara, I knew with great certainty that I could be of the highest service by creating a new series of audio CDs and booklets that would help others experience many of the healing approaches I'd found so effective in my own personal and professional life. I'd just gotten a fresh, first-hand reminder of the healing power of deep relaxation, guided imagery and affirmations, especially when combined with Love, the most powerful healing force of all. Now I knew it was time to share my deepened learning.

This insight ultimately led to the creation of my award-winning *Relax into Healing* series. Looking back, it's remarkable to see the perfection of the timing in which each step unfolded. This is not to say there wasn't a lot of hard work, long hours, tenacity and perseverance. But through it all, there was always a sense of rightness. Through my seeming adversities, I'd been blessed with such deep learning and growth, and now I was able to share it with others in such profoundly meaningful ways. I knew I was playing at least *one* of the roles I've come here to play.

*****

"All the world's a stage, and all the men and women merely players... "
—William Shakespeare

*****

Our life dramas are really pretty similar to those we see performed by actors on a stage. To me, the mark of a good theatrical production is that it makes you think, feel and reflect. It makes an impact. It changes you in some way.

My cancer healing journey had had all the elements of good drama— conflict, suspense, romance and more. Once my physical healing journey was over, at the same time I felt compelled to begin sharing what I had learned with others, I knew I first needed personal time to integrate the profound experience I'd just been through. After many months of *doing,* what I wanted most was to have time to myself to just *stop.* To draw inward, reflect and integrate.

*****

Some of the most profound healing occurs after the treatment has ended.

*****

Over the course of the next several years, *many* changes continued to occur in my life. My primary relationship very lovingly transitioned during this time period, and by September of 2004, I was engaged to be married to Ken, the wonderful man who's now my husband. Another amazing Synchronicity afforded me an opportunity to spend several months in... Iowa!... getting my massage license. More Guidance led me to become steward of *The Healing Sanctuary*, a nine-acre property with home and studio space. It was the place I'd visualized for years, and finding it when I was least looking for it was yet another blessing.

This sacred ground has become a *Healing Sanctuary* not only for me, but also for many clients and workshop participants... not to mention neighbor dogs and repairmen. More often than not, the latter seem to find reason to stay and share their personal life stories after their appointed task is finished. Of course, I've also been told that I could draw the life story out of a monk who'd taken a vow of silence!

I've had several big burly sorts of guys wander back to their trucks after having told me some pretty intimate stuff that was going on for them, shaking their heads and saying, "How did I get into telling you all *that*!?" Simply *listening* with compassion to someone's story can be surprisingly healing... for all involved.

*****

Writing a chronicle of life events like this, with timelines so condensed, it becomes even more evident that life just keeps on going: births and deaths, weddings and separations, high points and rough spots—such is the stuff of life. During this time period, I also had the privilege of acting as "spiritual midwife" for my dad as he made his transition with colon cancer. As anyone who has helped usher another into the Light knows, it was an indescribably rich and beautiful experience.

Through it all, life affords such rich learning, no matter how that lesson is "clothed"—sometimes it's like a tattered old T-shirt on a Saturday afternoon; sometimes it appears in the finest regalia. From rags to riches, life so elegantly presents us with the lessons our soul most needs to learn.

The outer stuff of the next year or so was mostly "tattered T-shirt" kind of learning—just the stuff of everyday life, devoid of "Big Ones" for a change... a lovely time of grounding and integration. And then, in early February, 2005, the "T-shirt Learnings" gave way once again to another round of Big Ones. I was about to be faced with the type of challenge that made even my own cancer healing journey pale by comparison. I was about to hear some of the most dreaded words that a mother could ever imagine...

*****

In March of 2005, after 11 days of "Hospital Purgatory" awaiting a definitive diagnosis, my otherwise radiant, always-before-healthy nineteen-year-old daughter, Annamieka, was diagnosed with Hodgkin's Lymphoma. In the time span of a couple months, I watched my gorgeous, healthy daughter turn into a literally unrecognizable "sumo wrestler" look-alike. With a large tumor obstructing return blood flow via her superior vena cava, the situation was quite serious and the immediate answers lay squarely in the allopathic (western medical) arena.

My "nature girl" daughter, who had not taken so much as an *aspirin* in her life, was now suddenly relying on prednisone and sleeping pills to do two of life's most basic things: breathe and sleep. Given the imminent danger of the situation, I welcomed the steroid drugs that normally I would have strongly opposed. This was the first of *many* drugs that would enter my beloved daughter's body that I would never have believed up to that point I'd be so grateful for.

I am also extremely grateful for the many alternative and complimentary healing approaches we implemented. I spent many hours helping Mieka deal with extreme itching and pain, using deep relaxation and hypnotherapeutic suggestion. We used guided imagery and affirmative prayer, sound healing and other energy healing techniques. Whole, healthy foods were brought in to augment or replace the hospital offerings. Various herbal, nutritional and enzymatic supplements helped support her immune system. Laughter therapy was integrated whenever possible! Many people, friends and strangers alike, prayed for her. She was surrounded and infused with the healing power of Love.

*****

My learning from Mieka's cancer healing journey was already beginning. One of my first lessons was to *Never say never*. Life can change very, very quickly.

Despite my strong leaning toward natural remedies and my general aversion to allopathic forms of treatment, these six months afforded me many opportunities to experience the life-saving benefits of *integrative* medicine. There were many soul searching moments for me along the way of Mieka's six-month course of chemo and radiation. Given it was her chosen course of treatment, we all put full energy into supporting and fully believing in the healing power of these western medical interventions, as we continued to support her healing with many adjunctive approaches…the most potent of which was Love.

Now five years (at the time of this writing) after Mieka's diagnosis, the learning and healing for both of us continues. Mieka is happy, healthy, and pursuing a career in the healing profession. My live presentations and my work with private clients, many of whom are cancer patients, have deepened in ways I could never have imagined. The healing experiences I went through as a supporter, survivor, and mom were direct and essential steps along the path of what I believe to be my highest calling.

I am unspeakably grateful that my CDs and booklets are "out there" helping people, mostly in ways I will never know. They are used in hospitals, pain centers, hospice care facilities, as well as by countless individuals, many of whom have let me know what "lifesavers" they have been. I am also

Aaron, Nancy and Mieka

blessed to work with amazingly courageous private clients who open their hearts and lives to me, as we share the struggles and triumphs of their journeys together. I *sing* with joy and gratitude, literally and figuratively.

My primary role as a "healer" is to be a conduit, helping to guide clients into the sacred place of deep stillness inside where all healing begins. My role as "speaker/teacher/author" is to use words and stories to inspire that same soul-awakening. Similarly, as a "performer", my most fundamental role is to touch and open audience members' hearts and minds, so that deep Wisdom may be revealed.

Nancy Hopps

I would not be doing what I'm doing without having gone through everything I have. I think of my cancer journeys as Divine gifts. If cancer or some other major challenge is a part of your Path, please remember:

*****

Our biggest challenges are also our biggest blessings.
The paths are many. They all lead Home.

*****

Whatever your circumstances may be, whatever challenges you may be facing—for we *all* have challenges of one sort or another—I acknowledge, and thank you, for your courage. True healing of any sort takes deep honesty and extraordinary courage. The healing that each of us does, we do for the greater whole. We are, indeed, all in this together. In time, you *will* emerge from the deepest struggles with unimagined wisdom and invaluable gifts to share.

Blessings on your Journey.

Behind the Story

While many of the stories in this book were found by following a trail of bread crumbs from one author or acquaintance to another, I discovered Nancy Hopps' story literally in my own back yard. Nancy lives and works at *The Healing Sanctuary*, just up the hill from my parents' five country acres. My mom often told me how she would hike up to Nancy's place for yoga classes or massage. I was always intrigued by this neighbor who had a yoga studio and healing space adjacent to her home. As a fitness instructor myself, I had a similar dream of opening my own private exercise gym.

For a birthday gift one summer, as I was "home" visiting my parents, my mom arranged for me to have a massage therapy session with this fascinating woman. Nancy was calm and spunky at the same time as she gave me a tour of her "Healing Sanctuary." I was definitely feeling a combination of envy and inspiration as I saw how beautifully she had developed her space.

When she guided me into the massage studio, I noticed her *Relax into Healing CDs* carefully placed on the window ledge. Immediately, they reminded me of my own desire to help people heal and a discussion about her work, and mine, ensued. After hearing of her journey through not one, but three episodes of cancer, and how she was able to serve others through what she had learned and developed from these experiences, I asked Nancy to be part of this book. She smiled and warmly said "Yes... this feels right!"

Since that day I have come to know Nancy better and even read the first draft of the book she wrote as a result of writing this chapter for me. It has been rewarding to witness Nancy's ever-growing opportunities to share inspiration and healing with others.

For more information about Nancy, including the full-length book on her personal journey(s) through cancer, (title still TBA as *The Triumph Book* goes to press), her award-winning *Relax Into Healing CDs* (on cancer, surgery, pain, sleep, healing affirmations, deep relaxation and related topics), as well as information about her current public appearance schedule and more, please visit: *www.RelaxintoHealing.com*.

Twelve

The Walker

Author: Carlos Diaz

In 1995 I was diagnosed with Multiple Sclerosis or MS, as it is commonly known. MS affects people in many different ways. Some have short periods of blindness in one eye or the other; some have pain in their extremities, while still other people function normally so that you would never know they have MS. My version of MS affects the entire left side, from my arm down to my foot. Having balance and an ability to walk on my own has been reduced to using a cane and an electric scooter when I have to walk longer distances, such as in the mall. I suffer from extreme fatigue and chronic pain. I have often asked my wife, Janet, and especially God, in my dark and alone moments, "What am I supposed to do? Why am I here with this heavy burden?" The answers are almost always "To inspire, and to encourage others to LIVE life one day at a time." Somehow, someway, God has found a way to use my *abilities* and not allow my *disability* to get in His way, so that my life can inspire others to live each day to the best of their abilities and encourage them to "lean not on their own understanding, but to trust God."

My MS causes severe weakness on my entire left side. I wear a brace on my left foot due to a "drop foot" condition, affecting my gait. My left hand is constantly curled into a closed fist; I have aches and pain in my body and loss of balance. However, I tell people who don't know me that I have MS, but it doesn't have me.

For me, MS started with a small cramp, then numbness in my left leg, leading to limping on that leg as well as being thirsty all the time (due to the diabetes I was also diagnosed with a year later). From the diagnosis until about 2000, my MS and diabetes were manageable and my afflictions were no more than an inconvenience; but they were about to become much more debilitating. In 2000, my limping and loss of balance became worse; the weakness, fatigue and body aches became severe. Then one morning, in 2004, I was not able to get up out of bed at all. My wife had to help me that day to do everything. I had what was called an *exacerbation from MS*. I took three months off from work in order to recuperate. When I tried to return to work, I was not able to because the company said I could no longer do my job and it was being eliminated anyway. This was at the beginning of the financial downturn in America.

While this was going on, I was becoming depressed and angry. The more my wife pointed out that I was frequently grumpy, angry and generally in a bad mood, the more depressed and angry I became. I have always been a happy, funny, easy going guy, so I didn't know where this grumpy old man was coming from. What I knew is that I had to find a way to pick myself up and not let my family down, especially my teenage daughters; so I started on a quest for a college degree in Web Design. I also kept busy by volunteering with small things at church, in my daughter's high school, at my wife's elementary school and by making simple, healthy, family meals. I have found that keeping busy, serving others in whatever little way I can, helps keep me from focusing on my woes. It is not always easy for me to do basic things like getting out of bed, tying my shoes, loading or unloading my electric scooter into our van and especially making meals for my family. Because of this, I know that it has not been me doing all these things with my own abilities at all. My strength and perseverance comes from the Grace of God. This is powerful knowledge to have, for without God's Grace my abilities would not be so clear, in spite of my disabilities.

My girls and wife have learned to deal with MS and my lack of mobility, along with all the other little obstacles that this disease throws into our lives. No one has taught my daughters how to make accommodations for, or how to serve, people that have special needs; but I have observed them handle these potentially awkward situations with great compassion and love. For example, when they see persons with a disability, instead of ignoring or turning away from them, they approach and ask "How can I help you?" or "Do you need help?" They handle these situations better than I ever did as a teenager or young adult.

I recently graduated from college with a Bachelor of Science degree in Information Technology/Visual Communications. I purposely set out to obtain this college degree to show my daughters that we can do anything we put our minds to, that nothing can prevent us from reaching our goals, even a disability such as mine. With the help of God, all things are possible, "if he goes before us who can stand against us?" My accomplishment, I hope, has left them no room to fear and instead has instilled a driving desire to do their best in college, life, and to constantly set their sights higher. But I am human and weak, and every so often, when I feel I am going into the "woe is me" frame of mind, God quickly sends me either a swift kick or an embrace and I continue, with my family, to fall forward!

Last winter I had just such an occasion. My MS took a turn for the worse and I was having difficulty walking with the cane. It was becoming dangerous for me, as well as people around me, because at any moment I could lose my balance and either squash someone on my way down or hit them with my cane as I landed on the ground with a thud. I had purchased a walker, but it sat in the corner of the living room, daring me to use it. Every day I lumbered past it, I told myself, "I'm not going to be caught outside using this walker!" To be seen in public using this device would be the most embarrassing and un-manly thing I would ever have to do… or so I thought. I continued to struggle for weeks, if not months, with my balance, lack of ability to walk with just a cane and with my fear of what people will think when they see me coming with a walker in front of me.

I was having "Woe is Me" moments quite regularly. I was allowing my male ego, what others might think of me and my disability, to bring me down to a dark and unhappy place. Like I mentioned previously, I am normally a happy, pleasant and funny guy, but I was becoming a mean, crotchety, whiny old man of 48 years. I didn't want to go outside my house; I did not want to be around people. I was forcing myself to become more and more depressed. Because of my stubbornness and big, macho ego, I was making not only myself miserable, but those around me were suffering as well.

Then one night my daughter, who was working at a retail store while going to college, called to say she was having car trouble. She made it to work safely, but the engine oil lamp was on. I told her "Okay, we'll have to look at it when you get home." But in my gut, my mind and my heart, I knew that the right thing to do is hop (or struggle) into my car, drive 10 miles to where my daughter works and check on it because she would not be getting out until around midnight. Just that morning I had been praying, asking God to give me the courage to use the walker, to not be ashamed, to not worry about what others were thinking, and to start using me in life like he used to, because I could not do it by myself. I did not have the strength or courage.

In my mind that night, after hanging up the phone with my daughter, I kept hearing these words "When you are weak, I am strong." So without telling anyone where I was going or what I was doing, I grabbed my cane… and then I grabbed the walker just in case I needed it. I first drove to the local auto parts store in order to pick up some oil. When I arrived at the store, I was in luck; there was a parking right in front of the building! It would be easy enough for me to step up over the curb, pull open the heavy doors to the auto store, go in, grab a basket, pickup five quarts of oil, some rags, a funnel, pay for all of this and walk out using just my cane. I could avoid the embarrassment of fumbling with a walker in the auto parts store, a place that was full of other "manly" men. I was sure I would be able to do all of this without falling, dropping something, or being noticed by anyone else. But then I heard in my mind "I didn't bring you this far just to let you fail. Now grab the walker and go inside!" So I sat outside and wrestled with myself (maybe even with God) and waited until there were very few customers inside.

I finally had the courage to get out of the car with the walker. I easily moved up to the curb. I was beginning to wonder how I would open the doors with this walker in front of me when all of a sudden the young guy working in the store spotted me, jumped out from behind the counter and held the door open. In my mind I was thinking, "Darn, he spotted me. Now everyone will know I'm here." Then the next thing I knew, the guy was asking me what I needed, how many quarts, what type of oil, and before I could even tell him "I can get it for myself" he gathered everything I needed. It was at the counter, bagged and ready for me just to pay. He then, without comment, effortlessly took my bag of merchandise and asked if I needed help carrying it out to the car. I responded by saying that I could do it because I could easily place it on my walker and secure it so it would not fall. Just as I was thinking "Great, I'm going to make it out of here with no other guys seeing me except for this young man behind the counter!" a couple of tough-looking biker men were walking through the doors. As they approached the entrance, they said "Let me get this for you (meaning the door)" and "How ya doing?" After a brief "hello, goodbye, thank you very much", I rolled out to my car and put the auto supplies and walker in the back seat. As I got into the driver seat, I smiled and chuckled to myself, "That wasn't as bad as I thought it would be; thanks God!"

I drove to the place my daughter's car was parked, by the retail store where she worked. As I parked my car beside hers, another fearful thought entered my mind. I would have to go into the store and ask for her so that I could get the keys to the car. As I approached the front of the store, a young man that worked there held the doors open and greeted me without staring or asking why I was using the walker. He even asked how he could help. So I explained to him that I needed to see my daughter and get her keys. I thought for sure he would get on the loud speaker and call my daughter to the front of the store by saying "Hey Vicky, your handicap dad and his walker are here looking for you." Instead he spoke into his wireless radio and quietly told my daughter through her ear piece that I was there to see her.

After getting the keys, I walked out the door again, smiling and chuckling to myself, "That wasn't as bad as I thought it would be either; thanks again God!"

The next big mountain to climb was going to be crossing the street where people would see me getting to the car, opening the hood, checking the oil and then pouring it in with this walker beside me the whole time. "Not only will people be staring," I thought, "but it's going to be hard having the walker in the way." It took me about 25 minutes to pour three quarts of oil into my daughter's car, start it up and ensure everything was okay. It took quite a while for this simple task, but it wasn't made any more difficult by the walker. My left hand had not been working very well and caused the delay. In fact, the little seat on the walker actually helped by holding the oil cans, rags, and funnel while I worked. When I was done fixing my daughter's car, and it was running; I felt pretty good inside. Instead of people staring at me, they were willing to help. Instead of other men pointing and making me feel less manly, they just did whatever they could and assisted with my challenges.

The car was running; I knew my daughter would be able to go home safely; the walker was becoming a non-issue. All I needed to do was cross the parking lot, go into the store, give my daughter back her keys, and go home. As my daughter came to the front of the store and I returned her keys, I asked (as I normally would), "Have you had your dinner or lunch break?" the whole while thinking to myself, "I hope she has already had her break, otherwise I'll have to go to dinner with my walker." As it turned out, she hadn't had her break and we were able to eat together. We chose to have lunch at a little Mexican restaurant. As we pulled up to the place, I said to my daughter, "We can find a fast food drive-through; otherwise we'll have to go inside and be seen with my walker."

Again, I struggled my way through, pulling the walker out of my car, up the curb, and into the restaurant to find a table. After we sat down and ordered our food, my daughter said to me "Why are you so hung up with the walker?" Taking a deep breath, gritting my teeth together and trying my best to hold my emotions in check so that my daughter would not see the weakness in me, I told her, "I'm ashamed to be seen in public with this walker and feel that I am less of a man." Then my daughter said some things to me that I'll never forget.

She said "Dad, all the years I was on the water polo team, or whenever there was an activity at school where a parent should be supportive, you were always there. I would be in the water at a game, and could look up and search for that little yellow scooter, and I knew you were there. I had to be at practice at 5:00 a.m. and you drove me every time. Whenever there was a reason for you to be at school supporting me, and my sisters, you were always there when other parents who had no disability or handicap wouldn't show up to cheer for their kids. Dad, you were always there!" She looked me right in the eyes and said "Dad, we don't see your disability, we don't care how you get there; we love you and we just care that you are there for us." We finished our dinner and I drove my daughter back to her job, holding back tears of joy the entire time.

As I drove home that night, I thought about that morning when I prayed to God to give me the courage to use the walker, to not be ashamed, to not worry about what others were thinking. I prayed for Him to start using me in life like he used to, because I could not do it by myself. I was almost chuckling to myself out loud thinking that God has a real sense of humor. He knew what I needed; he knew how to give it all to me. I had just not asked for help yet. But as soon as I did, all the answers to my questions and my requests came falling into place. Now that I could look back on the last few hours that evening, it all seemed funny. What was the big deal about using the walker? There wasn't a big deal with the walker. It was just me focusing on my disabilities and not on my God-given *abilities*. As my daughter so lovingly pointed out to me, there is so much that I can give to others, sometimes just by being there to support them.

I don't take for granted what I have to offer people around me anymore. It may just be a warm smile, a handshake, or a friendly hello. And it's not just people who know me and love me who are blessed simply because

I'm there. Sometimes it can even be a stranger in the store, on the street, someone who may not have planned on serving another human being that day, until I showed up and they saw I needed a helping hand. Perhaps others, with or without disabilities, need to know that their presence is valued and needed by another person. There is no sitting around licking my wounds anymore. I have been a Christian all my life and Jesus is where I find my strength to go on every

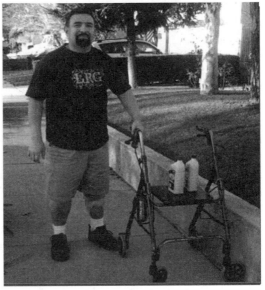

Carlos Diaz

day. I take whatever life throws my way and have confidence that I can overcome life's challenges. With God on my side, what can be against me?

Behind the Story

Carrie Svozil is the graphic designer who created the man-holding-the-book silhouette and designed the cover art of this book. While searching for stories, Carrie mentioned to me she had a good friend from high school, Carlos Diaz, who she knew was struggling with illness and who she recommended as a great person to contact.

I met Carlos over the phone and we talked for more than two hours. He told me his MS story; how the illness began and what a great loss his physical abilities were to him because he had been a talented athlete. Carlos shared that as he lost his physical abilities, he also lost friends. He said it wasn't always his illness that caused them to be distant, but his own difficulties in dealing with the painful and unwanted changes to his body. He spoke of reaching low points and finally realizing that he was giving up on himself; and that he shouldn't. His message to me that day was full of hope that he could yet regain some of what he had lost... and that we must never give up. I was excited and encouraged as I listened to his story. I told Carlos if he could write exactly what he had just said to me, it would be perfect for *The Triumph Book*.

In the narrative you have just read are elements of the story Carlos told me that day, but the main events of the story he officially submitted for this book are *even more profound* than I was anticipating. Carlos has shown that there is tremendous purpose in our tragedies, not only through the heightened ability to serve others, but particularly by being someone others can serve! In many ways, this is the hardest way to serve and feel purpose, as the rewards are often greatest for those actively giving the service. Therein lies the power of becoming a recipient of service as a result of tragedy... it allows people around you to rise above their own challenges as they think of others. As someone in need of help, the gifts and opportunities you present to others can be the most meaningful life possesses. There is great and lasting joy in giving service.

I am truly grateful to Carlos for providing a twist to the concept of serving others through tragedy by showing there is purpose in absolutely every situation we may be in!

Thirteen

The Rose Ceremony
Author: Benjamin Scott Allen

Soft petals on lips hold the story of three lives lived and lost; three different colored roses give testament to each of their lives. How do you celebrate life in the midst of the grieving process? When someone close to you dies, or another loss of great magnitude enters your life, what do you do to bring healing and closure? Sorrow and loss can either freeze a moment in time or it can become the catalyst for their loving presence touching your life in a deeper and more meaningful way. The creation of the Rose Ceremony offered me a sacred place to honor the lives of my wife and two children; and helped me move into a different relationship with what is lost and what remains.

It is October 4, 1996. I collect one yellow, one red and one violet rose and find my way to Half Moon Bay for an honoring ceremony. It begins a ritual of remembering the gifts I received in being a husband and father.

Although each was born on a different day, and died under a different sky, it is this day, October 4, 1982, during the birth of our first child, Matt, that Lydia received a blood transfusion. Had we known the blood contained an emerging virus yet to be called HIV, would we have had our second child, Bryan, two and half years later? We knew something was wrong; we just didn't know what.

We got the call from the blood bank asking us all to be tested in September of 1985. Bryan was four months old then, already struggling

165

for each moment. Matt was one month shy of three. Lydia was thirty-two; and I, the only one to test HIV negative, was twenty-nine. Over a thirteen-year period, we journeyed the unfolding of life towards the timekeeper's inevitability of death.

Bryan died on February 2, 1986. I choose the yellow rose for him. Lydia died on February 28, 1992. Her rose is violet. Matt died on November 10, 1995. For him, red.

On October 4, 1996 I began the ceremony of taking one rose for each of them to the ocean's edge; the same ocean where, one mile out, their ashes drifted from my hand into the waiting sea years and months earlier. I remove one petal at a time, in time... beyond time. With each petal I think of a beautiful memory and swirl that memory around my soul and my senses, then kiss the petal and release it onto an ocean wave.

Yellow comes first. Bryan was the first to die so I start with his memory. Although Bryan lived only eight and a half months, we shared a full life. For life is a collection of moments, not days, not years, just precious moments. Bryan was the first to teach me the true value of moments. I hold the first petal in my hand and I thank Bryan for this gift of truly living in the now. This came to me as I held him against my chest, rocking him in the stillness of candlelight, resting my head as close to his soft skin as possible so I could feel him, for just a moment.

I kiss the petal. It feels as soft as his skin did to my lips. I release it onto an incoming wave. I pluck another petal from the rose and wait for another memory to emerge. I have never gone looking for moments to remember, for I know the right one will find me. Even though Bryan had eight and a half months of moments, he never crawled or held his head up by himself. He was born two and a half months before his due date. To wait any longer, the doctor said, was impossible if Bryan were to live. The emergency cesarean left both mother and child in a fragile state. Bryan spent his first month of life in the intensive care, just as Matt, his older brother had spent his first month and half of life in intensive care.

The vibrant yellow petal between my fingers brings me the moment I first held Bryan. It was not at the delivery. There was no time for me to give Bryan a welcoming embrace to this planet. If he was to live, they needed to get him to the intensive care immediately. The first time I touched Bryan, wires leading to monitors covered his tiny body. The intensity of care by the medical staff was equaled by the concern we parents had sitting on the edge of our seats... sitting on the edge of life and death. The experience of scrubbing antiseptic soap under my fingernails, donning light blue paper gowns, rubber gloves and mask to enter a room filled with tiny cots and machines that would tell me whether my son was to live or die, was all too familiar. Lydia and I sat for a month at Matt's bedside under the same conditions.

I found a variation of John Donne's famous line, "No man is an island." I discovered that no moment is an island as well. I could not sit next to Bryan's bed without the collective anguish and toll it took to sit by Matt day in and day out during his time in intensive care. However, I sat differently next to Bryan. I was different. I no longer had the innocence and uncertainty of the first experience.

"We are not afraid of the future. We are afraid of the past repeating itself," is a quote that came to me when I held Bryan in my arms, his body against my paper gown. I held something back. I was unable to hold my youngest child the way I held his brother two years earlier. In holding Bryan, I was afraid. I sensed Bryan was much sicker than Matt. His soul did not sit in his body the same way. And I have to live with the fact that I did not sit well in the true weight of that defining moment.

The yellow petal still rests between my fingers. I remember with gratitude that Bryan taught me about the limits of my soul. Every time I held him, I knew the transitory nature of our collective moments, and, sadly, I held a piece of me back.

I kiss the petal and thank Bryan for being the first to teach me to never hold back, never let a previous moment dictate my response to this moment; and to try to let this moment be an entity within itself, unencumbered by the self-imposed boundaries created by 'the familiar'. Bryan taught me how much I lose when I think I already know all that this moment holds. In reality, I am blinded more by what I see than what I don't see. I remembered the horrendous pain of holding Matt and partially translated that into my experience with Bryan; fortunately, not entirely. It was a small portion that I held back, but enough of me to know that I lost an opportunity to live deeper in the expanse. I let this petal go in between the waves and out to sea.

I examine another petal as it leaves the stem. As if it can give me a clue to the next memory that will rise to the surface. Bryan gave me the gift of love's transcendence. On most occasions when I rocked Bryan, I would sing the Simon and Garfunkel song, 'Old Friends'. It might sound like a strange selection, but it made perfect sense to me. It speaks of two old friends sitting on a park bench late in life. Some of the words are *"Time it was and what a time it was. A time of innocence. A time of confidences. Long ago it must be. I have a photograph. Preserve your memories. There all that's left you."* Of all of us, Bryan was the oldest soul within our small celestial sphere. His eyes told of the depth of his journey. His perfectly shaped body and sweet facial features emanated a depth of spirit. When I held him, I felt him holding me. Our journey in the rocking chair took me to places uncharted. He was strong and tough. He had to be to endure what he endured. The pain medication, prescribed in four-hour intervals, lasted about fifteen minutes. For the next three hours and forty-five minutes Bryan would cry and his body would tense to the point of exhaustion. He would sleep for an hour or so and wake into the same pain.

I would hold Bryan and visualize pure love flowing from my heart, encircling his entire physical being, caressing his soul. Bryan gave me a deeper understanding of the gravitational pull that creates time and space. In fact, isn't the theory of relativity based on gravity actually creating time and space? Love transcends gravity, transcends time, transcends space. When I rocked Bryan I would imagine that we were on a train platform. The train was slowly pulling from the station and we were running alongside, speeding up in sync with the carriages. I wanted a smooth transition for my son, so when he entered the experience beyond time and space he would already know it. He would be able to say, "I know this place. This is love. I experienced this in my mother and father's arms." *Time it was and what a time it was. A time of confidences....* I bring the petal to my lips and release it to in the watery expanse.

Another memory rises from an additional touch of a yellow petal. The gift of experiencing what is mine and what is another's. Bryan had a central line—a tube that went straight to his heart and protruded out of his chest. Lydia, with her nursing background, helped train me in the art of cleaning the area around his central line. Everything had an exact order to ensure sterility, from the opening of the packets that contained the antiseptic solution and the white gauze, to the final step of washing my hands and the way I put on the sterile rubber gloves. The sequence was necessary because what was touched had potential consequences. Even the circular motion of wiping the area around where the tube went from his skin to his heart had a procedure. If the central line became infected, it could kill our son.

One day Bryan and I were alone. I had completed the process and taken off my gloves. It was then that I realized that the clamp securing the tube had come off. Blood was spurting over the changing table. In my panic I tried to hold the tube shut with my fingers, but it was too small to fully secure. I instinctively placed my finger over the end of the tube. I found another clamp and stopped the blood flow. Then I realized what I had done. My first thought was whether my finger had anything on the end of it that could kill my son. Looking back, it was probably an illogical question. The blood was flowing out, not in. However, at the time logic was not part of the equation. All I could think about was whether my action might take the life of my child.

Guilt is an interesting phenomenon. What I've observed in my own journey is an inverse relationship between the intensity of guilt and the degree to which I'm living in the depth of the moment. The greater the sense of guilt, the less deeply I am living. I had guilt for going to a school in an area where there was a higher incidence of HIV. It was my fault they were infected. I had guilt for being HIV negative (survivor's guilt is one of the deadliest of all). There was guilt for not being able to save them, or take away their pain. Guilt for moments I wanted to live. Guilt for the other moments I wanted to die, and watching how much they wanted to live made me feel more guilty still. That was how I felt when I was swimming on the surface of life—guilt ridden. For me, guilt was often a defense to push people away and isolate, to wallow in self-pity. And yet guilt has also been a catalyst for healing, for entering inner sanctuaries that bathe me in forgiveness. Guilt has been a beginning point which, if I am true to my path, can take me into the expanse where compassion flows freely in all directions.

But in that moment, when I held Bryan wondering if my actions might lead to his death, I stood frozen in guilt. What had I done? This was a tipping point for me into a deeper understanding of what's mine and what's another's.

I have no doubt my actions have consequences; and these consequences interplay with those around me. On the other hand, what is the journey of another? What is their spiritual contract with life? What did he or she come to experience on this planet and where do the events that shape their moments intersect with the events that shape mine? I can only see a small section of the 'grand scheme' (and my assumption is that there is one).

It's a paradox that we are all connected and separate at the same time, born from the same dust yet die separately. The day before Matt died I asked him, "When do you want to die?" because he was lingering in such anguish. In a whisper, he said, "I want to die when you die." As a father, it was the one thing I could not give him. Ultimately, we all die alone. His journey was not mine.

Bryan's presence was the beginning of my lesson in what is my path and what is another's. As I held him after cleaning the central line, he taught me how powerless I am over the plight of another, and how, in many ways, I am powerless over my own plight as well. He also showed me the ultimate paradox of finding even greater power within such surrender. I thank Bryan, kiss the petal and let it join the others that drifted beyond my reach.

Of all the yellow petals and moments of gratitude I kiss this day, the greatest one I save for last. Bryan gave me the gift of standing on the edge of eternity at the place where life and death meet and metamorphoses into the spectacular.

I was not with Bryan for his last breath, but he waited. Whenever Bryan was admitted into the hospital either Lydia or I stayed with him constantly. This particular time, I had to go out of town for several days and Lydia stayed by Bryan's side while the grandparents stayed with Matt. When I returned home, I convinced Lydia that she needed to come home that night and we could leave him for one night. All his vital signs were the best they had been in a long time. She reluctantly agreed, knowing we would be back first thing in the morning.

As we were getting ready to return to the hospital that next morning, we got a call from Bryan's doctor asking us to come as soon as possible. We were out the door in seconds, Matt in tow. It was a Sunday morning and the streets were pretty empty. I sped, paused at intersections, before running red lights. Lydia sat silent next to me.

When we entered the hospital, I took Matt to the playroom. Lydia went straight to Bryan's room. I settled Matt in and followed her. I opened the door to see Bryan resting on Lydia's chest like a thousand times before. Lydia's eyes told me what her voice only echoed, "He's dead."

When it was my turn to hold him, his body was still warm and supple. I could feel the wisdom in his eyes behind his shut lids. His countenance was calm and peaceful. The moment carried a weightless depth and timeless expanse. I felt a part of me enter such a space where moments melt at the meeting place of life and death. His presence was palpable. By invitation, Bryan offered me a glimpse into the love I spoke of earlier. The love I had with great intention showered him was the love he now bathed me. His spirit waited to love me, to give me a place to rest before continuing the journey without him. The theme of Bryan's bedroom was rainbows. That moment, where life and death met in Bryan, was my rainbow. The promise made; the promise delivered.

I kiss the last yellow petal and free it to join the others that circle a small corner of a massive sea.

After all the petals have gone, what remains is the thorny stem. It protects the lifeblood of the rose and her petals, and yet in between the thorns it is smooth and lusciously green. I spend time slowly running my finger across the stem before I kiss the thorns and release it to join the petals out to sea.

Ritual is both remembrance and renewal. Ritual gives me a place to return the sacred of each moment back to sacred's origins. It is an opportunity to empty myself—the beautiful, the painful, the ugly, the blessings, the forgiveness... all of my humanity into sacred's essence, the essence of healing. I remember what I have been given and a deep experience of renewal widens my path.

Lydia's violet rose is my next offering. The first petal is my thank you to her for coming into my life. It carries me to the time when we sat on the grass in front of her apartment and laughed into the night. I had known Lydia since I was eleven years old, but at the age of twenty I found I loved her. She was strong and wise, a woman of depth packaged in one hell of a body. Her warm brown eyes camouflaged a piercing power of discernment. I kiss the violet petal and the wind takes it to rest with the yellow petals floating on the waves.

The next petal does not bring me a memory. It leads me to a place of gratitude for Lydia's pragmatic wisdom.

I don't know why Lydia entered my life. I don't know why we traveled the paths we did. To question "why?" is ultimately a futile endeavor, but that never stopped me from tormenting myself with its hollow refrain. I guess I felt that if I could answer the question why, and make sense of these senseless events, then all the pain and suffering would have meaning. The question why was the Minotaur at the opening of the labyrinth—the twisting passageways that lead me to nowhere, and further away from the only way out. Nevertheless, I found myself over and over asking the why.

Lydia taught me to stop asking why and ask "what now?" I would *think* a lot. Lydia would *do* a lot. Not that she wasn't a thinker, I just believe she was better at multi-tasking than I was. She preferred manifesting her thinking with her hands. Some of that was due to her expansive heart and the necessity to channel what she was feeling into something tangible.

My fingers find a petal that honors the moment we got the call from the blood bank asking us all to be tested, and I remember her motherly instinct to protect her children. Another petal touches my lips and I remember how we dressed Bryan in a little sailor suit before we placed his cold body in the casket. Another petal brings the memory of her standing up for Matt to get him into school. I remember how she could barely get out of bed, but would walk resolutely into a PTA meeting as if nothing was wrong, so her child could live in some semblance of normalcy. Still another petal reminds me of how she walked into death with such grace and dignity.

One petal that I caress longer than others is for the conversation we had several weeks before she died. She knew she was going to die before Matt. She never truly recovered from the death of Bryan. There are multitudes of difficult circumstances that people go through in a lifetime, but one of the most difficult experiences anyone can go through as a parent is enduring the death of a child, and then to be dying of the same illness that will ultimately claim the life of a second child. How painful it is to have to leave that child behind, knowing he will also endure the same agony and die without you.

In this particular conversation, Lydia and I talked about the meaning of life. I shared with her my view that I believed we had come to *experience* life more than *do* life. After we traveled through some of the experiences we collected together, we talked about whether there was some ultimate learning achieved. Lydia said that she felt she had come to experience letting go—letting go of her life and letting go of Matt.

Also in this conversation, I asked her, "What do you think is on the other side?" She answered, "I don't know. All I know is that I will surely know my babies."

This petal is more than kissed. I gently rub it across my lips before embracing its beautiful touch with my return kiss. Lydia gave so many things that have shaped me, but this and one other left me with the wonderment of a woman that could step into the unknown with love and feel a certainty that the adhesive of the universe, love itself, would bind her to what and who was most precious in life. Where Bryan gave me a rainbow, Lydia offered me a peek into the eternal essence that sustains every molecule and every moment.

I save the last petal for the ultimate gift she gave me—the gift of the night Matt died.

Forgive me as I go out of sequence, but memories, like grief itself, are not designed for linear motion. I already spoke of Matt in the midst of Bryan's petals. I could go on with the interweaving of stories and memories. Grief, in its natural habitat, lives in the wild. It has its own rhythms. My experience is that when I let go into 'what is,' it will take me to places where grief heals, but never on a pre-determined path. I have never found a way to manufacture healing by one of those paint by numbers formulas. My most healing moments come when I draw outside the lines, being guided by love's higher intent. Sometimes it's incredibly painful. Sometimes it's unbelievably hilarious. But never is it boring. So, the last violet petal that marked my homage paid to my wife and the mother of our children involves Matt's last breath.

Matt was an avid reader of Greek Mythology from the age of three to his death. One day, weeks before his death, he said to me, "Herod is the goddess of wind and the goddess of love." I knew Herod was neither, but the dementia was becoming a more prominent feature of our waning moments. So I simply agreed. Then he asked, "Who do you think will come first?" I said, "I don't know, Matt. Maybe Mercury will come first. Or maybe Mama will come first." He quickly responded, "Mama will come first." I remembered a conversation Lydia and I had about me being on one side of life and her being on the other side waiting to meet Matt. I said to Matt, "Yes, Mama will come first."

I thought Matt had one more day. I always wanted to believe we had one more day. I had been up with him since 2 a.m. and it was around 7:00 that evening. I was lying next to him when I dosed off to sleep. Outside a thunderstorm raged. At 8:30 that night a huge gust of wind slammed against the window. I awoke, startled, unsure of my surroundings, but just as I turned to Matt he had two breaths left. Lydia kept her promise. She woke me before Matt was ushered into the next part of the journey. Had I slept through the death of my son, I would have been devastated. It was horrible enough as it was, but she gave the gift of not looking back on that horrendous moment with regret.

I kiss the last violet petal and let it softly drift downward, a plethora of yellow and violet petals swims beneath me.

Now it is time for the Rose Ceremony to turn to red. Matt and I were extremely close. There are no words I could choose here to describe what is ultimately the indescribable. He was the greatest teacher I've ever known. Most parents get to teach their children how to live. My task was to teach Matt how to die. Part of Matt's journey was to teach *me* how to live. He was a very old soul, still not as old as Bryan's, but a soul nonetheless immersed in an ancient wisdom that I've witnessed in other terminally ill children. They are a unique breed of humanity and I was well aware that Matt was one of them. I hope I was able to honor his path in this plane of existence as much as he brought me the gift of experiencing life beyond boundaries and within the multi-layered moments dreams are truly made of. It is from this place of gratitude where my first kiss of a red rose meets the waiting yellow and violet petals.

I caress a red rose between my fingers and 'rowdy night' rises within me. There was a massive thunderstorm on that particular Friday night. Matt was three. We had just moved to another state. I had lost my job and Bryan's life still dangled by a thread. The lightening seared the sky and it took only seconds for the thunder to rattle the windows of our new home. I didn't want Matt to be scared of the thunder so I suggested we have a slumber party. We folded out the coach, made some popcorn and snuggled under the sheets to watch the show outside. With every crack of thunder we would squeal in delight. When Lydia walked by, we were just in the process of 'roughhousing'. She said, "You guys aren't having a slumber party. You're having a rowdy party."

From the age of three till the week Matt died ten years later, every Friday night we would have a rowdy party. Rowdy night became snacks and a movie. When I touch the red petal to my lips, I am smiling.

Another petal takes me to a photograph Matt took around the age of three and a half. It still sits next to my meditation pillow. Matt was on a trip with my mother and father to Mt. Vernon, George Washington's estate and gardens. They had already toured the historic site and gone outside when Matt asked if he could take a picture. His grandmother handed him the camera expecting him to take a picture of the grand structure. Instead, Matt turned to the landscape. The picture reflects both moment and meaning. The green manicured lawn stretches out to glimpses of a river lined with small trees, but one large tree stands as a sentry in the middle. Closest to the camera is a row of slender iron posts, connected by a single chain that extends beyond the frame of the photo. Resting on the chain is a single butterfly with its wings straight up, ready to fly.

Here was Matt capturing a moment, not of historical significance, not a house of history, but a moment of meaning. I think often of the chains I have that fence me in when there is an entire landscape unfettered by my self-imposed restraints. I think of a butterfly that has so little time in this life to fly, which has come through so much to finally find itself ready to take flight.

I kiss the red petal and thank Matt for showing me the limits of my sight and for the gift he had to see what is really important that lives well within my reaches, if I only chose to see it.

I have an orchard of red petal memories that could unfold in this moment, but that is not the purpose of this chapter. I was asked to share along the theme of triumphing over tragedy. In truth, I don't really know what that means. I do not see my life as a triumph, a victory over something. Nor do I see my life as a tragedy.

A friend once told me, "I can tell you my life and make it sound like the most horrible, painful life you've ever heard. I can tell you the same life and make it sound like the most beautiful, wonderful life you've ever heard. And it's the same life." No, my life has not been tragic. It has been blessed with a multitude of experiences that have taken me on priceless adventures. I was honored to be taught by three remarkable people, to journey alongside them and countless others that have been woven into the fabric of me. How did I come to meet my moments in this way? For I know that I could have easily fallen into bitterness and anger. I did travel through those states, but I am so deeply grateful I continued the journey beyond them. I feel there are several insights I found along the way that have helped me to celebrate life, laugh and enjoy this moment, absorb life to the best of my ability and give back to life as much as I can in deep gratitude for what I have received; and perhaps, most importantly, moved on to other chapters of my life within the embrace of love.

It is my hope that our remaining moments together will leave you with a resonance highlighting some of our potential common experiences and ways to retrieve them. Certainly it is not an exhaustive list of possibilities, but maybe, just maybe, there is something here that will renew a way of approaching your own journey with a fresh perspective. I say that because I doubt you were drawn to this book in any other way than through a deep personal experience with the long and persistent shadows of sorrow. We come together to share moments like this because of the nature of being in moments like this.

Here are some of the important lessons that have become the wind-shapers of my life:

First, I learned to lean into life no matter what. I resisted the 'is' of life for a long time. I wanted to fit reality into my fantasy and it just wasn't working. When I resisted, I found myself engulfed in self-pity, entitlement and a hell of a lot of anger. *Life was doing all this to me. What did I do to deserve this? The world owes me!* All of those feelings were extremely detrimental to my healing. As for the anger, I'm a big fan. I've got no problem with anger and I had a ton of it. The challenge I faced was keeping the anger fluid, finding healthy outlets to let the anger flow. My experience is that if I lean into life regardless of what I'm feeling, and I keep it fluid, it will always lead me to a place of healing. I met a dear friend who had gone through the enormous loss of a stepson to a motorcycle accident, a murdered husband and later an eighteen year old daughter to cancer. She gave me some sage wisdom. She said, "Keep your finger in your heart and never let it close." When I found myself in so much pain that I could barely breathe, 1 leaned into her advice and never let my heart close. After each tsunami of anguish, I found myself with greater compassion for the world around me, and within me. Lean into life. It's strong enough to support whatever anyone goes through.

Second, I don't fight; *what is, is.* I read in a book, the phrase, 'don't push the river'. I was pushing a lot of rivers and I'm here to testify that it didn't work very well. I also don't agree with Dylan Thomas' famous poem "Do not go gentle into that good night." I want to go gently into every moment. I assume Thomas was really saying 'don't give up.' I agree with that, but easing gently into each moment is like slowly sinking into a lovely hot tub on a snowy night...*ahh!* What I resist, I become. I find that to not fight offers me more options and allows me to fully experience what the moment brings.

Another lesson I'm practicing is to live within my own personal economy of energy. If I can do something, I will. If I can't, I won't. Watching Bryan, Lydia and Matt and experiencing the exhaustive nature of traveling with them through it all gave me this gift. I needed to pace myself, to do only the important things in life, like watch cartoons with Matt or sit next to Lydia and watch a sunset. In utilizing the economy of energy perspective, I found I was molding myself into a state of authenticity. I didn't have the energy or inclination for trivial pursuits or not being who I truly am. If it didn't make me happy, if we didn't laugh or cry, if that moment didn't come with the inner layers of meaning that every moment has on offer, then why do it?

Which leads me to another mainstay of my being, I needed to find a spiritual path that worked for me. I'm not talking about a particular religion. I have nothing against religions. I believe we are all looking for a way to describe the indescribable that comes from a spiritual articulation of life. As feeble as those vocabularies are, there is still a place for me to try to express spirit's expanse.

The best definition of spiritual I've found is "that which gives meaning." I needed to find meaning. I've walked with quite a few people through the living/dying process, both professionally and personally. The subject of what happens when we die always seems to come up. In fact, I've noticed it comes up for us all. My theory is that whatever one believes happens when we die, overwhelmingly dictates their actions, thus the manifestation of their life. I've seen terribly destructive belief systems that suffocate so many priceless moments with fear, remorse and anxiety. I've witnessed other spiritual articulations that soar in the expanse of spirit itself. I needed to find my own spiritual path that was authentic for me and I felt to be healthy and whole. I think it is the greatest gift I've been given—to find meaning in what I can give to life rather than what I can get. My hope is you find meaning.

I'm coming down from my soapbox now. I hope it is received as sharing experience rather than giving advice, for that is my true intent. And it is part of the final piece of experience I will relate. I found the need to find another to speak to. I needed to be heard by at least one other human being that knew what I was going through. As much as I hated to admit it, I needed others to help me heal.

When Matt died, I had already arranged to take him to a crematorium and put him in the oven myself. As his father it was my duty and privilege to go the distance. I found a tender, loving mortician that worked it out with another mortician to use their oven. It was about 50 miles from where we lived and he died. She drove her Suburban with Matt's body those 50 miles in darkness and I followed in my car. I was given the gift of carrying the body of my son into the crematory. His naked body was wrapped in a white cloth. The oven itself was chest high and the gentlemen mortician asked me for permission to hold one end of the cloth, while I held the other. With tenderness, we put his body on the slab.

I brought the ash and bone out of the oven and poured the remains into a Ziploc bag, then placed the bag into a cardboard box. It was late at night when I placed the cardboard box next to me in the seat where Matt always sat. In the distance was a silhouette of city lights. It was the city where life was lived and, on a windy night, life had ended. Thirteen years, three deaths, and a box next to me; there was only one person I wanted to see in that moment, one person I wanted to talk to; she was the only one that would know what I was feeling at that moment. I yearned to see Lydia. She would know. She would know. I wanted someone there that knows.

I'm not exactly the poster child of reaching out, but life has gifted me with people that have entered just at the right moment. People that have either gone through similar experiences and know, and other people who have not shared the same experience but still have the capacity to sit with me in an authentic space of unknowing, which has equal value to me.

As much as I wanted to contract every fiber of my being into solitude and isolation, I found sharing life to be an absolute necessity for healing. There is a place for being alone on my path, but there is also place for shared history and present tense community. To have somebody that truly knows is invaluable and to truly say to another "I know" heals us both.

Perhaps that is why this book has found you and you have found this book. It is my hope that you find the kind of avenues that will lead you to a place of peace. It took, and takes, great intentionality for me to open up to life on a moment by moment basis, but it is worth it. What a shame it would be not to honor the gifts I've been given by shutting down, living in the past, or shrinking my present experience by holding on to what was rather than living in what is and opening to what will be.

For many years I went to the closest body of water to do the Rose Ceremony. Every birthday, every death day I would go through the same ritual, sometimes with the same memories, sometimes new memories. It was always one rose for one person. Only on October 4 would I do three. There were a lot of roses, a lot of memories and a lot of healing. But as the years passed, I began to question whether it was time to let it go. Would it be a betrayal to the testament of their exceptional lives to not go to the water's edge on those still significant dates in my life? Would I be turning my back on them to not keep going? Was it wrong to 'move on'?

I realized I was asking the wrong questions. It wasn't about moving on or betrayal. What I discovered was that by leaning into life and feeling each moment, I had come into a space where I am experiencing their place in my life as being an integral part of the entire landscape of my being. I don't think a day has gone by that I still don't, at one point or another, think of one, if not all, of them. But now they are blending into the totality of my present tense, so interwoven in the context of all my life that I no longer have the need to distinguish between then and now. It was time to let *time* go. It had nothing to do with letting them go.

It is such a beautiful sight to see all the yellow, violet and red rose petals move in the rhythmic dance of the ocean waves. Some petals drift out to sea. Some inch onto the beach. Petals, like memories, like life itself, go where they will. And because of the blessings I've received in this life, so do I.

Benjamin Allen

Behind the Story

Through a unique path of bread crumbs, I discovered Benjamin Scott Allen and his profound story... and storytelling ability! It was a radio show host who brought us together. She'd interviewed Benjamin on her show a few months prior and was deeply touched by his story. She wanted to support Benjamin in getting his message out and so, when I spoke with her about being on her show and sharing the vision of this book as well as my bereavement program, I knew Benjamin's story must be in *The Triumph Book*!

As a grief recovery specialist and author, Benjamin draws from the depth of his personal experience with grief and loss to serve others. Over the years he has supported many in the healing journey of grief. In his inspirational non-fiction book, *Out of the Ashes*, he tells his full, heart-wrenching story which is truly one of the most skillfully and beautifully written I've had the pleasure to read. He leads us on a journey through the many landscapes of grief, and ultimately into a place of deep healing and transcendence.

His book is available at: *www.thegiftofgrief.com*.

As a sought after speaker, Benjamin has delivered keynotes to thousands of people on topics relating to personal growth and the soul of business. With his wife, Rachel Flower, he also co-founded Senssoma LLC, dedicated to supporting people in living their authentic self and true purpose. Benjamin and Rachel offer programs and resources to promote wellness, healing and rediscovering a deeper sense of meaning in life; for more details visit: _www.senssoma.com_.

Fourteen

Cody's Legacy

Author: Sharon Southern

Texas Parks and Wildlife Department requires that every hunter born on or after September 2, 1971, must successfully finish a Hunter Education Training Course. Cody had successfully completed the course in his youth. He loved hunting and exploring the outdoors. When he was 17 years old, he was in Clay County when a Texas Game Warden happened upon him. Cody was proud to show the Game Warden what he had shot….a few birds including the field lark, which he then found out was a protected song bird in Texas. That bird cost a $250 fine and a few hours of community service. The story is funny now, but when it happened, it wasn't very humorous.

Cody was born July 22, 1985 in Lubbock Texas. He was my only child and son. He was quite a charmer with a million dollar smile. He loved the 4th of July and would save his money from mowing lawns or any other chores just to buy a huge supply of fireworks. He also loved Halloween, but on Tuesday, October 31, 2006, Cody lost his life. While working road construction in Lubbock, TX, Cody was hit by an 18 wheeler.

I was at work when I got the news of Cody's death that afternoon. I had been preparing for my trip to Las Vegas Nevada with my fiancé, Gary. We were flying there on Thursday November 2, 2006 to attend the PBR Finals (Professional Bull Riders) and be married on Saturday November 4, 2006. A co-worker had been teasing me all week about getting married in Vegas and my reply was always, "anything could happen." Well, the worst did happen....my baby boy was killed.

Instead of flying to Vegas, we spent Thursday November 2nd making funeral arrangements and picking out a casket. Cody's funeral was Saturday, November 4th, and if you can actually say a funeral was beautiful, his was indeed beautiful. Cody's service was performed by the retired minister who had conducted his baptism, with the help of the current minister of the First Christian Church in Wichita Falls. We had an emotional slide show depicting Cody's 21 years of life, accompanied by inspiring music. The co-workers from his company, as well as Texas Department of Transportation (TxDOT) employees, made the four hour drive to the funeral which was held in the First Baptist Church of Bowie. It was especially touching when Cody's co-workers placed roses on his casket at the end of the service.

Gary and I made new plans to get married the following month. We were married by the retired minister that delivered Cody's eulogy while the current minister served as a witness. It was very special to me that the same ministers who performed my son's funeral also performed my marriage. So here I was, newly married, relocated to Mineral Wells, Texas with my new husband and grieving the loss of my son. I don't really think Gary knew what to do. Then my new sister-in-law, Debbie, told me about a grief support group at a local church. I called the facilitator, Cindy, and talked to her. She too had lost her son in an accident, so she was someone I could relate to and ask if the feelings I was having were normal. She assured me they were. The group she conducted was called F.R.O.G.—Fully Rely on God—and they were starting a new session soon… thank goodness! On the first night of the new session, I headed to the church where the group was meeting. It was located off the beaten path. I actually got lost, cried and thought about going home, but I was determined to seek help. Walking alone into the church was difficult, but proved to be the best steps I took toward understanding my grief.

Losing a child is heartbreaking. It is indeed the worst pain I've ever had to endure. The first year was especially difficult. While many things are blurry from that first year, I do remember that every Tuesday and every 31st of the month were struggles. The first Thanksgiving, Christmas, Valentine's Day, Easter, Mother's Day, July 4th and then Cody's birthday came along. It seemed like the "firsts" would not stop. Then the dreaded "one year anniversary" of his death approached.

When the accident happened, I told my friends and family that I would never set foot in Lubbock, Texas again. I figured it would be too painful and heart wrenching. Well, never say never. A memorial was planned at the site of the accident by some of Cody's co-workers and they invited the family as well. On October 30, 2007, Gary and I drove to Lubbock and visited the site for the first time. The space is marked by a cross a co-worker built and erected on the day of Cody's funeral. The next morning, October 31, 2007, Gary and I arrived at the site about an hour early. It was very cold and windy. While we were sitting in the pickup, several TxDOT pickups drove up simultaneously with their emergency lights on the top of their trucks flashing. The TxDOT employees all got out of the pickups at the same time and put on their orange coats. It gave Gary and me a chill seeing this. Then Cody's co-workers started showing up, along with his dad and other family members. What we thought would be a small gathering turned out to be about 60 people meeting at Cody's cross. KCBD News Channel 11 had a crew there to film the memorial and I was interviewed. They asked me what message I wanted to send out and I told the anchor I wanted people to slow down and watch for these guys working in construction zones. I reminded all those watching to remember the TxDOT slogan in work zones....*Give them a brake.*

After the memorial service, I knew I had to do something more and that I could turn the negative of Cody's death into something positive. I was put in contact with Amy of the Fort Worth TxDOT office and started donating my time speaking at TxDOT safety meetings. The first time I was desperately nervous and really did not have anything prepared, but I knew whatever I said had to make a meaningful impact to help employees be more aware of the dangers inherent in their jobs. Like the story about Cody shooting the bird, I tried to convey that you can be the best trained person, but sometimes distractions or simple mistakes can happen. I wanted them to know how the tragedy of death can hurt families and friends. The day after I spoke to the Weatherford TxDOT employees, I received a call from Amy with TxDOT that one of the men in the meeting had a close call. He had to run for the ditch when a truck came bearing down on him in a work zone. He was fine, but his TxDOT pickup had been crushed by the truck. Miraculously, he had not been inside his pickup. In addition to speaking at TxDOT safety meetings, I was also invited to speak for a major oil company. Sharing my story and hopefully making a difference to employees so that the next time they are in a work zone, they will stop and think of Cody, gives me a great sense of purpose.

Speaking at safety meetings is not the only avenue that has helped me through my grieving journey. After Cody's accident, I found myself scanning online newspaper obituaries for other families that had lost a child. Sometimes I reached out to the family and offered the chance to talk to someone that can actually say they know how it feels. It gives someone great comfort to hear those words because they often feel like the only one who has suffered a loss of their child. It seems that everyone else's children are getting married, having children of their own or celebrating other moments of happiness in life, while my child's body is lying in the graveyard. It's not that you want others to lose their children; it's just such a great feeling of loss and "what if."

If I could say a few things that I wish everyone could read, it is "Please do not avoid parents who have lost a child. Please let them talk about their children and share their memories. And if you don't know what to say, just express that you don't know what to say. That is a greater comfort than you could ever know."

In May 2008, I read in the newspaper that a 21 year old man had died in a motorcycle accident. I felt compelled to reach out to the mother, so I stopped by the funeral home and left a note for her about Cody and my phone numbers in case she wanted to call and talk. A while later Laura called and we discussed our losses and our feelings. I invited her to F.R.O.G. which she attended. That is how Laura and I bonded as friends.

In December 2008, I was at the local Walgreen's pharmacy drive thru picking up our prescriptions. The pharmacist asked me if I was still involved with the grief support group. I told her "yes" and she said she would like me to comfort a mother who had recently lost one of her twin sons at birth. I told Becky to give her my name and number as I would be happy to talk to her and invite her to F.R.O.G. Later, one Sunday, Gary and I were visiting local churches and on our way that particular morning he asked me where I wanted to go. I told him "First Christian Church." We sat on almost the last row and, of course, my tears flowed. A woman behind me handed me a box of tissues. After the service, I turned around and thanked her. I felt like I needed to explain why I was crying. I did not want her to think I was some big sinner crying in church. I told her I had lost my son two years ago and then she said, "I lost my son four months ago." I asked her how old her son was and she nodded toward the baby on her hip and said it was his twin brother. I said "Oh my gosh, you are the woman I had been told about!" Afterwards, Jennifer came over and visited with me so we could talk about losing our sons. We formed a great friendship and she too joined me and Laura at F.R.O.G. Jennifer later admitted to me that on that particular Sunday, she did not want to come to church but had anyway. I told her that God had brought us together.

Everyone grieves differently and grief has no time table. I truly believe that in the journey of grief, you should not bear it alone. I know without

GOD, family, friends and a grief support group, I would not be nearly as strong today. My faith has been a vital anchor in this journey. My faith never faltered, even though for over two years I could not attend a church service. The music tore me up so much and I was embarrassed because I cried, but I've finally became strong enough to get back to church. I still shed some tears over the music and even a few of the sermons, but I think I have it a little more under control because I am stronger.

Cody Green

Last summer, my husband and I were at a friend's ranch sitting on the dock at night. I prayed for God to give me a falling star for Cody and a few minutes later, I saw a falling star. I prayed again, and again another falling star. I prayed the third time and again another falling star. I then told Gary about my praying and the three falling stars. I'm sure he was a little skeptical because falling stars are rare and especially three in one night, here in Texas. So, I prayed again and asked that Gary might see the next falling star. After a few minutes or so, he too witnessed the next falling star. I was very grateful to God for giving me those falling stars in memory of Cody.

A plaque on each end of a newly constructed pedestrian bridge in Lubbock has been placed. I recently went to Lubbock to see it for the first time. It is very beautiful and a great tribute to Cody's memory, for which I'm deeply thankful.

Cody Green

Pedestrian Bridge which contains a memorial plaque for Cody at each end

The Plaque

Behind the Story

The trail to Sharon's story was laid by Autumn Ater (***Robert's Story***). Through Autumn's bereavement program, *A Hole In My Heart*, she has met many grieving mothers with exceptional stories. After speaking with Autumn about sharing her story, I asked if she knew of any other stories which might fit *The Triumph Book*.

Cody's Legacy, as well as the story following this one, came through Autumn's recommendation. What impressed me most about Sharon's story is how she naturally and instinctively began *actively* looking for others to serve as a way of healing her pain. She is the epitome of the message in this book.

Fifteen

Strength to Live with Purpose

Author: Veronica Lowery

I have had many challenges in my life. Most difficult of all have been the losses over the years of my eldest son, my daughter, my first grandchild and my daughter's fiancé. I would like to share with you a little about my life's greatest sorrows, and how they have given me the strength not only to go on, but to live with hope and a sense of purpose.

During my senior year in high school I became a teen pregnancy statistic. Scared and unsure of life ahead, I chose to keep my baby and marry my boyfriend, Robert. I was afraid, being so young, of becoming a mother and of becoming someone's wife. I knew that my life was forever changed. I knew that I would not make all the right choices, but anything other than keeping my child was not an option for me. I feel that there is not one correct choice and that each of us has been given the gift of decision for a reason.

One's choice is not necessarily the right one for another. Of course, there were typical comments like "Oh, you had to get married." But I just never saw it that way. Especially since I loved Robert and could see our future together. I was determined to be the best mom and wife I could be. Though school administration was attempting to persuade me to go to school homebound, I chose to stay and graduate with my class. I see this not as an adversity, but as a starting point for my determination and future life course. I have been with my husband Robert 25 years this year, through all our life challenges, our love has remained strong.

After graduation and the birth of our first son, Michael, I quickly learned the ropes of being a stay-at-home mother. I was, quite honestly, excited and terrified in the same breath of being such a young new mom. Looking back I see that I was overprotective of my son. I embraced the idealistic "50's era stay-at-home moms stereo-type." Michael Wayne was an adorable, caring child, one full of love and creative imagination. He filled my life with love and hope for the future. Pictures and drawings have filled our home for years which serve as a testament to the joy he brought into our lives. Memories of him make me smile and will forever remain in my heart. My stories of the brief and blessed time he was with us will be passed on throughout my life. One of my favorites is how he said his name. "My name is Dikel Wayne Lowlee and I'm free." I was seven and a half months pregnant when I lost him, so one of my other fond memories was how he would help me get and put on my red tennis shoes as it was difficult due to my extended belly. Then he would tell me how pretty I was. "Pretty Mommy" he'd say.

He loved trains and I can still hear him say "choo choo train Mama." He loved his Dad's motorcycle and would always tell him, "Go vroom Daddy, go vroom!"

Though I loved Robert and choose to think we would have eventually married, I know that the pregnancy of Michael played a large part in our path together. We share our love for Michael, our pain upon his death and the continuous trials and testaments upon our life. Having lost a child so quickly and so young has impacted our lives in ways that can't always be put into words.

So many things go through your mind when facing a tragedy. One obvious question is, "Why?" And another—being the most prominent is, "Why didn't I just..." The questions are endless, the guilt unbearably overwhelming, not to mention the hurtful things others say or do that unwittingly add to your grief. For example, I happened to be in the grocery store when I overheard someone talking about the little boy that just drowned and how they heard everyone that was out there had been drinking and let the boy drown. Or the door-to-door witnesses that wanted to make sure I knew that my son was in a better place, the exact words were, "Aren't you glad that your son is in Heaven with the Lord rather than here on this Earth?"

It is very difficult to not only hear this information, but dwelling on it can become consuming. Michael had just celebrated a perfect third birthday party on July 2nd. Then a few days later, we began what was going to be a great holiday, spending the day out at the lake with our friends, swimming and enjoying everyone's company. It was a fun day. Toward dinner time, we decided to take a break from the water activities and go up a block to a friend's house to eat.

With me being pregnant, we chose to drive. After eating we drove back down to the boat dock. Robert helped our children (we had two boys by then) out of the car. I remained behind with the difficult task of putting my shoes back on.

The next thing I remember was walking up the boat ramp which led to the large party dock with sparklers in my hand, Michael's favorite. I recall asking "Where's my Mikey?" Someone responded "You didn't pass him?" In an instant people were jumping in the water on both sides, looking for my son. I remember screaming and feeling as if this wasn't happening to me, like I was in a dream state. This just couldn't be real. I remember running to people and screaming "Where is my son?"

Michael was found, but someone screamed to keep me away, and that they were doing CPR. *This just isn't happening!* I thought. The ambulance came and I remember my husband helping me into the car. We followed the ambulance so close we could almost touch it. I can recall the paramedics, one was a woman, looking out at us through the back window and shaking her head. I remember people not pulling over for the ambulance, *"What were they thinking?"*

When we arrived at the hospital a nurse called us into a room and there was no Michael. Then the doctor came in and told us our son was gone. My husband punched a cabinet. I asked to see my son and was led into a cold, darkened room. My son's body was there, but he didn't look like him. I remember looking into his eyes and he wasn't there; that's when I knew he was gone. I remember the pain, the hurt, the longing for this not to be true. Please to not let this be happening. The funeral home was ready to take my son's body, but my husband told them that he was the first person to hold him when the doctor brought him into this world, and that he wanted to be the last; no gurney would take our son out of the hospital.

The next few days were blurred. I don't remember exactly who was taking care of our other son, David, only that I was told he was fine. Boxes and boxes of chicken were sent as people tried to force me to eat for my baby. I just kept thinking *"You're kidding me, right?"* I just wanted to roll up in a ball and die myself. I already missed him. And who the heck were all these people? All these people that were in my house, that were making me try to eat all the time? I remember the horrible feelings of having to meet the pastor and pick out the casket. *Were we supposed to be doing this?* It all just seemed backwards, parents aren't supposed to bury their children. *Again, why us, why him, what had we done, not done?*

I remember feeling nauseous as the pastor touched my shoulder, telling me how much God loved me. God, *He loved me? Then why did he let this happen to us, to our son, our beautiful little boy who we adored? Some children suffer through illness, abuse, loveless homes. Why take our healthy, happy, loved child from us?* These were questions that would haunt me for years. Not to mention the dreams; there were endless vivid dreams of my son falling in the water and calling for me. Living was torture, pure torture.

Life goes on, so to speak. I chose not to crawl up and die. Not to bury myself in a hole. Not to give up on my life. My middle child, David, the child growing within me and my husband, Robert, all needed me. The truth is, I needed them as well. I'm not sure where all my strength came from, but I do know that my faith in God, my friends and family guided my path.

Upon the birth of our daughter, Jaime, I could see a light at the end of the dark endless tunnel. She was a difficult birth, but excitement filled the air to learn that we were having a daughter. Michael used to pat my belly and tell us he was having a "lil sista." He would touch my belly and loved when an elbow or foot ran across it. He would push and try to pinch it. Having a girl helped ease our sorrow.

When Michael was 18 months old, the addition of our son David Lee made him ecstatic. He loved his new baby brother, born on Christmas Day. Our two boys were inseparable, with the occasional squabble, which is to be expected. Life was good. During this time I also invited the Lord Jesus into my life. I believe strongly that without my relationship with God, at times during my life, I would have truly felt alone. Though family and friends are supportive and loving, sometimes healing comes totally from within oneself. My relationship with God, progressive through the years, has definitely been the basis of my healing.

After the birth of my youngest child, Jaime, I decided that instead of remaining a stay-at-home mom, I needed more to focus on. Being a natural nurturer, I chose to enter college on the road to a nursing degree.

Still healing from the loss of my son, I was unaware that the college counselor had placed me in the wrong program for my BSN intention. Therefore, I received an Associate of Science as well as my Bachelors. At the time I was quite upset with the added time, stress, work and expense of the mistake. As the years have progressed, however, I see that time as necessary to my healing and life course.

In 1997 we lost our home and almost all of our possessions by a house fire. I was home at the time and was terrified I would not make it out alive. This event was devastating as we lost almost everything we had, including possessions which were tied to the memory of our first son, Michael Wayne.

I reflected often on life and its meaning after the fire. It is definitely frightening and humbling to find yourself suddenly without material possessions. However, the recognition of the things that can't be taken away from you, like memories and your relationships with family, friends and God, is priceless.

Several years later I was in a car accident and sustained paralysis below the waist for approximately one year. I depended on others for my care. I was wheelchair bound and had to wear adult diapers. At the time I was a Nurse Manager at a rehabilitation hospital; so now I was *the patient* for approximately one month. I experienced the care of my staff first-hand. Due to incapacity, my position was reassigned. Therapy and the pain were intense, but I was determined to walk and regain my prior health status.

With time and tremendous hard work, I regained my ability to walk and returned to work. I began serving as a home health nurse, which I enjoyed. However, I took a sabbatical when my mother-in-law, who runs a small family business, was in need of my assistance. So I began working for her. Being able to take a step back, I reflected on my favorite part of nursing... teaching. I made the decision to return to college and obtain my teaching certification. Due to my high level of science education, I began the program with the intent of teaching high school science.

When my middle child, David, was a senior in high school and preparing for a career in the Marines (heavy in ROTC since middle school), he had a life changing accident. While jumping his dirt bike, he landed wrong and crushed his ankle. As a nurse, I was able to assist during his rehabilitation. I have been troubled over the years with the effects of our life's challenges on our children. For David, he has not only lost siblings (he has changed order several times, from being the youngest, to the only child, to the oldest, to being the only child again) but he has experienced the loss of our home, the difficulty of dealing with an injured parent, traumatic personal injury and the death of multiple loved ones. I know for him these have been extremely difficult challenges.

As a parent, it is our greatest desire to protect our children from both mental and physical harm. Guilt and enabling can become quite an inhibitor to healing. This has been a difficult area for me. My natural instinct is to hover and protect. My son, now 22 years old, has to gently (and sometimes not so gently) remind me that he is an adult; requesting that I don't cut the strings, but let them out a little bit. As a Mom, it is difficult to do that when your family has been through tragedies.

Some wisdom I would share with you from my experience is that we must understand how preventive strategies are important for safety, but life happens and accidents occur. Don't be afraid to be you and to live life to the fullest. It's important to understand that everyone handles difficulty and stress differently. Unlike me, who loves to share and talk, my husband is very quiet and self-reflecting. Not all people you care about or know will understand the depth of your sorrow or know exactly what to say or do. I think this realization has helped in my healing process. This has become more apparent to me upon my latest life changing event.

Recently, I lost my daughter, Jaime (pregnant with my first grandchild-Heaven Nevaeh/Salvador, Jr.) and my daughter's fiancé, Salvador, in a hit and run drunk driving incident. Jaime was a typical 18 ½ year old. She had moved to Fort Worth approximately 45 minutes away from us and began attending beauty school. Since she was a child, she loved everything about hair, makeup and fashion. Jaime was always one to be different and to think outside the box. She had an imagination and creativity that was sure to take her far in life. Jaime was very adamant about being herself. In fact, one of her favorite sayings was, "to be yourself in a world that is constantly trying to change you is quite an accomplishment." She proved this from the time that she was born.

Growing up she had difficulty with her weight, yet she chose to believe in herself and her individuality. She loved dancing and theater arts. She was excited and proud to keep up with the smaller-built girls. She even graduated from high school a year early to accomplish her goals. We had recently found out that she was pregnant. I was both nervous and excited about becoming a grandmother. Jaime and Salvador (her fiancé) were making plans to become a family. Life was in full circle. It was déjà vu for my husband and me. You naturally want your children to have an easier time of life than yourself; we prayed for this for our children. We were supportive and did our best to ease their worries.

I was excited to be involved in Jaime's pregnancy; taking her to appointments, shopping for maternity clothes, etc. I had no doubt that Salvador was going to be an excellent husband and father. My husband also knew that being married early in life, with a child arriving so quickly, would not be an easy task. In the last few days of Jaime's life, she chose to spend time with us at our home. She was excited, going through the baby things we had bought together. Her Dad and I were proud that she wanted to spend time with us since, being her age, it was often difficult to get her to take time out to visit. Our memories of those last few days are precious. We feel blessed to have them. We loved seeing the beautiful smiles, watching movies together, shopping, going out to eat, having Jaime sleep in her own room again and even going with me to my college campus.

Finally it was time for Jaime to go back home. She missed Salvador and reminded us that she was an "adult" and of course had things to do. We drove her back home; enjoying the time together as a family. She knew that we loved her very much and that, though the pregnancy was a surprise, we would help her all we could. When we got to her apartment, it wasn't long before she said, "You can go now, because I'm good." So we said our goodbyes. The next day I tried to text Jaime and there was no response. I knew she and Salvador had gone out, so I wasn't too worried that I didn't get a response. I knew she probably stayed out late and was sleeping in, especially since the pregnancy was exhausting her. When I was unable to reach Jaime the next day, however, I was growing concerned. Her roommate said that she had not come home the previous night. She thought maybe Jaime had just stayed the night at Salvador's; but I was unable to reach Salvador either.

As the day wore on, I became more and more concerned. I continued to call Jaime's roommate at work. She said that she was also unable to reach Jaime or Salvador. The roommate said that she couldn't leave work, so I called the apartment manager. I told her to go to the apartment and to check on Jaime, thinking maybe she had fallen. There were countless horrific ideas running through my mind. During that time, the roommate arrived home and said that she still hadn't heard from them, and that there was no evidence Jaime had been home. None of their friends had heard from either of them.

I was hysterical with worry. I remember thinking, *This isn't happening to me again!* At that point, my husband and one of Jaime's friends drove up to Ft. Worth to find them. In the meantime, my sister helped issue an Amber Alert. We were extremely concerned for their well-being.

I was exhausted and fell into a fitful slumber. The next thing I knew I was wakened with my family circled around my bed. I remember them saying they found my Jaime. I was so excited and wanted to know where she was. I remember getting out of bed, my husband reaching for me and telling me it wasn't good. They weren't sure, but two unidentified burn victims were in the morgue. He was sure it was them. All I kept thinking was *It just can't be happening again. Not twice, not again, not my Jaime, Salvador and my grandbaby. NO!* It was confirmed through dental records that it was indeed Jamie and Salvador.

This time, I didn't question God or lose in my faith. This time I just hurt. The pain was unbelievable. The hole that was left in my heart was immense and immeasurable. I just couldn't breathe; couldn't imagine my life without one of my closest and best friends. We were as close as a mom and daughter could be. Even when she wasn't with me, we would call, text and even watch movies and shows together. Horror movies and Gilmore girls were some of our favorites. Going shopping or to places we used to be together, and the things we would do or see, was so painful, my chest would hurt. I cried about everything. I was on medication for depression as well as anxiety. The panic attacks were mortifying to me. One time, at a department store, someone rushed past me with a buggy and I completely panicked. I remember feeling that I was such a freak, nobody could understand my grief. I wanted to save everything of Jaime's, no matter how silly or menial it might seem to someone else. I didn't even want to wash her dirty socks or pillow because, for the longest time, they smelled of her. I couldn't bear to throw her old toothbrush or broken flip flops away because they were hers.

Eventually, I gathered enough strength to begin separating my memories from physical possessions, but it still can be difficult at times. I know that my husband, son, and other family friends felt the pain as well. It was like my world was ending, all over again. Only this time it was more difficult for me to even want to see any type of future. My husband and I went to grief counseling together and I chose to receive personal grief counseling on my own. Every new step/goal/obstacle I overcame, I chose to view as an achievement; just going to Jaime's favorite restaurant, shoe store or even grocery store, provided immense challenges for me. I would always wonder what I would have bought for her. Sometimes I would still buy things for Jaime because it made my loss seem not so real. Two and a half years later, I still have to stop and catch myself. One thing that did happen with the loss of Jaime was that my *Michael nightmares* stopped. I believe it is because I know she is with her big brother and I now feel more at peace with the loss of him.

When my daughter died, I felt the world had finally come to an end and life was without purpose. Luckily, the college semester was at its end and my finals were forgiven. After a short healing break, I made the decision to return to school the very next semester. I knew that my daughter wouldn't want me giving up after working so very hard. She had told me how proud she was during our last days together (she had even visited my campus with me).

After Jaime's death, I felt that it would be unfair to my students, and to myself, to continue on the path of high school teaching. Therefore, I made the decision to become an elementary teacher. I changed my plan to EC-fourth grade. Finding a teaching job was stressful and difficult, but I was blessed with the perfect fit. I absolutely love it! I am a fourth grade teacher in a Title 1 (under-privileged) school. I became the RN consult to assist my school district with health care services. Thankfully I get to work with an excellent LVN (licensed vocational nurse), teachers, administration, staff, parents and students all of which I respect and adore. I also work four days a week for the MASH (after school program) assisting students with tutoring and extracurricular learning. Last year was quite difficult juggling my job responsibilities, MADDvocate (Mothers Against Drunk Driving Advocate) duties and college simultaneously. With the completion of my teaching certification, I am looking forward to an excellent year.

I am quite a bit older now; my faith is much stronger. There has been no *why me* this time, only *what am I learning and how can I use my situation to help others?* I look back on my life and all its trials and realize that one of the main purposes I have found in life is to share my hardships and triumphs with others. I want to show that though life can be filled with much adversity, it's all about how we choose to perceive what's happened. It is not up to me to question the

Veronica and husband, Robert Mitchell Lowery

purpose, but look for the strengths I have gained from the experiences I've been through and how I can share and help others fight similar battles. I have chosen to pick myself up and lead those around me to a brighter future which might otherwise be dark and without hope. Through sharing my pain, coping skills and achievements, I can help while I yet continue on the jagged path of healing.

Journaling, sharing with others, becoming active in causes I believe in like MADD, consistently working on self-improvement, lots of "me" time for healing and reflection (I have a cry party if I need it—and realize it is healing), these have been important steps on the healing journey. I give love and kind words freely and accept them back with deep appreciation;

Michael Wayne Lowery

David Lee Lowery

I don't just think or say... I do! I don't take my days for granted and try to have a positive outlook on my life. The number one thing I realize is that each day I actually *do* make a difference in the lives of others. It's an awesome feeling!

Through all that I have endured in my life, which at times seems unbearable, I truly feel blessed. Our family, friends and the Lord have been an infinite source of comfort and affirmation. I miss my loved ones every day without fail. Memories flood in, often prompted by a favorite spot, saying, commercial, etc. Some days my thoughts of them completely envelope me; then there are other days when memories of them give me a smile and a tear simultaneously, as if they are still here. I often think that living without my loved ones is the hardest part, but now I have much more to offer this world because of these experiences and I know that one day we will be together again.

Jamie Leanne Lowery

Jamie and Salvador, Jr.

Behind the Story

Autumn Ater (***Robert's Story***) introduced me to Veronica Lowery. Knowing people like Autumn, Veronica and all the authors in this book, has been life-changing for me… a truly joyful part of experiencing tragedy!

Those who endure sorrow often find a common understanding; a shared desire to rise above their grief and to lift others up alongside them. There is a unique society or culture which can be formed out of adversity. Membership in this *Society of Survivors*, though hard-earned, is like belonging to a *City of Angels*; those who feel this sweet association never want to be without it.

Veronica's story is a powerful lesson in adversity, purpose and hope. In this book so far we have read stories of death and loss, of disability, and of searching for a lost child. Veronica has endured ***all*** of these and still speaks with hope and acceptance. What might otherwise cause someone to be severely depressed, angry or suicidal (even if only spiritually) has left Veronica stronger and more positive.

Veronica finds her healing through active service, as well as her faith and positive attitude. She is a teacher with an after-school program called MASH which, as Veronica describes it, is "Time for students to receive tutoring and mentoring through creative instruction and activities." She is also the schools registered nurse as well as consultant for the school LVN (licensed vocational nurse). As Veronica says, "I definitely wear many hats, but that's okay because I'm into fashion!"

Veronica is a MADDvocate and has introduced a bill into the State Senate. I have asked Veronica to describe this bill and her success in the effort:

The bill that I helped initiate with the help of Senator Kip Averitt is (Senate Bill) SB521. The bill allows more than one victim to be placed on a Texas Department of Transportation memorial sign. After my daughter, her fiancé and my grandbaby were killed by a drunk driver, we wanted to place memorial road signs at the accident site. At the time, only one person or family name were allowed on these signs (the baby wasn't allowed on the sign) which were $300 a piece (our cost). Due to the importance of spreading the word about drinking and driving, along with *preventing this tragedy from possibly happening to others, we chose to place signs.*

It was very difficult during this time emotionally and financially to have to make this decision. In initiating this bill my hope was to prevent other drunken driving accident victims families/friends from having to go through the same struggles. I was very excited when I was invited by Senator Averitt to attend and speak at the Senate Committee meeting at the State Capitol in Austin. It was an awesome experience.

The bill has traveled quite a path that you can follow on the Texas Legislature online website. I am proud to announce that the Governor signed the bill into law in June 2009 and it became effective in September (my daughter's birthday month). Awesome! I haven't found out if the law will be named after my daughter, but that would be very cool. I am proud to be able to say that one person can make such a difference. The main idea I would like my students to get from this is that they too can make a difference in our world.

Sixteen

Surviving Cancer

Author: Laura Pasley

"There it is," the young doctor said. I was lying on my side on a hospital bed at the Gastroenterology Department at Baylor, Dallas. The room was cold and unfeeling. I began chattering nervously. I had no idea what was coming out of my mouth. I guess it was just mindless prattle in an impossible task of breaking the tension that was growing in the room. I felt a woman's soft hand gently patting the top of mine. The nurse that was the upper part of that hand gently said, "Be quiet now, let the doctor work." Fear gripped my heart. "There what is?"—"Let the doctor work on what?" Frantic thoughts filled my head. I had learned a long time ago to relax to the point I could actually take my mind out of a scary situation. It was just a matter of deep breathing and having my thoughts go somewhere else. I closed my eyes, took a long slow deep breath, and my mind began to drift...

I'm not sure any particular illness had been in my thought process. I knew I was sick; very sick. It had been ten long months of vomiting, diarrhea, constipation, emergency room visits and constant calls to the doctor. I was eating anywhere from four to six very large cups of shaved ice from the local Dairy Queen. I could not get enough. I drove through the drive-thru many times every day ordering only shaved ice. Because I am avid about researching medical issues, especially mine, I knew craving ice meant anemia. My arms were turning brown with large patches up and down both of them. My body had blown up like a hot air balloon. I would alternate between going for days without having a bowel movement to diarrhea so severe, I would be unable to stand up. The vomiting was violent and caused sharp pains which felt as if my upper extremity muscles and neck were literally being ripped out of my body by the roots.

I called the doctor's office many times during late 2001 and early 2002. My doctor, a handsome young man who looked a lot like an All-American football player, had insisted I had Irritable Bowel Syndrome. I was only 47. The doctor kept assuring me I was too young for Cancer and did not have a family history of Cancer so he could not get an approval for a colonoscopy. Besides, I didn't have Cancer. I just had problems with constipation. I had been bulimic for the better part of my life so I decided this had something to do with the damage I had done to my body with years of binging and purging. Or, it probably was due to stress. I had spent 25 years working for the Dallas Police Department. In doing so, with a typing speed of 120 wpm, I had destroyed the muscle tissue in both of my arms and caused a disc in my neck to bulge on one side and a nerve to pinch on the other. Dr. Wayne Z. Burkhead, a world renowned shoulder specialist had operated on both shoulders and my left elbow.

My reward for working so hard for over half of my life was being assigned to a lieutenant with a serious lack of integrity and whose sole purpose was to get rid of me. He spent the last six months of my 25 year career harassing me to the point of nearly killing myself. Because I LOVED to work and LOVED my job, he assigned me to evenings doing nothing but answering the phone. He knew this would drive me crazy. I cried a lot. Because I cried, he requested a "Fitness for Duty" assessment. The Police Psychologist who examined me told me if he were in my position, he would cry too. He also told me I could take a few weeks off with this little harassment tool; so he removed me from my glorious "no job" for two weeks. There is actually a triumph in that story as well, but it took a while to understand how God was going to use that for good. I mention it now only to show you how much stress I was enduring during this time. Now, let's get back to the story at hand.

The Baylor Out-Patient Clinic sent articles to read about Irritable Bowel Syndrome and put me on every conceivable medication for that disorder. The doctor repeatedly reminded me I could have a colonoscopy when I turned 50. "It's only a couple of years away," I thought. "Let's just get my tummy well." I bit the bullet.

I took the medicine and spent many days vomiting violently and trying to have a normal bowel movement. I was growing weaker and sicker.

I need to stop here and give a little bit of my history for you to understand the magnitude of stress this illness was having on me. Colton Blake Pasley was born on January 26, 2001. He was my nephew and was born testing positive for opiate exposure in-uteri. Within ten minutes of his birth, he went into withdrawals. He was screaming "uncontrollably" and his little body was shaking with sharp jolts. His medical record reads "inconsolable infant." I was taking care of his brother, Dalton Pasley, age nine, and Tara Pasley, age six. We had traveled the fifteen minute trip to Kaufman Presbyterian Hospital to see the baby for the first time.

When we reached the hospital, the nursery blinds were closed and my brother was pacing outside, sweating profusely. I knew the signs. He was either high on methamphetamine or he was coming down. There was no in-between during that period. I secured the two little ones and looked between the blinds to see my new nephew jerking and screaming. I went to my brother, who stands quite a bit taller than I do, and grabbed his shirt with both of my hands. "What the hell is wrong with that baby?" "What is he on?" I implored. Doug's eyes were wide and full of fear. He looked crazy. I asked him again, "What is he on?" "Methadone" he said. My heart literally skipped a beat.

My chest began to burn with anxiety and fear. "How?" I thought. I reminded him that I had taken his wife, my sister-in-law, to a treatment center to "dry out" the minute we found out she was pregnant and using Heroin. I looked around and saw that the CareFlite team was there, apparently to get Colton, an innocent little baby who had done nothing but be born. I walked to the phone and called my brother-in-law, Robert "Bob" Looper. He was a CareFlite pilot at the time. The baby was being transported to the Dallas Presbyterian Hospital for more advanced treatment. Bob told me to make sure someone went to the hospital with the baby. Doug wrote a note and gave it to the CareFlite team that said, "My sister, Laura Pasley, is the only person with permission to be with my baby." This would cause me a great deal of grief with the entire family on both sides, but I was not thinking of anything but that child. I had a set of the children's grandparents take them to my parent's house. I got in my car and drove straight to Dallas. I would be there for two gut-wrenching days beside my new nephew as he went through some of the most hideous withdrawals I have ever seen.

Because Colton was born exposed in-uteri to opiate narcotics, and not having any pre-natal care, Child Protective Services was called. On February 13, 2001, I was ordered by a Dallas judge to be Temporary Managing Conservator of all three children and in March, 2002, it was changed to Permanent Managing Conservator. This story and the proceedings will be shared in another story as it has been a Triumph in my life as well. This information is crucial to the Cancer Survivor story because I was involved in an investigation, many court appearances and sick-as-a-dog during the entire time.

For days at a stretch, I would be so sick I could barely get out of bed. Colton was tiny and needed a great deal of constant care. I remember one particular day when I had vomited all night long while I sat on the toilet trying to have a bowel movement. All three kids were at home. I knew they were terrified, but my body was absolutely beating me to death. As I sat on the toilet dry-heaving, Dalton came to see if he could help. The fear on his face scared me tremendously. Dalton had to play "adult" so much of his life and I hated it, but this time, I had no choice. Between gags I managed to say, in about four syllables, "Jennifer."

Jennifer LeeAnn Pasley is my only biological child. I have raised her alone, except for the assistance of my parents. Her father was a Dallas Police Officer. He left us when she was only two. Jennifer is a beautiful brown-eyed girl who looked like a porcelain doll as a child and was, and still is, the light of my life. I suffered with endometriosis for a long time and the doctor told me I could not have children unless I went into the hospital and had the "patches" of endometriosis removed from my female organs. Her father had a vasectomy eight years prior to conception so we had a double reason why we "could not" bear children together. Imagine my shock when the doctor told me I was pregnant! Now Jennifer was a young woman with a job and home of her own.

Dalton went to the telephone and called Jennifer's number. She could hear me in the background with loud, violent bursts of what seemed like endless vomiting. By the time Jennifer had left her job and made it to my house, I was lying in my bed totally exhausted from hours and hours of trauma which my body would not soon recover from. My hair was soaking wet and my complexion was a white/grayish color. Jennifer took one look at me and said, "Mama, we are going to the hospital."

I do not remember where she took the three little ones; probably to my parent's home around the corner from mine. She loaded me up and away we went. I lay back in the seat of the car wondering *Why?* The Bible tells us, "God does not put more on us than we can handle." I remember thinking He was coming dangerously close in my case. I had nothing to pull myself up with. I had been deathly ill for months. Just going to the bathroom was incredibly painful and most of the time it was accompanied by nausea and vomiting. I was in excruciating pain and, nutritionally, I was vitamin depleted. My tongue was fissured and blistered. I was anemic; my arms were dark brown; I had no energy and I had lost my will to move forward. I can honestly say at that point I was broken.

In the emergency room, they hooked me up to an IV which addressed the symptoms. It was very much a "treat 'em and street 'em" approach. The IV fluids always made me feel better for a few days, but I had the same scenario play over and over again. I walked around feeling like a hot air balloon. I was swollen all over, particularly in my face. There were red patches on my cheeks. Another bout with the "flu" or "Irritable Bowel Syndrome" would knock me off my feet; then the IV fluids would pick me back up.

On April 10, 2002, one of the chiefs of the Dallas Police Department died of colon Cancer. I had worked for him. His death was sudden and a shock to everyone. As I was talking to an old friend about the Chief, it occurred to me there may be something more than Irritable Bowel Syndrome that was causing me so much illness. It had not occurred to me that I might *actually have* **Cancer**. The doctor had told me the chances of that were pretty minimal because of my age and the fact that nobody in my family had Cancer, with the exception of two grandfathers having lung Cancer from smoking so many cigarettes. Nevertheless, it caused me great concern. By Friday, April 13, 2002, I had worked myself into a severe state of worry. That weekend, I called the Out-Patient Clinic and left a message on the voicemail for my All-American-looking doctor. I told him about our police chief's death. Then I stated and meant, "If you do not schedule me for a colonoscopy, I will come up there and kick your ass."

I found out later that my doctor had called the Gastroenterology Clinic and literally begged Dr. Stephen Coates to perform a colonoscopy on me. Dr. Coates was a very affable guy. He was short and had dark hair. He was outgoing and I liked him a lot. Somehow between Friday and Monday of that next week, I was worked in for a colonoscopy with the clinic (who "did not do" colonoscopy's on Friday). Mine was scheduled for Friday, April 19, 2002.

One of my best friends, Martha (not her real name), was visiting from her home town. She had to be at her attorney's office so she dropped me off at the clinic. I had done the "prep" the night before, which was about as hideous as any procedure I had ever endured. I had this large jug of putrid tasting liquid which I had to drink until it was gone. It was a very difficult evening. I would choke down the liquid followed by going to the bathroom every few minutes. This would "cleanse" me for my test. In spite of this, I was in decent spirits by the time I got to the locker room to change into a hospital gown. Humor has always been my way of getting through tough times. This day was no different.

The IV team came in and hooked me up. This one was pretty easy. I had been poked and prodded so many times in the past; and some of them were fairly brutal! This one was not so bad. It was not long before I was lying on a gurney, being wheeled into the room. Nervously waiting for the "twilight" drugs to begin working, I asked Dr. Coates if he was going to kiss me before he used that tool. I remember him laughing and being very jovial. I was teasing everyone around me. After a few moments, it got very quiet in the room. It was uncomfortably quiet. The tension began to thicken. I felt the pat on the top of my hand. The soft voice spoke, breaking the tense silence. "Let the doctor work now" she said. At that moment, I was too afraid to speak. I lay there in utter terror. What was it they were not saying? In those few moments, I felt as if I had been lying there for an eternity.

All kinds of memories flooded my mind as I tried to utilize my "deep breathing" techniques, learned in a three week Pain Management Program at Baylor. They were an absolute life saver. When I was afraid or in horrible pain, I would close my eyes and take in long, slow deep breaths. It was absolutely amazing how the body could relax itself. On this particular occasion however, it was not working. I was truly terrified.

I was transported to the recovery room where people were avoiding eye contact with me. I could feel them talking to one another. I heard someone tell someone else to page my regular doctor. They asked me if anyone was there with me. I was trembling and shaking. "My friend should be here soon," I said. I was as concerned about what they were *not* saying as much as what they were saying. In a few moments, my doctor came into the room and stood by my bedside. He, Dr. Coates and two other men were standing in front of me. "There is a mass," one of them said. They told me they would not know for sure what it was until it went to pathology. I knew they knew exactly what it was. I could see it on their faces. "We have biopsied it, but it will take a few days to get the results," someone else said.

"I don't understand," I said. I was not ready for the "C" word. Without warning, there it was. "It looks like Cancer," said Dr. Coates. My body literally froze on the bed. "No, you are wrong. No, I do not have Cancer." I pointed to my regular doctor, "You told me I was too young." They told me the pathology report would be back on Tuesday. I was told not to eat anything all weekend. I was already hungry from missing supper the night before and breakfast that morning. I asked if I could use the phone. I wanted my dad. I called my little sister Julie Looper and asked her to page him. She asked me what was wrong and I just said, "Cancer." She paged my dad and he called right back. "Daddy, I am so afraid." I said. I could hear the worry in his voice but, being the ultimate positive person, he was upbeat. It wasn't long before Julie walked into the clinic. There was no color in Julie's face. Martha was finally there. I was surrounded by people, but felt very alone. Julie was whispering in my ear, "Don't leave me Lollie." It was all too much to soak in. This would be one of the longest weekends of my life, and it was only Friday.

Martha and I drove back to my house. We were pretty quiet, except for the small talk. Fear was taking over. I thought what I always thought when something went wrong; that God was mad at me and I was being punished. Well, this told me something had gone horribly wrong so God must be really ticked off at me this time. I bowed my head and as the tears began, I asked Him, "Why me, Lord?"

Once we reached my house, I came in, hung my keys on the hook by the door and went into my room. I began running a hot tub of water. No matter what the dilemma, a hot bath would fix it. I could clear my head with just the right temperature. The steam would flow upward as my body made contact with the water. Bath soap, with a gentle, delicate aroma, would soon fill the room. Add a few candles and I would be myself. I felt dirty anyway. A colonoscopy has to be the most hideous of all medical procedures; at least that is what I thought at the time. I would soon find out there are a multiplicity of hideous things that can be done to you in the name of medicine.

I slipped out of my clothes and slid into my bubble tub of steamy hot water. For the first time that day, I could let go. No doctors were in there. No nurses. No family, no friends. It was just me and my favorite tub in the world; and an emotional, gripping pain that was just too enormous to describe. I covered my face with my hands, and while tears rolled down my cheeks, the jerking sobs began. My shoulders were beginning to spasm. The pain in my heart swelled up, pressing against my chest wall. I have no idea how long I sat in that hot bath crying from the very depths of my soul.

In an effort to "pull myself together," I sent the kids to their grand-mother's house in Kaufman, Texas. Martha would be with me until the following Wednesday when she would be returning to her home town.

We decided to spend our last weekend together at home so I could "rest." I was instructed not to eat but to go home and wait for the pathology report along with a call from my doctor. There is not an emotion I did not experience throughout that weekend. I experienced a stage of denial, a time of laughing and cutting up with Martha and, of course, I was scared out of my wits. I had no idea how I was going to tell my kids. Jennifer and her best friend, Marjorie Stewart, had gone to Canada on a vacation. I absolutely hated the fact that I would be telling her I was sick at the same time she was coming home from her vacation. I swore her friends to absolute secrecy until I had the opportunity to tell her myself. I was the only parent Jennifer had.

Dalton was the next one I was worried about. I had been side by side with Dalton since he took his very first breath. In fact, I took a photo of him as they pulled him out of his mother's freshly cut abdomen. I was the person Dalton called to come get him and his sister when things got bad at home; he had actually decided on his own to live with me, at the ripe ole' age of seven.

And Tara! My little seven year-old, curly headed Tara. Nicknamed The Terminator, Tara had informed me when Child Protective Services had placed her in my home that she "took care of herself." I had been determined to prove to her she could trust me to take care of her. She was an absolute delight and as pretty as a picture.

I thought of Colton. He was fifteen months old and was in love with life. He woke up smiling and went to bed smiling. His grin was so huge; it looked like he slept with a coat hanger in his mouth. How in the world could I tell my kids? Where would I put them if I needed surgery? Jennifer had to work. Dalton and Tara had to go to school. I realized I had so many things to think about. My head was swimming.

Then, there was Moma! I knew Moma was going to be hysterical. She had never been able to handle it when one of us got hurt or sick. To write about Moma, I would need to start a whole new book. Suffice it to say, she got on the phone and told pretty much anybody that would listen that I was at death's door. Between her and my oldest sister, Deborah, I felt they already had me dead and buried before I had even been officially diagnosed. Deborah had run to my brother's house announcing my horrible plight. This was like an atomic bomb going off in our family and I was helpless to control it. I hid out at my house for the entire weekend with Martha, avoiding the telephone as much as possible. Martha was composed, supportive and so helpful. She was strong that weekend. I found out later when she got on the airplane to go home, she sobbed.

Sunday night, my Jennifer landed in Dallas. Jennifer had been to Canada once with me to do a talk show and she had always wanted to return. She was bubbly and excited when she got to my house. I was sitting in my bedroom in a recliner my parents had bought for $60.00 at a garage sale. My heart was pounding at the thought of what I had to tell my beautiful daughter. Before I could say a word, she took one look at me and said, "What's wrong Mama?" I looked at her gorgeous face, that looked like a blend between me and her father, and said, "I may have Cancer. We should know something no later than Tuesday."

On the morning of Tuesday, April 17th, my phone rang at home. I had attempted to prepare myself, no matter what the outcome, for the phone call. I know now that nothing gets you ready and if I had realized it at the time, I probably would not have tried so hard. The ringing of the phone made my nerves burn all the way to my fingertips. I picked it up and on the line was my All-American handsome doc. "Well?" I asked. He told me the biopsy was positive. "It is malignant" and I needed to pack my things and prepare to go into the hospital. He told me to be at the clinic at 9:00 a.m. the next morning.

I don't remember sleeping that night. I talked with Martha. We cried, we laughed, and did things best friends do when life is handing one of them a tough blow. The phone continually rang. I let most of them go without even answering. I had decided to let Bob and Julie keep Colton. He would need the most one-on-one care. Theirs was the perfect place for my littlest angel. Bob was retired due to his own Cancer so he would be with Colton all the time. Although I knew he was in excellent hands, my heart ached as I let him go. We had been joined at the hip since he was born, with the exception of his four day stay in foster care; and not having him beside me was one of the toughest things I had to do. Jennifer, Margie and the rest of their friends, took care of the other two. They got them off to school and picked them up when it was over. All of them tried not to show the other they were afraid. But, I knew they were terrified. I could see it in their faces. I felt it when they came near me to hug or kiss me. A mother just knows.

Martha and I got into the car with all of my things. Martha was going to drop me off at the Baylor Out-Patient Clinic and then she had an appointment with Skip Simpson. Skip was my attorney and following the disposition of my case, I began working for him. Martha was not only my

207

best friend, but she was a client of Skip's. To this day, Skip remains one of my dearest friends. And Martha—well that goes without saying.

I got to the clinic and was placed into a treatment room. I could tell by their faces they knew someone had dropped the ball. Besides, one of my new doctors told me that one of the nurses made the statement, "It was Cancer and we missed it." A couple of the nurses had become really frustrated with me during the previous ten months because my "Irritable Bowel Syndrome" did not seem to be getting better and I am sure there were days I behaved like a real b**ch. I sat on the end of the examining bed and felt as though I had lost the only friend I ever had. I asked again, *"Lord why? Why is this happening to me?"* After several moments, there was a light tap at the door. Without glancing up, I said, "Come in." I looked up to see a very handsome man in a pair of blue scrubs. He was wearing strange looking skids. He walked in and sat down on the little round chair. I looked into his very dark eyes and detected a little fatigue, but also a sense of great concern for this new patient he was seeing. His dark hair was neatly trimmed and the look on his face was very serious. He began asking me questions. He was concerned that I had been vomiting and nauseated throughout the weekend. He told me he was going to admit me right away.

Salim H. Jabbour, M. D. was in his last few months of his residency with the Colon Rectal Clinic at Baylor Hospital in Dallas. I would be one of his final patients before graduation, vacation to his homeland, Lebanon, and transition to private practice. He seemed more mature than his twenty-three years.

Dr. Jabbour asked if he could examine me. I told him, "Whatever trips your trigger." He gave me a half-hearted grin. I laid back and saw this doctor do something I had never seen a male doctor do. Before he put his hands on my stomach, he blew into them and warmed them. This little gesture may not seem like much to most people, but to someone who has been poked and prodded by all kinds of medical people, it was huge. For a surgeon to take a moment to make it just a little more comfortable for the patient was very instrumental in gaining my trust. I liked him right away; and he remains one of my doctors to this day. Before leaving the room, he patted me on the shoulder and told me he would get things ready for my admittance.

One of the nurses came into the room a while later and told me to wait at the Admitting Office in the Johnson Building. They were trying to "find me a room." It was a long wait. By the time a room was ready, my

Jennifer had come and Martha was back from Skip's office. The two of them were with me when I was taken to the Trauma Unit. The Colon and Rectal Unit did not have a place for me yet. As God is my witness, if it had not been for one simple truth I learned that day, I would have spent the past seven years wishing that I would have waited until a room on the right floor had opened up prior to going to the hospital. The Trauma Unit slapped me with a dose of reality and taught me a lesson I would not soon forget. I was not ready for the nightmare that was fixing to take place. On the other hand, it was where I discovered the answer to *"why me"* which I had asked God so many times in the days before.

I changed from my clothes into a hospital gown and got into bed. A short time later, and without so much as an aspirin or a warning, two nurses came in and literally crammed a long thin hose into my nose, shoving it all the way into my stomach. It was as barbaric as anything I had ever experienced. It took the breath right out of me! They did not explain what they were fixing to do, they just did it. "What the hell are you doing?" I yelled. I glanced over and saw sheer terror on Jennifer's face. I was helpless to comfort my daughter or ease any of the fear I saw in her eyes. Even Martha's mouth was gaping open. A cramping fear was griping my heart, causing my chest to tighten and ache. I suppose in the Trauma Unit, they are accustomed to emergency situations where this might be necessary, but I was utterly terrified.

By the time they were finished, my energy was gone. I had fought them, because I had no idea what they were doing or why they felt it necessary to play so rough. I was in so much pain, so afraid and it honestly felt as if someone were trying to kill me. After they had completed their "procedure," I did not utter a sound. I felt as if I had been attacked in a back alley and left to die. I felt hot tears rolling down both sides of my face. I am not sure whether I was more afraid than angry; or, so angry I did not have sense enough to be afraid. I know I was speechless. I began to feel a sense of utter despair. *"Why Lord?"*—*"Why is this happening to me?"*—*"Where are you?"* These are the only thoughts that continued to fill my mind.

It was not long before I heard a bit of commotion going on outside my room. My Jennifer had gone out to the nurses' station and pulled a "Shirley McClain" on the staff. *"Terms of Endearment"* was one of our favorite movies and it seemed Ms. Jennifer had the mother's role down to an art. She was even threatening them with our attorney, Skip. The only comment I remember was her telling them, "I bet our lawyer is better than yours!" It wasn't long before they brought me a shot for pain. But I knew at the end of that little bit of drama, this was not going to be easy.

I sent Jennifer home. I told her it was best she keep the kids as normal as possible. In reality, I did not need my daughter to see any more of this or be affected and I needed the little-ones protected as well. Jennifer was the only one that could do that for me.

The first gift I got was the cutest little vase with a couple of flowers in it. As it was being brought into the room, I heard a familiar voice saying, "Who sent those wimpy little flowers?" I could not believe my ears! Here was Skip, Jana (his wife) and Mollie (his secretary). I was a mess. My hair was going every direction and I had a hose in my nose and an IV sticking out of my arm. But the comfort of his voice and the smiles on their faces caused my heart to melt. Skip has always walked into a room and took command. This day was no different. I will never forget the look on his face as he read the card on those "wimpy little flowers" only to find they were from the "Law Offices of Skip Simpson." We all laughed together. Skip never seemed to accept the fact that I didn't need a huge bouquet of flowers. That he thought of me in the first place warmed my heart. And then to see him take time from work and come to see me within a couple of hours of being in my hospital room was amazing. It was a kindness I will never forget. Their visit seemed to go by too fast.

I hated the Trauma Unit. I was miserable. It seemed everyone around me was miserable. The nurses seemed to hate the Trauma Unit. The whole floor had a foul smell to it. As my wonderful attorney and friend, and his wife and secretary hugged and kissed me, then left, I looked around and reality stepped right back in. The patients in there were in the most horrible conditions: disfiguring car wrecks, horrifying accidents, violence of all kinds, leaving human bodies broken and crumbled. The very air in that unit was depressing. The room décor was bland and unfeeling. I felt myself slipping into my own depression. It has been several years since I felt depressed. I had been working with the False Memory Syndrome Foundation since the end of my legal action. I was helping families reunite all over the country and kept busy speaking out against therapeutic abuse. (See *"Misplaced Trust"* © Laura Pasley 1993, *"True Stories of False Memories"* and *Skeptic Magazine,* 1994 [both English and German version] for more information). I had been traveling the country speaking, doing talk shows, working with families and I loved it. My life was full by putting my heart and soul into helping people out of misery. Now I was in my own form of hopelessness and depravity. I felt myself slip into an abyss of discouragement and despair.

In my own sadness; I asked again, *"Lord, where are you?" "Why now?" "Why me?"* My heart sank as low as it could possibly sink. I closed my eyes and envisioned the end. I felt as if my life were going to be over and I had no idea what I would do with my 18-month-old baby boy, or, for that matter, all the rest of my wonderful children. Tara needed consistent parenting. Dalton needed me to be steadfast and strong—he depended on me. And my Jennifer, that poor girl had been hurt so badly by not having her father in her life and me in-and-out of all kinds of things that took me away from her. Does she know how much I love her? Do all of them know they are loved? Have I made that crystal clear to each of them? Somehow, I felt I had let everyone down. Now, I was in this dingy room giving up. I was letting myself down. I was letting my children down and I was continually letting Satan win.

That night in the Trauma Unit was my bottom. It was my low point. I bowed my head and asked my God one more time where He was. As if a fog lifted, my answer came almost in an audible tone. *"I'm right here. I never left you."* My problem was not that God had left me, I had left God. I thought because trauma had come into my life once more, I was going to be left to die. I closed my eyes and asked my Father in Heaven to forgive me for not knowing He was there. I prayed not my will, but Thine be done. I told God to use me any way He wanted to, throughout this entire ordeal, and confirmed that my life was His to do with as He needed. I prayed that God would open my eyes and make my life, and everything that happened in that hospital, be for His Glory. I gave up and let Him take the wheel. A peace passed over me that night so strong and so real, I did not panic another time. There would be some close calls. I ended up having blood transfusions and I would be pretty sick for quite some time. But, I knew from that moment, God had my hand and was holding me up.

For reasons unknown to me at the time, an orderly came and wheeled me out of that depressing room the very next morning. I was put on the Colon Rectal Unit on the 12th floor of Baylor Hospital. The change was as different as night is to day. I felt like I was being rolled out of the projects and into a fancy hotel. When I was rolled into my new room, I closed my eyes and thanked God. It overlooked the heliport so I could watch the helicopters fly past my window and land right out in front of me. There were big windows and the blinds were opened so I could see all over Dallas. It looked like a big Christmas holiday. I also discovered I could raise the bed almost to the ceiling. Doctors and nurses would come into my room and I would have the bed near the ceiling watching the beautiful City of Dallas below me. The nurses that came in were so kind and gentle and kept telling me if there was anything I needed, just let them know. It was the first time I had relaxed in a long, long time.

The room was already filling up with the most beautiful flowers I had ever seen. Two dozen red roses from my parents, pot after pot of fresh flowers, plants, little trees, and even a huge bouquet of pink flowers (roses and carnations) from Dr. Wayne Burkhead, my orthopedic/shoulder doctor. There were text and email messages being sent from all over this country and several others. Pam Freyd, Founder of the False Memory Syndrome Foundation, and Janet Fetkewicz, Retractor Coordinator, and the staff sent flowers and a card. Many of my FMSF Family sent flowers, telegrams, cards and general well wishes. Doctors, lawyers and educators called and sent messages of hope and love. I even got emails and text messages from friends in the United Kingdom. I had never felt that kind of love from that many different people. Families I had helped put back together, following tragic therapeutic situations, sent letters and cards. The phone never stopped ringing. My room was overflowing with the most beautiful flowers I had ever seen. The smell went down the halls so far that other patients were coming to see them. People were sending the names of one church right after the other that had pledged to lift me up in prayer during my entire stay as well as during the surgery.

My surgery was scheduled for the day after I had been transferred to the 12th floor. That day, Dr. Jabbour came to my room very early and sat down on my bed. He had a concerned look on his face. He patted my knee and told me they had to reschedule my surgery for the following day. This was difficult news. I had been prepped (which for a colon procedure is pure hell in and of itself). I had been praying and people all over had been praying and committed to stopping what they were doing to pray that day. I was discouraged. It was not until later that I found out that because the surgery was rescheduled to include one more day of prep, my colon was so clean, I would not need a colostomy bag attached to the outside of my abdomen following the surgery. God knew what He was doing and that incident alone taught me another lesson about questioning His timing.

The morning of the surgery, I felt secure and safe in the arms of my Heavenly Father. I was asking surgeons, anesthesiologists, nurses and whoever else was in charge of my care, if they got enough sleep, if they had drank the night before, or if they were having marital problems. "If so, be gone!" I told each and every one. I was facing and experiencing one of the scariest surgeries ever with a peace that passed all understanding. I literally felt as if I were being held up by thousands of angels. It was the most awesome, surreal moment of my life.

When I was wheeled into the operating suite and hooked up to the machines, the nurse over my care took my hand and asked if she could pray with me. We closed our eyes and she said the most beautiful prayer I had heard in a long time. She was putting herself, as well as the rest of the treatment team, in God's hands. She was also lifting me up to God and asking that He protect and watch over me while the team did their work. Talk about feeling a sense of absolute peace! Dr. Jabbour came in and when he asked me if I was ready, I smiled at him and said, "Let's do it." A moment or two later, I fell into an induced deep sleep.

It was dark when I was wheeled back into that beautiful room with all the flowers. I had another hose in my nose, tubes and IV's were sticking out of my hands and arms and a central line was in my neck. I opened my eyes, then closed them, over and over trying to gain a little idea of where I was or if I was dreaming. The minute the transport team left my bed, nurses came in and were checking my vital signs and adjusting tubing and bedding. I do remember looking out to see a beautiful CareFlite helicopter coming straight towards my window, turn quickly and circling around and down onto the helipad below. It was breathtaking. I did not speak. I knew I was very weak. I remember my family was there. I don't remember seeing anyone but Jennifer. They only let her see me following the surgery. My other children were too young to come back, but I was so relieved to see her. I could see the fear on her gorgeous China doll face. She took my hand and told me she loved me. My beautiful Jennifer; the girl I fell in love with before she was ever born; the extension of myself, was helping me through this. My heart swelled with pride and love. Looking into her eyes made my blood warm and the comfort of having her near me was overwhelming.

The next few days were touch and go. At one point, I looked over from the hose running down my nose to see my mom and dad sitting in the chairs. Neither one of them was speaking. They were just sitting, being there, as they had always been, quietly worrying about their middle child. I could see it on their faces. I closed my eyes and slept during their entire visit.

When the pathology came back on my Cancer, it was described as "adenocarcinoma." It is said to take 10 to 15 years to grow and starts as a polyp. I had a colonoscopy in 1999 and it was not discovered. By the time it was removed, it was nearly breaking through my bowel wall. It was so large, there was an opening the size of a pencil head for any waste to leave my body. If I had waited until I was 50, as suggested by the doctor,

I would be dead. I lost about a third of my descending colon. In being persistent with my doctors, I was instrumental in saving my own life.

When the hose was finally removed from my nose, I had a sense of relief like no one can understand unless they have been there. Much to my chagrin, the nose hose would go back in a few days later. I had arranged for Dalton and Tara to come to the hospital to spend the night. It was Friday and we always had family night on Friday. They came to my room and we watched cartoons. After they had fallen asleep, I began dry heaving and the hose had to be put back down my nose. It was a setback. The following Monday, the doctors told me I needed a blood transfusion. I would have a couple of good days and then a bad day. I am not sure I realized at the time just how sick I was. One of my physicians was a family friend we had known since he was born. Dr. Amit Patel told the nurses to give me anything I asked for. I remained in good hands throughout my hospital stay.

When it was finally time to release me, I was so happy to go home. I had literally been gutted. I had a large incision from my belly down through my abdomen. There were staples that were probably more painful than the

Laura Pasley

actual incision. But I had come through this very serious illness with more assurance of God's love than when I went in. The doctors told me I needed six months of chemotherapy. That would be another saga of illness and fatigue beyond anything I could have ever imagined. My veins had been blown so badly in my hands and arms, they had to put a port into my sub-clavian artery to access my veins for chemo. When the port was surgically put in, I complained it burned when it was accessed. The nurses told me it was just new and I wasn't use to it. On a night when I was rushed to the emergency room, a very smart tech decided to roll me under a CAT scan to discover a broken port and that the medications were spilling out, in essence, burning the tissue of my left sub-clavian area. Demerol and Phenergan had set me on fire, not to mention the chemo. I had to endure an additional surgery to replace the port and a third one to remove it following my chemotherapy.

I had moments of despair, as anyone who has suffered with Cancer knows well. But, after that life changing night in the Trauma Unit, I always saw the light at the end of the tunnel. As I write this story late in October, 2009, it will be seven years since I finished chemo. Seven years! At the time I was going through this ordeal, I had to literally put one step in front of the other. But I can say today, with God's help, I beat Cancer. I not only beat it, I kicked its butt. I know much of my peace and enduring the ordeal was because people loved me enough to pray me through it. People I had never met were praying for me from all over the world. And, most of all, God made sure I saw His love and His mercy. I saw it in the medical team that took care of me; doctors, nurses, medical techs, IV Teams and I especially saw it in my chemo nurse, Margaret. Every single Monday, Margaret came to me with a warm, loving smile and a caring heart. So many people, many of them strangers who reached out and expressed compassion and love, made a huge difference. So much of overcoming something like this is attitude. My family and faith helped this become a triumph in my life. I can honestly say at this point, "Why not me?"

Laura's family: Tara, Justin, Jennifer
(baby in tummy: Zayla Marie),
Keaton, Dalton, Colton.

Behind the Story

Laura Pasley has been a good friend of mine for many years. She is an avid storyteller and they are most often tales from her own life. Laura usually begins her stories with the phrase: "I've had more than my share of life's experiences...!" after which she relates the most amazing chronology of events. She has endured far more than most people I know, as a collective group of varied adversities. For this, she is quite an entertaining and wise narrator and I have often told Laura, "You should write a book!"

I grabbed the opportunity to share a glimpse into the epic tale that is Laura Pasley by including her in *The Triumph Book*. As a regular beneficiary of her storytelling, I know first-hand the value of what she has to share!

Seventeen

The Refining

Author: Ronda Knuth

Between life's first lusty cry and death's final labored breath the story of life is written. Each story unique; each filled with joy and sorrow, hello and goodbye, triumph and tragedy. It's true of my tale; no doubt, it's true of yours as well. Who I am today is a direct result of my life experiences, my choices in them and the grace of God. I've learned to laugh and I've learned to cry all within the safety of His embrace.

At eight years of age, afraid, and feeling very alone, I lay in a hospital bed in the neurological unit of Children's Hospital in Denver, Colorado. Partial paralysis from an inoperable, terminal *brain stem glioma* laid claim to my body. The prognosis for recovery was dismal at best, "Take her home and love her," the doctor said to my sorrowing parents, "She'll be gone within a year." The news shattered their world, but being people of faith, they found the courage to believe for a miracle.

Though I did not know the seriousness of my illness, I did know that whatever was going on in my body was making me very, very sick. I experienced partial paralysis, and sometimes the headaches were debilitating. Word spread about the little girl who was dying, and many joined in prayer for a restoration of my health. Much to the amazement of my doctors, I did not die. Instead of getting worse, I got better.

A hothouse plant, though beautiful, is never as strong as one subjected to the elements of nature. The harder the rain, the greater the wind, the deeper the roots must go if it is to survive. I was a hothouse plant. In my

217

early twenties, I was taken out of my cozy, warm greenhouse existence and set down in the midst of a ferocious storm. The testing was severe. Often I despaired as the winds of affliction ravaged me tossing me this way and that intent upon destruction.

The testing began innocently enough during college. On Friday and Saturday nights, I joined a number of other students to volunteer at a drug rehab center in Dallas, Texas. My introduction to the "real" world was daunting. I knew nothing of illicit drugs or depraved sexuality.... absolutely nothing.

I did however discover a niche with my name written all over it. I loved working with the children. The summer after my freshman year, I stayed on in Dallas joining a team conducting children's crusades in the low-income projects of north Dallas.

The summer passed in a blur of activity. Plans were underway to open a home at the rehab center for needy girls in the area. Willing workers were needed so at the invitation of the director, I stayed on rather than going back to school that fall. It was a decision I lived to regret.

Eddie W. came to the men's program after a life-changing turn-around for the better while serving a sentence in the state penitentiary in Texas. Upon release, he applied for and was accepted into the program at the drug rehab center.

He was a nice looking, dynamic man. I respected him. I admired his gentle demeanor. He was a favorite whenever he shared his personal story. His words brought hope to those whose lives had been ravaged by illegal activity and drugs.

In time, Eddie completed the rehab program and was asked to join the staff. He threw himself wholeheartedly in to his new life. Eventually, we began dating. When Eddie asked me to marry him, I quickly said yes. Perhaps that assent that made him feel invincible. Twice before moving back to Denver to ready for the wedding, Eddie forced himself upon me sexually. The first time he invited me to his room, "C'mon up, I want to show you something." The second time was on a lonely stretch of highway between Dallas and Denver. Both times I said please don't. Both times my plea fell on deaf ears. Nevertheless, I denied that what had happened to me was rape.

To acknowledge it for what it was presented a dilemma I was not ready to deal with. Instead, I put a new spin on it—one that was more acceptable then rape. I blamed myself. *I must have done something to cause this.* I could deal with immorality much easier then sexual violation. I could not, would not, tell anyone what had happened. If I did, what would they think of me? Would I be sent home in shame? I convinced myself that since I was tarnished and no longer a virgin, no one would want to marry me. Therefore, it was in my best interest to follow through with the wedding. I would forgive him, forgive myself and put what had happened in the past. My secret proved a shaky foundation upon which to build a marriage.

Eddie and I married in Denver, Colorado on Valentine's Day, 1975. As part of the ceremony, I sang a song of commitment to him, "Until the twelfth of never, I'll still be loving you." I chose to love him and to commit myself to him for a lifetime.

The first year or two we were relatively happy. I cried when I wasn't pregnant the first month after our marriage. More than anything, I wanted to be a mother. When I finally conceived, my joy knew no bounds. Our first-born son, Paul, was born nine days after our first wedding anniversary. Oh, how I loved him! He completed my life. Perhaps, in spite of a rocky start, we would still be able to realize a storybook life.

We lived in a comfortable, one-bedroom, furnished apartment in Grand Prairie, Texas. Eddie worked at an area factory as a welder on pressure vessels, and I immersed myself in motherhood. I was quite content to play the role of homemaker, mother and wife.

Days after Paul's birth, Eddie was involved in an accident at work. The pressure vessel he was welding on shifted, shooting the wedge used to anchor it in place into the side of Eddie's face. An "nth of a degree" either way would have killed him instantly. His injuries were severe. The week following his accident was touch and go. I found myself on the road constantly driving to and from the hospital. I was torn between needing to be with him and wanting to be with Paul.

This was not how it was supposed to be. A couple at the church we attended offered to take care of Baby Paul until Eddie was released from the hospital. Many nights, after making the long drive from Dallas to Grand Prairie, I would drive by their home, sit outside in the car, and cry. I wanted to be with my baby but I couldn't. Physically I was exhausted. After several days, my body cried *foul* and I began hemorrhaging sending me to my own bed for a much needed rest and time of healing.

Once Eddie was stabilized, he was allowed to return home. Baby Paul soon followed and for a few weeks, we bonded as a family. It was a happy, happy time. Eddie's accident was devastating financially, and he chose to file a lawsuit against the company. Needless to say, his return to work was without welcome and when at last the dust settled he was without a job. We did the only thing we could think of to do... we moved to Colorado to be near my family.

Eddie was restless, frequently moving from job to job. We moved several times that year, never settling for long in one place. One night he rattled my world when he came home to tell me that he had enlisted in the Navy. Because of his criminal record, his acceptance into the Navy required a series of concessions taking many weeks. When approval was finally given, Eddie was shipped off to boot camp and baby Paul and I moved in with my parents. I missed him dreadfully. After basic training was complete, Eddie was sent to San Diego for schooling, and then to Millington, Tennessee.

On one of Eddie's leaves from school in San Diego, I became pregnant with our second child. Once his schooling was finalized, Paul and I joined Eddie in Millington for several weeks. It was good to be back together. Morning sickness gave way to unmitigated excitement as my pregnancy progressed. In December, we received orders to Eddie's first duty station in Norfolk, Virginia. Four months later a beautiful baby girl, Diana Lynn, joined our family. We were about as poor as poor could be, but we were content. We lived in low-income housing a skip-and-a-jump from a major freeway and regional airport. I adjusted to the constant sounds of traffic and airplanes just outside my window. An older couple who lived in the apartment beneath ours befriended us. They became my saving grace during Eddie's frequent times at sea. During the longest periods, I would pack our bags and Paul, Diana and I would fly home to Denver.

A subtle change took place in Eddie during those years. He was never abusive, never unkind but he became increasingly depressed. When he was home, he was distant and aloof. He stopped going to church with the children and me. One night he told me, "I always lose the things I love the most." Most noticeable to me was his withdrawal from intimacy. We were "roommates"—nothing more—during our final year in Norfolk.

His behavior was confusing at best. I suggested counseling and he said that no one would understand what he was going through. He implied grief over his father's death, a father who had abandoned him as a young boy. Near the end of his first four-year term with the Navy, he was arrested for window peeping. He denied the charge, saying that he had gone for a walk, had become disoriented and took a short cut through a neighborhood. He was sentenced to a weekend in jail. I knew he was troubled, but criminal? No. There was no way that he would return to that kind of lifestyle.

Eddie served his sentence and, shortly after, he chose to re-enlist for another four years with the Navy. We were sent to Kingsville a small military/college/oil town in southwest Texas. I breathed a sigh of relief hoping that a new start would allow Eddie to overcome whatever personal demons he was battling. For a short while, it seemed to be just what he needed. We settled into a comfortable two-bedroom duplex. I found work at a medical clinic across town. We started attending a local church and life settled into a reasonable routine.

We rarely saw one another since Eddie worked nights and I worked days. Before long, Eddie's unrest returned with a vengeance. He refused to attend church with the children and me. He began drinking and smoking pot. Once again, he withdrew. We'd been married almost seven years. I wasn't exactly sure what was wrong, but something was. *Maybe it's me.* Why was the man I was married to intent on holding me at arm's length? What sense of worth I had evaporated like a cool morning mist on a blistering hot day.

Eddie's behavior became increasingly unpredictable. Soon after school began, Paul fell on the playground equipment at school and broke his arm. I rushed to the school to pick him up and immediately took him to the medical clinic where I worked. X-rays were taken and it was determined that a specialist who could perform surgery was needed. The closest major hospital equipped to handle his injury was in Corpus Christi, an hour's drive north/east of Kingsville. I stopped and picked up Eddie so he could go with us. I desperately needed his support. On the outskirts of Kingsville, he instructed me to pull over and let him out. No explanation. He just changed his mind. It was later that evening before he made his way to the hospital to be with us.

Then there was the incident with the "nighty." On a lark, the girls at work gave me a sexy nightgown as an early Christmas gift. Thinking it might be just the thing to spark my husband's interest; I donned it that evening and modeled it for him. He looked at me, simply said, "That's nice." then rolled over and went to sleep. Can you say, *demoralized?*

Near the end of November, I found myself praying one morning on the way to work, "God, I don't know what's going on in my marriage, but something is. I can't fight an enemy I can't see. Please bring it to light even if it hurts to know."

The answer to that prayer took place a few weeks later one late afternoon, three days after Christmas. Though it has been thirty-seven years ago, I can still remember that deadly blow with clarity.

For the most part, Eddie helped with chores, which made it much easier for me in the evenings. After a busy day at work, I stopped by the daycare to pick up Paul and Diana and then made my way across town to our little bungalow. We'd worked out a system a few weeks earlier dividing the household chores since we were working opposite schedules. This particular afternoon I walked in the door to find the house exactly as I'd left it the night before. I was miffed knowing I'd have to pick up before I could start dinner for the kids and me. I sent Paul and Diana out to play and rolled up my sleeves, ready for a quick house clean.

When the telephone rang, I answered and was shocked to hear the voice of Captain Gomez from the Kingsville Police Department. "We've picked up your husband and are questioning him in the kidnap and rape of a young woman in town. We're finished for now. Would you like to come and get him or shall I arrange for someone to bring him home?"

My initial response was one of disbelief. *Rape? You have to be kidding. He hasn't touched me in a year.* The truth is I knew nothing about rape. My only experience had been with my own violation at his hands and that I had redefined as something for which I bore the blame. I did not know that rape is a crime of anger and not of unrestrained passion.

I did not want Paul and Diana to know what was happening so I told the Captain to arrange a ride home for Eddie. I fed them supper, readied them for bed, and tucked them in for a good night's rest. It would be best if they were sleeping when their father came home.

All too soon, Eddie walked through the door. A detective from the police force accompanied him. He did a cursory glance around the house, asked a question or two, and then he left.

The obvious first question out of my mouth was, "Eddie??? Did you do this?" He denied involvement; said it was a case of mistaken identity and it would work itself out. We dressed for bed and crawled in, side by side.

"Don't you think we should pray, honey?" I asked.

"You go ahead," he encouraged.

I countered, "No. No, I think you need to pray." He prayed something about God being with us in this difficult time, rolled over and went to sleep. That settled it in my mind. *He can't possibly be guilty. If he were, he'd be worried instead of sleeping.*

We hadn't been in bed long when there was a knock at the door. "Who's there?" I queried.

"Open up. We have a warrant for your husband's arrest."

It didn't take long for Eddie to join us in the living room. He was cuffed, read his rights, and walked from the house. The detective told me that if I tried to hide any evidence they would arrest me. I was told to stay put and not to go anywhere. He said they would be back in the morning to search the house. Then they were gone.

For a few minutes after Eddie's arrest, I was alone in my living room. I randomly called an attorney and asked what I should and should not do. I called my folks in Denver. Then I called my minister. Pastor James, and his wife, Delores, assured me they were on their way. The children were asleep as I knelt to pray. *God, be with us. This is all a case of mistaken identity*, I reasoned, *nothing more than a terrible interruption in our lives.* Little did I realize the events that were about to transpire.

Delores stayed with the children while Pastor James and I drove to the city jail. On the way there, the thought crossed my mind that while our world was crumbling at my feet, the rest of the world was going on as if nothing had happened. I was so thankful for pastor's presence in the car with me.

I hoped that I could see Eddie for a minute and get a feel for what was happening to us. While sitting in the waiting room, a couple of officers walked by deep in conversation about the recently arrested rapist. "You know what I think they ought to do to him?" one said to the other. "I think they ought to take him out and string him up."

A rush of emotion swept over me—shame, anger, and searing pain. Someone said, "That's his wife sitting there." An awkward moment of silence followed. The officers glanced my way then made a hasty exit. My belief that Eddie was innocent began to wane.

We had a few minutes together. A detective apologized for the officers, and then he left us alone. Eddie reiterated that he was innocent. Then he made a very odd request, "Honey, there's a gun. It's behind the bed. Get rid of it, okay? I'm not supposed to have it." *Why is he asking me to do that if he's not guilty? When did WE get a gun?*

After returning home, James and Delores left so she could get her nightclothes. She was determined to stay with me, and I was so grateful. After they left, I got the gun and put it in the attic. I wasn't getting rid of it as Eddie asked but, still wanting to believe he was innocent, I decided to make it less accessible. If the police were thorough in their search, they would find it. At least I'd made an effort on Eddie's behalf.

Twice I received obscene phone calls. News traveled fast in the little town. The first caller asked, "Mrs. W.? How does it feel to be married to a rapist?" The second, Delores intercepted. Kingsville felt more ominous by the minute.

In the morning, I readied the children for daycare. I did not want Paul and Diana to be there when the police came to search the house. They had been sleeping when their daddy was arrested and I hoped to spare them the news of his arrest for as long as possible. I was weary having slept little the night before.

Paul slipped into my room as I finished last minute preparations. "Mommy," he said, "Where's my daddy?"

"Daddy is downtown, Paul." The jail was there and it seemed enough to say at the moment. I was surprised when he countered with, "But I thought I heard you tell my uncle during the night last night that my daddy is in jail!"

My mother-heart knew that Paul and Diana were going to need to know in the coming months that they could trust me. I made the decision at that moment to be as honest with them as I could be. The information I chose to share would be simple and appropriate for their ages. I reasoned that if they were old enough to ask, they needed to know. I pulled Paul onto my lap, wrapped him tightly in my arms and gently whispered, "Daddy *is* in jail, Paul."

Ever the precocious one, he probed for more information, "Why?"

"Because the police think daddy did some things he shouldn't have done."

"Did he?" he queried, looking into my eyes. I hesitated a moment, then looking deeply into my son's big, brown eyes whispered honestly, "I don't know sweetheart. I don't know."

Returning from the daycare, I found the police already in our home having entered through an open living room window. Pastor James met me on the walk in front of the house. Texas Rangers were posted on the front lawn, rifles in hand. I was told I could go in, but Pastor could not. In that moment, I reached heavenward and took the hand of God. Together we went inside.

The police were going through everything; nothing was sacred. I felt as if I were standing naked in a room full of strangers. Our lives were laid bare as they systematically searched one room and then another. What little self-esteem I had was destroyed that day. I sat on the couch, read the search warrant and told myself, *There is no way Eddie could have done these things.*

The front door opened and a detective came through. At the sound of his voice, I lifted my head. "Don't say anything," he said," just nod your head." At his side stood a beautiful, blonde, teenage girl; they walked into the living room and I instinctively knew that she was the one accusing my husband of rape. I hated her. I wanted to demand an answer to my unasked question, "Why are you doing this to us?" Instead, I hung my head in confusion and shame. She nodded her head in response to several items that were pointed out to her, turned and left.

I moved from my sofa so pictures could be taken for the investigation. Eddie had brought this young woman to our home and had raped her repeatedly, near the Christmas tree, close to the picture of our young children. Using an old sermon tape and a cassette player, he recorded her violation. Later the police found the tape stuffed in an eggnog carton in a trashcan in front of our home. Polaroid snapshots, taken while he violated her, were also found.

Slipping into the children's bedroom, I sat on the edge of one of the beds and began to weep. I loved that sunny little room and the memories it held. *God, what is going to happen to us?* The police captain came into the room. Cold, professional, he spoke, "You know I've noticed that you have a number of religious books and tapes. Could it be that you expected too much of your husband? Maybe he couldn't live up to your standards." Then he said, "You're the only one who knows what went on behind your bedroom door. Could it be that you made demands on your husband that he couldn't meet?" As he turned to leave, he said, "Remember if you are hiding any evidence we'll file charges against you too." In the space of two minutes, he had questioned my faith, my integrity and my moral character. In his accusation I heard, *you are responsible for what happened here.*

With a few choice words, I was destroyed. Local newspapers for miles around carried the story of Eddie's arrest, complete with our address and the fact that we had young children. Sensing that we were in danger, I asked my parents to come from Colorado for Paul and Diana. It would be several weeks before I would be free to join them. The police were not convinced that I was not involved. Later I was told that in many rape cases, the wife (or girlfriend) is present at the time the victim is violated. Putting our things in storage, I moved in with Pastor James and Delores.

The first Sunday after Eddie's arrest, and the day after the children were gone, I went back to the church I'd come to love. Slipping in after the service started, I fought the tears threatening to overflow. I didn't want people to notice my presence. With the final song, the congregation rose and began to sing, "Have doubt and fear come against your mind? Has your faith been sorely tried? Just lift your head, here cometh your help, it is Jesus for you He has died. Rise and be healed in the name of Jesus. Let faith arise in your soul. Rise and be healed in the name of Jesus. He will cleanse and make you whole. He will cleanse and make you whole."

I slipped from my place in the center of the pew, and walked to the front of the church, tears streaming down my face. As I knelt at the altar, a host of fellow parishioners surrounded me, laid their hands gently on me, and began to pray. I was so broken. I don't know what I prayed, even if I prayed. I simply wept.

At the close of the service, as I hurried to leave, a woman stopped me. She pressed a bottle of bath oil into my hand and said, "Here, honey. I want you to have this. I have a feeling you are going to need it in the days to come." I don't know her name, but I never forgot her kindness.

On Wednesday nights, I routinely attended a home-fellowship group made up of folks from the church. In an intimate setting, we shared our lives and prayed for one another. James and Barbara made sure each member felt welcome in their lovely home. I debated attending that first Wednesday, but I desperately needed to be with others who would support me.

The group had joined with another group that evening. I should have left, but I didn't. During prayer, a woman from the visiting group requested prayer for "that sailor who raped that young girl. He was used of the devil!" Rage filled my heart. How dare she presume to know anything

226

about *that sailor* or his family? We knelt to pray and another visiting woman, slipped her arm around me and said, "Honey, do you know Jesus?" It was too much. Choking back a sob, I rose from my knees and headed for the front door.

Barbara intercepted me and I'm so glad she did. She drew me into the shelter of her arms and whispered in my ear, "Honey, hold your head up high. You've done nothing to be ashamed of." So many times in the months that followed, I pulled her words close in an attempt to maintain my dignity—what was left of it anyway.

In the weeks that followed his arrest, I learned that Eddie had led a sordid, secret life that stretched back almost to the beginning of our marriage. I also learned that Eddie was in actuality a serial rapist who had been raping women for a number of months, possibly years. It was suspected that he had been raping while we were stationed in Norfolk. Eddie had expertly hid his double life from us. We'd been married almost seven years... how long had I lived unknowingly with his betrayal? No wonder he had pulled away from Paul, then five and Diana, three... and me.

Clearance from the authorities finally came and I caught a flight home to Denver. One cold, blustery night not long after Eddie's arrest, I found myself sitting alone in front of the fireplace in my parent's home where the children and I were staying. I watched as the flames performed a waltz of death, leaping impatiently from one rough-hewn log to another systematically reducing what had once been a majestic tree into a smoldering mound of ash. A deep sadness blanketed my bruised heart and I felt smothered by the weight of a love gone wrong.

I could not escape the insidious darkness assaulting my emotions. My dreams lay shattered at my feet, and I knew that, for me, life would never be the same. A tear, then two slipped silently down my cheek and trickled off the edge of my chin. "I'm just like that log, Lord." I whispered, "I've been destroyed, and there's nothing left of my life."

I wept until there were no more tears to weep. It was then that the greatest of all counselors came and wrapped my wounded spirit gently in His arms. The Holy Spirit ministered to me, whispering the words of Isaiah 61:3 to my shattered heart, "To give them beauty for ashes, the oil of joy for mourning, the garment of praise for the spirit of heaviness that they might be called trees of righteousness, the planting of the Lord, that He might be glorified."

I, in turn, whispered a prayer to Him, "Here, Lord: ugly ashes, in an ugly bucket. That's all I have left. I haven't known what to do with them, so I tossed it about in my mind and decided to bring them to you. They're not very pretty. I'm sorry, so very, very sorry. I started out meaning so well, wanting so much for you to be proud. But look at the mess I've made. I wanted to bury them so no one would know what had happened, but I couldn't. So here they are. I've heard that for them you would give me beauty. If you will grant me your beauty for these dirty ashes, I'll give them back to you through my life. And this time, Lord, this time I'll be a planting for you that you might be glorified."

I battled depression, uncertainty, daytime terrors and insidious nightmares. One night I woke abruptly from a troubling dream to find my mother at my bedside. She knew, as perceptive mothers are prone to know, that her grown-up-daughter-child was afraid. She laid a reassuring hand on my arm and spoke a few words of comfort before returning to her own bed. I heard her talking to my father and a deep peace settled over me. I knew that they were praying for me.

Because of a plea bargain, Eddie received a sentence of thirty years in the State Penitentiary in Rosharon, Texas. I struggled with the idea of divorce and after a period of time proceeded with the necessary legalities to obtain one. I, who believed in the sanctity of marriage and lifetime commitment, found myself a broken, devastated single mother of two.

Laid bare and deeply wounded, I sought out a pastor for counsel. During my third or fourth session he said, "You know, Ronda, you're just like the prodigal son. You've sinned and now you've come back home." It was several years before I dared to speak with a pastor's wife at a church I was attending, "Ronda," she said, "You must never speak about these things. As you do, you relive them." The first accused me, the second said, in essence, "I don't want to hear it!"

It would be many years before I found healing in my life. I tried other counselors but found none who understood the depth of my pain. I desperately needed someone who would ask the difficult questions and draw my story out of me.

The recovery for me was long and hard. There were times when I wanted nothing more than to die... it seemed preferable to the dark days that stretched endlessly before me. Even in the darkness of those days I remembered my promise to God, "I'll be a planting for You that You might be glorified." And, He has never forgotten His promise to me, "I'll give you beauty for your ashes."

There were other precious "rememberings" as well—Barbara's admonition to hold my head up high became a gentle thumb in my back that pushed me onward. The precious gift of bath oil reminded me of the care of others and the importance of reaching out to one who is hurting.

In time, Rob Knuth came into my life. He was everything Eddie was not—honest, kind, committed. He loved my children and me as we struggled for wholeness. After our marriage, we were blessed with two sons, Andy and Ben. Our family was complete... and we lived happily ever after.

Not really! The testing continued. Over a period of seven years, we were to lose many in death. Of those, eleven were family. Of those eleven, two were flesh of our flesh. One baby we lost as the result of a miscarriage. The other baby, William, was stillborn.

The conflict in my life has been vicious; the battles not imaginary, but real. Scarcely would I have time to catch my breath before another test would come. I found myself stuffing the hurt just to survive; there simply wasn't time to grieve each loss, or so I thought.

Then, through a series of events, I found myself at the breaking point, desperate before God for a complete healing. I doubted His presence in my life. I felt so alone and at one point despaired of living. Wanting to present the image of a strong, Christian woman, I stuffed the closet of my heart with package after package of pain. I took great care to wrap my "uglies" in colorful paper complete with pretty ribbons and bows. It was important to me that no one knew what was really inside those packages.

One day I went to put another package in the closet and discovered, to my dismay, that it was full. I opened the door and everything came tumbling out. I quickly tried to slam it closed, but the door wouldn't shut. It was time to do some housecleaning. With great emotion, I began rummaging through, sorting and tossing and making order out of my life once more. Through it all, as difficult as it has been, God has begun to do a work in my life. My inner strength has grown, along with my character, compassion and faith. God, who was the beloved of my childhood, has become Lord of my life.

God's reputation is not at risk because of my brokenness. In fact, as I am able to become increasingly honest and vulnerable, His redeeming work in me becomes more obvious... to me and hopefully to others. The emphasis has moved from me having it all together, to God having it all together. Though God did not protect me from pain, He has been faithful to enter into it with me and to touch me at my deepest pain.

A book was written several years ago detailing my experiences with my ex-husband. Written by Rocky Mountain News Reporter, Kevin Flynn, it is entitled, "The Unmasking: Married to a Rapist." (Used copies can still be obtained through Amazon.com) The author was fair, and truthful. The process was more painful than I anticipated but became a crucial part of my healing. The book is very graphic in parts and that transparency has been difficult for me. Nevertheless, I have seen it used repeatedly to speak to women who have experienced abuse, rape etc. In recent years, through writing and speaking, I have shared the "rest of the story"—the story of restoration and redemption. I have been given far more then was taken.

Ronda Knuth

Many opportunities have come my way to share: Phil Donahue, Sally Jesse Raphael, the 700 Club, Inside Edition and a number of radio programs. The Rocky Mountain News (Denver, Colorado) ran excerpts from the book in their *Life Style* section over a period of several days. I've spoken at area retreats, luncheons, high schools, and MOPS (Mothers of Preschoolers) groups in the Rocky Mountain region. Everywhere I go I meet those who are encouraged by my sharing. A fellow guest on the Sally Jesse Raphael show wrote, "While in New York, I planned to take my life. After meeting you and your daughter I knew if you could make it, I could make it, too."

Perhaps, most fulfilling of all has been the completion of a website sharing my story and the lessons I've learned with those who are in a life storm of their own. In addition, I have compiled an extensive (and ever-growing) resource page with the intent of placing helpful tools into the hands of those who suffer. The site, "Ronda's Resting Place" can be found at *http://rondasrestingplace.net*.

God has been faithful, and out of the testing of my life has come a love for Him and an intense desire to come alongside others who are sorrowing. I have learned to glean joy from the difficult seasons of life.

My heart's desire is to pour into others what God has poured into me. What an honor that He has called me His own.

Should you find yourself in a situation similar to mine, may I give you some wisdom to help you along:

- Hold your head up high.
- Find a safe person willing to hear your story and your heart. Don't stuff the pain and shame. I would have benefited from wise counsel.
- Be kind to yourself.
- Don't give up. The sun will shine again. It won't always hurt as it does now.
- While I cannot give thanks for the experience, I have learned to give thanks for God's faithfulness to me. I would never willingly go back through those times of trial; neither would I trade the valuable lessons I have learned. I am who I am today because of the testing.
- Keep a journal. Learn all that you can from your
- Experience; someday it will be your turn to walk with compassion with someone who is hurting.
- Run into the safety of Christ's embrace and let Him hold you. Indeed, on those days when you have no strength to walk; let Him carry you.

You are not alone. God is Sovereign. Even in this dark night, He is mindful of you. There is life on the other side. Life will never be as it once was, but God will give you a "new normal" filled with opportunity and hope. Never give up!

"Endurance is not just the ability to bear a hard thing,

but to turn it into glory." —William Barclay

Behind the Story

This is Ronda's second story. Her first was *The Gift that Changed My Life,* or *Story Three.* I wanted to include both of Ronda's stories separately because they each are a truly powerful message by themselves.

What I appreciate about this story is that it represents a unique tragedy for this book, and yet one which is unfortunately familiar to many. Regardless of the abuse, there are many who suffer guilt and loss of self-esteem due to the actions of another. To carry this burden of remorse for something a person is completely innocent of is a regretful tragedy, and one which, like all adversity, can carry a light of hope and a destination of triumph as Ronda so aptly demonstrates.

Eighteen

My Chuck
Author: Angela Dvorsky

October 8, 2005 was a beautiful day. The sun was shining, weather was perfect and I was looking into the eyes of the man who was about to hear me say "I do." We were staring at each other thinking it was the best day of our lives. We were so in love and everyone knew it. I didn't know almost three years before that day, when we began dating, that Chuck was "the one", but it became clear to me not long after. I had never met anyone like him. He was such a gentleman, always opening the door for women, standing up when a lady entered the room, speaking respectfully to everyone and it wasn't one bit fake. Chuck was the real deal. He was cultured, educated and a wonderful cook. I couldn't believe this prince charming was interested in me! He had the cutest little smirk that I couldn't resist. There must have been something special about me as well because he fell hard, very quickly.

I didn't fall *as* fast, but one night Chuck cooked me a very special dinner with wine and dessert. We talked for hours about our lives and memories, personal things... we couldn't believe how easily we gave up such intimate details, some that we never shared with others. He told me he loved me and that he had loved me soon after we met, but hadn't revealed it yet for fear of scaring me away. I fell in love with Chuck that night.

We went through some hard times while we dated; things that tested us. Chuck had the most difficult time finding a good job and at one point he had no job. The poor guy had a few horrible jobs that he was over-qualified for. Some people warned me that he would never get a good job or make any money, and I should cut my losses. I could never have done that! I told him he would get his dream job someday; the trick was to never give up. He lived at an apartment with my brother and parents... talk about testing a relationship! His pride was hurt a lot.

We made it through! I think enduring and surmounting those challenges made us stronger. It also caused us to realize: *We could do anything as long as we had one another.* One night, when he was living at my brother's apartment, he asked me something that changed my world. I was sick and looked like hell; I hadn't had a shower and was cranky. Chuck rubbed my feet to make me feel better, which he did a lot during our relationship. He told me how much he loved me, how beautiful I was and that he wanted to take care of me forever: to buy us a home and have kids. I told him that would be great but he had to get a job first. We both laughed and then he got down on both knees and asked me if I would fulfill his dreams by becoming his wife. I began to sob. I didn't expect a marriage proposal while I was sick on the couch! Then I realized *if he can love me like this, he is the one*!

We moved into my mother's house so we could begin saving for the wedding and an apartment. Let me tell you, if you ever want to know if your relationship will last, move in with your parents. It wasn't easy for any of us! We shared one bathroom and one television in the living room. My parents were smokers and we were not... it was hard! I am grateful to my parents for letting us stay because I know it wasn't easy on them either. Right before our wedding, we received good news. Chuck got a job working for *The Adolphus* in downtown Dallas.

Chuck was hired to work security on the night shift. At the time we were just excited for him to have a job. The night before our wedding, I stayed at a friend's house. I lay in bed and couldn't sleep, *Was this actually real? I am marrying a beautiful man who is crazy in love with me, makes me laugh constantly, makes delicious meals for me, rubs my feet, and just does everything for me? Wow! How lucky am I?* Chuck sent a text to me late that night to tell me he had killed a giant water bug and that he couldn't sleep either. I remember giggling. I sent a text back telling him that I loved him and couldn't wait to be his wife. He replied that he loved me too, and couldn't wait to be my husband and take care of me. I eventually fell asleep, feeling happy and refreshed the next morning.

October 8, 2005 was my wedding day. It was a beautiful day! It rained a little that morning, but I heard that rain was good luck on your wedding day, so it didn't bother me one bit. When I arrived at my cousin's home,

Chuck was already there making the food for our guests. I know the bride and groom aren't supposed to see one another, but he was cooking and I was putting up decorations... we couldn't help but see one another. It worked out fine. We set up our wedding cake and grooms cake, and then set out champagne as well as sparkling cider for the kids. Pumpkins, big and small, were set up on the tables and lawn.

Our decorations included gold and cream balloons. They were perfect for fall. My bouquet was made up of bright orange and rust colored flowers with white roses; it was all breathtaking to me! Chuck prepared some Italian meatballs and pasta, lasagna, chicken parmesan, different breads, his favorite cheeses, fresh fruit and much more. I was so proud of his ability to cook and the way he arranged the food on the serving tables. His presentation was so beautiful; people couldn't believe he catered it himself.

When the day was said and done, we were exhausted. We tried to stay and help clean up, but everyone was shooing us out of there. We got to the hotel late and were so tired we went right to sleep. We woke early the next morning and made up for it!

When we came back to my parents that weekend, we started looking for an apartment. We found one in Garland, TX and began moving right away. We were so happy! At last, we had our own little place, were married and both working. But things wouldn't stay rosy for long—that December proved to be hell. Chuck began having severe pain at work one night and they let him go home early. By the time he made it home, he was doubled over crying. It scared me to death! I begged him to go to the emergency room, but he said we couldn't afford it. I thought he was either crazy or maybe his pain wasn't as bad as he was letting on. I didn't know what to do or think. Eventually he went to sleep, but when he woke, the pain was worse than ever. It was the middle of the night; he couldn't sit still but said it hurt to move. He was gasping for air and I told him we were going to the hospital. This time he agreed.

The closest, and only, hospital I knew of at the time was a local community hospital. It's not known for giving good care. It had a bad reputation throughout the Dallas area. I was in a panic and needed help fast. Chuck was almost screaming in the car. He was not admitted quickly and once he was, I think we got the dumbest doctor on staff. She didn't listen to his symptoms. She didn't ask where the pain was coming from. She didn't ask when the pain had started. I kept thinking, "Is this a joke?" She eventually gave him some medicine which we found out later was for an ailment Chuck didn't have. The next morning I begged our way into our family doctor's office who told us he felt Chuck had a kidney stone. To be on the safe side, he wanted Chuck to get an x-ray.

Well God bless him for that because his x-ray showed a large mass on his kidney. We were devastated to hear the words *kidney cancer*. We were grateful to find we were in the hands of the best doctor in Dallas. We immediately made an appointment to have the kidney removed. When we left Baylor, we decided to get a shake and burger from Jack in the Box. We were in the drive-thru talking about how lucky we were, even with what had been thrown at us, when I got a phone call from my boss and another from a friend. The salon where I worked as a hairstylist was shutting down that month. When I got off the phone, I looked at Chuck and said, "Enjoy your food. We may not be eating for a while."

I couldn't believe it... we just moved into a new apartment and now my new husband had cancer and I was losing my job! I looked at Chuck and asked the most obvious question, "What the hell are we going to do?" He told me, "You are an amazing stylist and your clients love you! You'll find a job. We'll be okay." He was great! He was the one who was sick, and he was telling me that everything was going to be okay. God love him.

His co-workers understood when they learned that Chuck was sick. The Human Relations department, on the other hand, gave us a lot of grief. *How many days will you miss? We can't pay you for this. You need to make sure you do this and this and this...!* I came home one day to find him on the phone with one of those idiots. He was so angry; his Jersey accent was coming through along with all the hand gestures. I'd only seen him that mad a couple of times; this was not good.

The week of his surgery, I got another job. What a God-send it was! I didn't know at the time how much this salon and the women in it would mean to me in the coming days. Diana, the owner of Chambre Salon, had me come in for an interview. I thought, *Oh crap, she is going to think I'm unstable! Just wait until I tell her, "By the way I need off my first week because my husband has cancer."* I don't know why, but she gave me the job, gave me the week off, and sent us flowers at the hospital.

The day of the surgery I was very nervous. I thought *what If I never see him again? I don't want to be without him!* While Chuck was in the six hour surgery, I waited with my family at my side. When the doctor came out and told me everything had gone well, I felt relieved. I knew God had heard our prayers and had always been there. As soon as allowed, I went to Chuck's room to be with him. It felt like it had been days since I'd seen him. He told me, going in to the surgery, that he thought he would never see me again. He was so sure he was going home to Heaven. I was so happy to see him. We cried together and prayed.

Getting him well enough to go home was hard. Chuck couldn't do anything on his own, which made him grumpy. Eventually we did go home and began trying to recuperate. It was hard. We were drowning in medical bills. Chuck was pressured to go back to work before he was fully healed. Although we were stressed and didn't get to see each other as often as we liked, we still had each other. Chuck and I always had one another, "There is no one else I'd rather be under a bridge with than you, if we go broke," we would say.

Chuck's close brush with cancer made us want to start a family right away. We looked at baby clothes in stores and talked about names. A year later, I still wasn't pregnant and we were beginning to wonder why. We decided to give it another year. At the end of that year, we still weren't pregnant. We were so sad! We thought about going to a fertility doctor but Chuck said if it was his fault, he wouldn't be able to handle it, so he didn't want to know. We considered becoming foster or adoptive parents, but it was so expensive and we didn't like the idea of someone being able to take our child away. Besides, we were living in a small apartment, barely making ends-meat. We knew we wouldn't be approved as the powers-that-be would surely think us unable to provide for a child.

Chuck struggled for years in his job. He had come to hate his employment more than anything. One day he said, "I have to get out of this place; it is killing me little by little. I am having a hard time being grateful like I once was." He told me he was depressed and that was why he was playing his computer games so often. He wanted me to know he was trying to escape the reality of being an underpaid worker, living in a tiny apartment, being overweight and not able to have a baby. Chuck was one of the most positive people I knew and it was painful to hear him say those words.

Chuck was always the one telling me that God hadn't forgotten us, but this time he was the one that needed to know things would be okay. I told him I knew his dream job would come and that if we didn't have a kid, it was alright. In July of 2008, things were hopeful. A close friend mentioned that there was an opening for a job where she worked. We both said, "We have to get Chuck this job, he'd be great for it!" Chuck was able to secure an initial interview with DART (Dallas Area Rapid Transit). He was called back for additional interviews and they all went well. We were on cloud nine. The last thing he had to do before he got the job was to pass the drug test. Chuck quit his job that day. We knew if that was the only thing standing in his way, then that job was his! It took them a day or two to call us and let us know that they were 100% certain. Chuck finally had his dream job!

We celebrated for a week! We bought Dallas Stars tickets, went to eat at our favorite restaurants, went to the movies, on and on. It was so nice to do the things we couldn't afford for so long. When we officially got the call that the job was his, we knew life would be better than ever. He couldn't believe that overnight he went from almost 20,000 a year to 50,000. To me that was rich, to him it meant a little home for us to grow old in.

More than the money, he was happy to finally have a career. He loved his job, his bosses and his co-workers were amazing. I can honestly say that every day he came home happy. About a week before our third anniversary, I found out we were pregnant! I called Chuck at work and told him. He was silent for a second or two and said, "Are you sure?" I told him I had two more unused pregnancy tests; he encouraged me to take them! He said he hoped I really was pregnant and to call him right back. All of my tests turned positive right away. I told my mom and we both cried. I called Chuck back and said, "You're going to be a daddy!" I had dreamed of saying those words to him one day, but I didn't know it would feel so good. He told me he was the happiest man alive and I heard him tell his co-workers. I could hear words of congratulation and cheers in the background. Not long after, we moved in with my brother to save as much money as possible. Everyone was so happy for us; everywhere we turned, people were giving us the most wonderful baby gifts.

It was like living in a fairytale! I didn't have any morning sickness at all. My two best friends were pregnant as well; we couldn't have planned it better if we had tried. It seemed like there was nothing in this world we couldn't do or have as long as we had God and each other. The months went by quickly. Doctor appointments, baby showers—my tummy kept growing. Back when we were dating, Chuck decided that if we had a daughter one day, he wanted to name her Annika Marie in honor of his grandmother Anna, and his mother Mary. Every night Chuck rubbed my belly; he even talked and sang to her. I knew he would be an amazing father. Chuck couldn't believe he could love someone he didn't know so much. We became closer than ever during my pregnancy. He was always serving me or keeping me from doing things. I was glad he was protective, but geez! The first time he saw and felt her move was in the parking lot at Chambre. He was excited to feel her follow his hand. He kept staring at my belly in amazement. I knew he was going to be Annika's fool.

She was going to get whatever she wanted from her daddy. We began looking at homes in Rowlett, but were continually outbid by investors. I kept thinking, *Finding a home shouldn't be this hard!* I know now that it was a blessing in disguise. We found ourselves back in Garland in a nicer apartment than before, with more room. We started furniture shopping because Lord knows we had none. This time we were able to buy nice things for our place. We wanted a comfortable little place for our family until we found a home.

I was in my last month of pregnancy and it started not being fun anymore. I was hurting and couldn't sleep in any position. I had terrible acid reflux and was ready to get this baby out. I remember crying because I barely fit in the tub and I couldn't shave or shampoo my hair. Chuck helped me shave, washed my hair and rubbed my feet. Monday, May 18, 2009, I woke when Chuck did so I could spend time with him while he got ready for work. I did this every morning! He felt fine when he left for work. I had no idea he was never coming home. I got a call from him not long after he left saying he was hurting very badly. I asked him if he was coming home early. He said he didn't know. I went back to sleep thinking maybe he had eaten something bad. Later I got a call from his friend letting me know he was at Baylor Hospital.

I said, "Oh my God, is everything okay?" He told me they didn't know anything yet. I asked him if Chuck wanted me to come and he said "no." I should have gone, but I went back to sleep. After the second call, I decided that I would go to the hospital no matter what. When I got there, I felt terrible that I hadn't come sooner. I felt like a horrible wife, but I was so exhausted.

Chuck didn't look good. His face was so sad; it makes me wonder if he knew. I thanked his friend for his help. The poor guy could have left, but he didn't—he had been with Chuck all day. I sat down, started folding his clothes and noticed he wasn't exactly wearing his best undies. I kind of laughed and asked, "These were the best you could wear today?" Normally he would have smiled, but he just barely turned his head to me. I thought, *Man this is really bad!* At the end of the day, the doctors still weren't sure what was wrong, but they thought he had pancreatitis. No one could believe that he did not smoke or drink alcohol. That night he was given a room. He wasn't allowed to have anything but ice.

It was the last night I would ever hear his sweet voice. I wish now that I had talked to him more, but he couldn't talk since he was in so much pain. The next morning we were told the doctor was ordering exploratory surgery to see what was going on inside of Chuck. I told him that I was going to run home and feed the cats.

When I returned to the hospital, he had been taken to the ICU. When I saw him, I was in shock. Chuck was hooked up to a respirator and under anesthesia. He had a tube that was removing bile build up. I couldn't believe that Chuck had gotten so bad, so quickly. The doctors told me he was very ill. He had many doctors and nurses all working hard to save him. They said it didn't look good because his lungs had shrunk to the size of baby lungs and he couldn't breathe for himself. His bile was backing up quicker than they could remove it, and his organs were beginning to fail.

Each day that passed, I was closer to losing him… and closer to having Annika. Here I was in my *last week* of pregnancy, dealing with my husband rapidly slipping away from me. I prayed night and day, day and night. I stood by his bed with one picture of us at our wedding and one picture of Annika's sonogram. I talked to him, I sang to him, I prayed over him, I begged him, "Please don't leave me. We need you! Annika needs her daddy! Please wake up Chuck."

Friends and family came every day and sat with me. They prayed over him at the hospital, at home, at church. My Chuck was on so many prayer lists across Texas, I was sure he was going to come home.

One night my friends came to the hospital to see me and Chuck; and I was given a very precious gift. Visiting hours would soon be over and they were saying goodnight to us. Tracy put her hand on Chuck's and said, "You need to wake up—you have lots of diapers to change!" She mentioned that Annika and I were there with him. As soon as he heard Annika's name, his eyes fluttered and opened. He began looking around. I guess he thought Annika had been born and that she was actually in the room. Once he saw me, he managed to tell me that he loved me. With all of the tubes in his mouth and nose, I can imagine it wasn't easy for him to say those words. His eyes closed and never opened again.

I was so happy that one last time we could say "I love you." I was hoping that it wasn't the last. I looked at Tracy and her face was white. He frightened at least ten years off her life. It wasn't scary to me; I was grateful to her... but she needed a drink and a smoke badly!

The night before Chuck passed, the doctors told me to say my goodbyes to him because he would not make it through the night. I refused! I told him, "Get your ass out of this bed! I won't say goodbye to you, I love you too much." I sang, *You are so Beautiful, If You Leave Me Now,* and a couple of Christian songs. I told him that they were making me leave until 9:00 a.m., but that I would be back.

I had two spiritual friends with me that night. We went to the chapel where I prayed and sang. I prayed that God would heal Chuck in a supernatural way that the doctors couldn't explain. I prayed for Annika's health because I was under so much stress and not sleeping well. I thought God could use Chuck as a testimony to show His power. I prayed that God would show how mighty and loving He is by healing Chuck.

The next morning he was still with us and I thought, "Hooray, he didn't leave me last night. There is still a chance!" I was asked to leave at 6:00 a.m. and told I could return at 9:00 a.m. I left to feed my starving cats and promptly headed back to Baylor. As I was parking at the hospital, the phone rang. It was Chuck's doctor. He asked if I was driving. I told him that I was and then I asked if Chuck was gone. He said, "Just let us know when you're in the building." I told him I was pulling into the parking garage. I asked him again "Is my Chuck gone... Is my Chuck gone??!!"

"Yes, Mrs. Dvorsky he is gone."

I hung up and screamed in my car. Then I ran into the hospital. When I turned to the hall where Chuck was, I saw people outside his room. The walk down that hall was the longest of my life. The closer I got, the harder I cried. It was Tuesday, May 26, 2009. Chuck's poor body was exhausted and couldn't fight anymore. I sat in the nurse's chair while everyone held me and allowed me to scream and cry. I looked in the doctor's eyes and painfully asked him, "Why? My poor baby... her daddy's dead."

"Why did He take my husband, Annika's daddy?" "Why Lord?" I continued crying and questioning until they let me see him. Then, just for one moment, I stopped crying. I was in complete and utter shock. There, before me, lay the body of a man I wanted to grow old with, raise Annika with, and just be together forever. I kept touching his body. It was so swollen, it didn't look like him. His poor little fingers were purple from all the poking. His skin was discolored from the backup of bile.

Family and friends began to come to the hospital. Together we cried and cried and cried. It had been a long horrible week for us all. I kept rubbing my belly, telling Annika I was so sorry. When they took him from the room, it hit me. *He really is gone.* One day later, Thursday, May 28, 2009, my precious Annika Marie was born. I cried so much, I didn't know which were happy-tears and which were sad. Much of her birth, Chuck's service and the funeral, is a blur to me. I don't know if it's a good thing or a bad thing. I just remember bits and pieces. Like during Annika's birth, while I was pushing, I wondered if Chuck was with us.

At the viewing, I was so glad that Chuck looked better than he did in the hospital. He looked more like my sweet Chuck. Any minute I expected him to do his impression of my laugh, which would make me laugh all the more. I thought of how all his music, flowers and pictures were perfect.

It's been seven months since I lost my beautiful husband. I miss him every day. I don't know how I made it seven months, but somehow I am here. I am slowly trying to get my life in order. I am learning how to pay bills, take care of Annika, budget money, and rebuild my hair clientele. I am still trying to learn to cook and just live everyday life. I became a widow, a new mom, and single parent within a day of one another.

Every day is hard; I won't lie. But, there is hope too. Every day I see Annika's little smiling face I want to live. Every time I want to kiss Chuck, I kiss her little sweet face. When I look at Annika, I see Chuck—his smile, his eyes. It's amazing to see him every day in her. I love being her mommy, just like I loved being Chuck's wife. Both are an honor. She is such a good little girl and an enormous gift from God.

I still don't know why I was meant to go through this, but I know I can make it. At one time I didn't think I could. I am far from having a healed heart, but every day it is mending. I just remind myself of the saying, "Every day that passes is another day closer to seeing you again." My heart may be broken, but it is bursting with hope and love for my baby girl. I'm grateful for the seven years I had with Chuck, for our child, for my friends and family who stayed with me and helped me during the most difficult days. I'm thankful for the doctors and nurses who fought for him. We are really blessed! So many people gave me their deepest kindness and generosity.

I know my future is bright. Someday I will own a home, make new friends on my journey, and meet someone with whom I will have a strong connection and love. With all my heart, I know Chuck would not want

Annika and me to be alone forever. A lot of healing has come from my faith, friends, and family. They have all played a part in dealing with my loss and enjoying my gain. Seven months ago I couldn't imagine that I would be writing about my journey. I went from absolute devastation to knowing that I am on a path to happiness.

Angela and Chuck

I have started pulling my life together by working on improving myself. I have begun going to the gym; I'm learning to cook; I'm wearing make-up again and dressing up more. I also began going to church and spending more time with my family. I want to honor Chuck's life and the things he believed in and stood for. Living my life to the fullest, giving God praise every day, and raising Annika to be an amazing woman, is what he would have wanted.

Going through this whole ordeal has been a reminder to me that we are not promised tomorrow. There are no guarantees in life, so make every day count. I am so thankful to be a part of this book. To share my story with so many people in the hopes that someone will read this and be touched by it. If I am able to help one person come through their own difficult situation, it will all be worth it. Thank you to many people who helped me in any way!

Behind the Story

I met Angela when she participated in the bereavement program I was creating. Because her group was part of a pilot study, I was able to personally observe the meetings. One day Angela brought a photo of her daughter, Annika, who was born one day after Chuck died. It was a darling baby picture. The group asked how old Annika was when the picture was taken and Angela said, "Four months." Then she was asked how long ago the photo was taken and Angela replied, "Oh, it was taken recently." I am sure my mouth dropped open. She was attending this program only four months after the death of her husband! Naturally she was in great pain, but the level of peace and acceptance she demonstrated, being so recently widowed, was absolutely amazing!

The last night of the group meetings, I mentioned to the participants that there may be an opportunity to have the local news come and do a story about their *Author's Celebration* (the party where group members bring the storybooks they each publish as a crowning achievement of the process. The book contains their life-wisdom and Triumph Story. The party helps them share the book with families, friends and fellow participants and celebrates their accomplishment). Angela immediately and enthusiastically said she would love to participate as she wanted to help others any way she possibly could. The truth is, after hearing her amazing story during the course of the program, I thought it would be perfect for *The Triumph Book.* I hadn't said anything to Angela about it yet, though, because her loss was so recent. I wasn't sure if she would be ready for such a public platform for sharing her story.

Before we left that night, I spoke with Angela privately and asked if she would like to participate as an author in *The Triumph Book.* Her response was immediate, joyful and certain. She wanted to share her story, their love story, and what she has learned, and is still learning, about grief and triumph.

Because I asked Angela to participate near the end of my story-gathering, I needed to speak with her more, right away, about the purpose of the book and give some instructions. Angela is a hair stylist and so, to have time to talk more with her, I scheduled a haircut the very next week.

The salon where Angela works is built to resemble a darling Victorian home which serves as a comfortable gathering place for the clients and stylists. As I sat in the chair, not only was there an opportunity to hear more of Angela's story, but I heard from the other hair stylists who were there with Angela through it all. She has a wonderful family of "sisters" surrounding her who have helped her through the tragedy. One of the ladies was Tracy, the woman mentioned in the story that brought Chuck out of his coma to briefly say good-bye to Angela, simply by talking about Annika in his presence. It was funny to hear them talk about how this scared her silly... they were still laughing about it! I could clearly see that this network of loving, surrogate family has been an important part of Angela's strength and healing. It is wonderful to witness how service to, and from, others can make such a big difference.

Nineteen

From Hiccups to Hospice

Author: Betty Garrett

Nothing chills the soul quite like the word *cancer*! My husband, Gene, was the personification of health. No one in Gene's family had ever been diagnosed with cancer. So when we learned in April 2003 that he had esophageal cancer, we were stunned.

My emotions ran the gamut... denial, fear, sadness, terror. What caused Gene's cancer? Where do we go from here? When will treatment begin? Denial gripped me by the throat and threatened to choke the life out of me. Gene was my soul mate, my Rock of Gibraltar. How could this be happening?

I kissed a lot of toads before finding the man of my dreams. We were so close we finished one another's sentences. We cried singing the national anthem. We thanked God for sending us one another. Gene validated me, strengthened my self-confidence and gave me assurance that I was wanted and loved. There was a magnetism about him that intrigued me. I had never met anyone quite like him before.

When we began seeing one another, people cautioned me about pursuing a relationship with Gene. He was eighteen years my senior. I listened to what they had to say, but in the end I listened to my heart. I loved this man. He thought and acted like a man who enjoyed life and living. When he proposed, I had no problem saying, "Yes!"

Ours was a marriage made in Heaven. Fifteen years of wedded bliss and now this! I couldn't help but question, "God why have you allowed cancer to enter our lives?" Gene refused to wallow in self-pity, instead he held me close and said, "Betty, we are going to play out the hand that's been dealt us." Together as team-mates and soul-mates, we were going to fight this enemy tooth and nail with determination, side by side. I chose not to get caught up in the *what if's*. With all of my heart I believed that this was nothing more than a detour. We were going to beat Gene's cancer. This was only a hiccup in the middle of the road.

Gene had a "wow" personality that won people over. When he smiled, it drew people to him like a bee to honey. He was incredibly kind, never uttering a harsh word about anyone. He was tender, but he was tough. Step over a boundary, though, and the white ring around his mouth appeared, warning, "This far, no further."

Not long after we met, Gene had a quadruple by-pass. Walking so close to death made him realize just how much he wanted to live. He changed his eating habits and began to exercise regularly. After a while, the routine of walking and running became boring. He needed to change up his workout routine so he asked if he could join me in the Jazzercise class I was taking. Jazzercise is an exercise program that incorporates cardio, strength and stretch moves in a 60-minute fitness class giving the body a total workout. It was perfect for him!

At the first class, Gene was the only guy in the room, and the girls were immediately drawn to him. He took his place on the back row, while I moved toward the front where I could work my butt off undisturbed. Once, I glanced over my shoulder and saw a sly grin on his face... he had not even broken a sweat! To make matters worse, he was checking out all the cute girls from the rear. We finished our session and when he asked to join the class permanently I said, "Sure, on one condition. Your skinny little butt is going to be on the front row where you won't be just watching all the girls. That's not going to happen... not on my shift!"

Jazzercise was looking for testimonials from people who had been helped through the exercise program. A neighbor came over the day before the testimonials were due and asked Gene if he could tape him talking about the benefits of the class. The recording was submitted and Gene was selected! We weren't really surprised; since not many seventy-eight year old men were excited about the benefits of Jazzercise!

We were both invited to the company headquarters in California. When they saw the chemistry between us, they asked me to join Gene in an infomercial as well. We had so much fun! It was a privilege to meet the developer of the program and be interviewed on camera as well as filmed doing a class with sixty-eight other Jazzercisers. This was a win-win for Gene. He enjoyed exercising, and he loved being the only guy in the group. My friendly, joyful husband had a healthy appreciation for the opposite sex.

Gene told me every day how much he loved me. He constantly surprised me by subtle, sweet expressions such as leaving a card under my pillow. I never questioned the depth of his love. Not even when his ex-wife was in the final stages of melanoma and she asked to see him. Being the thoughtful man that he was, he felt immediate concern about how I would feel over such a visit. He needn't have worried. I encouraged him to go, "She's the mother of your children. You spent many years with her." I reminded him. I loved Gene even more when afterwards he said, "Betty, I need to talk to you. Was it alright to tell her that I love her?" We were one. I was not threatened by his expression of love. It was different than the love we shared. I said, "Of course! She was an important person in your life. I would be disappointed if you hadn't."

We married in 1989; Gene became sick in 2004. It wasn't long enough. We still had a lot of living to do! We always assumed, because of his history of heart problems, that when his time came, Gene would die from a heart attack. Such was not the case.

The beginning of the end started with a terrible case of the hiccups. Gene's voice became raspy, which we blamed on allergies. Initially, we also suspected his age may have caused his throat muscles to relax, causing him to hiccup. One night he had an unrelenting bout that was so bad he could not eat his favorite dish of black-eyed peas and cornbread. That is when I knew something was seriously wrong and he needed to see a doctor.

Gene's hiccups became more pronounced and frequent. We sought the help of a gastroenterologist who immediately scheduled him for an endoscopy. It was during this test that cancer was discovered. We were shocked! Never in our wildest dreams had we considered that hiccups could be a symptom of cancer! A second opinion confirmed the diagnosis. We took the first step that day on a journey we never wanted to take.

Though the prognosis was grim, neither of us believed Gene would die of the cancer. We went through treatment fully expecting success. Gene was in good health and did well with the chemo and radiation. Of course he was going to be all right!

Even though the tumor had shrunk, Gene's doctors felt surgery was necessary. I called our pastor and immediately requested that the prayer team at our church begin intercession on Gene's behalf. I told him, "Put Gene at the top of the list!"

Prayer does make a difference, and we experienced miracles! Ten days before surgery, Gene developed a blood clot that caused swelling in his legs. A filter was inserted and the doctors considered putting him on a blood thinner... not a good idea right before surgery. Two of his doctors were against it; one was for it. Gene had almost died once before from being given the drug, so before the order was written to give him the smallest dose of the thinner, one of the doctors said, "Let me look at his legs one more time." When they pulled back the blanket, there was absolutely no swelling—the clot had disappeared on its own. We all knew that we had witnessed a miracle!

When I returned to the hospital the next morning, after nine hours of surgery, Gene was semi-conscious. I was standing at the foot of the bed when Gene woke. Tubes protruded from his body and a breathing mask covered his mouth. It didn't matter to me, I was just happy to see him awake. He tried to speak but I couldn't understand what he was saying. I thought he might be in pain, or maybe needed his lips moistened. With every question I asked, he would shake his head, "No." Finally, the nurse attending him said, "Mr. Garrett, do you want to kiss your wife?" He nodded yes, and with this gesture, I felt sure that he was going to make it.

Gene was in the hospital two and a half weeks. His burly, rough-looking, teddy bear of a doctor came twice a day to walk up and down the hall with him. This doctor was a guardian angel! I needed to know everything that was happening. Gene's doctor patiently answered every question I asked. One day he said, "I've never done this before, but I want you to have this." He handed me a prayer card that I carry with me to this day.

Going home was oh-so-sweet. We were on the road to recovery, and best of all, Gene was cancer free! We had met the enemy and beaten him! We enjoyed six months of new-found freedom. Cancer no longer dogged our every step. It was a sweet reprieve.

But it wasn't long before Gene started having problems again. He wasn't gaining his weight back. New tests confirmed the cancer had returned, this time with a vengeance! It had spread to his liver, stomach and lungs. We both knew that we were in big trouble.

I knew I needed help. I needed information and I needed support! Support groups existed for cancer patients. I went to Baylor Hospital and suggested they develop a group specific to caregivers. I did not want Gene to be burdened with my challenges or pain; he had enough of his own. I desperately needed a safe place, within an understanding community who would support and care for me. I longed to be able to vent and cry and ask my questions without judgment. I had an insatiable hunger to learn all I could about how to care for someone with cancer. Everyone I asked countered with, "What do you want to know?" How was I supposed to know what I didn't know? I had never walked this journey before. All I knew was that if I was going to get us through this intact, I had to be at the top of my game! That meant I needed information and lots of it! I looked for it on the internet. Every brochure I came across that appeared to be helpful became mine. My ears perked up every time the topic was addressed, whether it was on a television show, the radio, or a couple talking loudly at a neighboring table. I drank it in. I felt so helpless. "Gene," I said one day when I was particularly exasperated, "This is criminal. There is a lot of information for the cancer patient, but almost none for the caregiver!" I had learned so much in caring for him and I felt a pull, a compulsion, to create something that would be helpful to others in my situation.

I made careful notes as I discovered what was helpful and what was not. I wrote systematic directions on how to take a blood pressure or flush out a feeding tube. When the hospital put in a portage pump to administer Gene's chemo, they gave us a yellow cover. I did not know if it was for Gene or for me! Turns out it was for neither of us—it was part of a *Chemobloc: Home Health Spill Kit*. It was not a poncho for me to wear! ☺

I learned not to let a doctor leave without understanding exactly what was said. If I did not understand, I would question and restate what I thought I had heard as many times as necessary until I did understand. I needed to take care of Gene and I intended to do it right! I had a hard time finding a balance between the demands of my schedule and the need of my heart to be with my husband. Twelve percent of my time was spent at the doctor, 33% was spent in the emergency room having tests and scans, and 20% was spent being with Gene while he went through chemo and radiation. The remaining 35% was divvied up between cooking, running errands, managing a business so we could pay the bills, and trying to sleep when I could. There just were not enough hours in the day to do all that needed to be done.

Gene was patient and supportive as I researched and gathered information for the book I knew I would one day write for caregivers. If I could light the way for others, it would be worth my own walk in the dark. Gene made me promise that I would finish the book, regardless of what happened to him.

I knew instinctively that this time Gene was not going to make it. I was tired, so very, very tired. My body, my mind, my soul, ached with fatigue. I loved Gene. I would do anything for him, but I no longer had the stamina to care for Gene by myself. It was incredibly frustrating. Time was limited and when it was exhausted, I was going to lose my soul mate.

The chemo did not help this time and it was suggested that we begin hospice care. When hospice is called in, there is generally six months or less left of life. I felt as if someone had stabbed me with a knife because I knew that hospice marks the final stages of life's journey. Initially the doctor thought Gene would not make it through the weekend—he made it two and a half months.

In the early days of hospice, I had a difficult time remembering when they were coming and when they were not. Sometimes I was alone in caring for Gene. We did the best we could. I gave him a bell to ring when he needed me and I was on the opposite end of the house. He encouraged me to maintain as much of my routine as possible.

At night I would go into the office and use my computer to write down stories and the "how-to's" I had learned that day. I kept a journal where I processed my thoughts and feelings. While some experience anger towards God, I did not. I felt acceptance. Often I remembered what Gene had said when we first started walking the cancer road—"We're going to play out the hand that we've been dealt."

Gene died in November 2004. Even a year after Gene's death, I continued attending the support group at Baylor. In 2008, I spoke at a gathering of case managers for hospitals. That event forced me to finish the book I had begun before Gene's death. It is designed to be simple to read, understand and access. It is titled, *From Hiccups to Hospice: a Survival Guide for the Cancer Caregiver*. In 18 months, we literally went from hiccups to hospice.

After publishing the book and making it available to the case managers, I developed a website. I wanted it to be a user-friendly resource for those dealing with cancer care-giving, a site where the information they needed was all in one place. Who has the time and energy to search through a myriad of sites, and read a dozen or more books when you have a loved one to take care of?

The book was published, the website up and running, but there was one more thing I wanted to do. I felt compelled to create an organizer with a calendar for caregivers. There they would be able to keep track of appointments and medications. I called it *Caregivers Companion* and it provides a place to keep important papers, constantly requested medical information, and phone numbers. A wonderful addition is a list of practical suggestions for people who want to help, but don't know what to do. Organization of these things frees up cherished minutes for the caregiver to focus on their loved one.

Taking care of a loved one who is ill is exhausting and overwhelming. It's easy for the caregiver to neglect his or her own health and well-being. The *Caregivers Companion* provides a space for the caregiver to journal and track emotions.

Gene and Betty

I walked through my grief to the other side where I was able to assimilate the experience into my life. Gene will always be part of my life story. I have a sense that I am on a mission from God. There is purpose in all I have experienced. I have developed workshops on setting up support groups for care-givers, and I have also developed a curriculum for oncology nurses and medical teams to help them work with the caregiver and patient as a family unit. Writing and creating support groups and curriculum is a kind of therapy for me. My joy comes from helping others.

Do I have a medical background? No. I do have a Master's Degree in the School of Hard Knocks and I own the love and information which I freely share with others. Because of the knowledge and skills I've obtained, I am better able to guide others on their journey through cancer. The skills I developed while caring for Gene were also useful when I needed to care for my father and mother in their illness and subsequent passing.

I've since had my own bout with cancer. When I was diagnosed with breast cancer I could hear Gene whisper in my ear, "Betty, you're going to play out the hand that's been dealt!" So I've come full circle. My *hand* is to continue living and helping those who are facing and caring for illness of any kind. It's a great hand to hold because this service truly brings me joy and a purpose I would not want to live without, and will never have to! I may lose loved ones along the way, but I will always have this *love* in my life!

Behind the Story

I met Betty when Keith Colley (author of **The Faces of Grief**) asked us both to speak at a bereavement event held for organizations across Dallas addressing pre- and post- bereavement. Betty was the pre-bereavement speaker and shared her story, message and books. Then I spoke about overcoming grief and finding purpose. We couldn't have been a more perfectly matched set of presenters and we had a sense of divine serendipity in our meeting.

Luckily, I found Betty's story at the eleventh hour, just before publishing. I had hoped to finish the manuscript for **The Triumph Book** many months before, but there were multiple challenges which arose right up until we met. Once I met Betty, she brought the number of chapters to twenty (I am much happier with a round number) and her story was added just weeks before the manuscript completion and publishing efforts began. Once I met her, everything finally lined up.

Sometimes we set a time-table in our minds for the things we want to accomplish and all too often it feels that life is working against us as we fail to meet those self-imposed deadlines. However, in almost every case, if we look back across the wait, we can see there was purpose in it. I love that about life. I am able to recognize this element of achievement more and more as I work passionately towards goals and dreams. It is always hard to be patient, but I have learned that if things don't go as well or smoothly as I hoped, there is usually a very good reason; one I will be grateful for!

I am thankful for Betty's tireless effort to help the army of caregivers in our world. I say army because cancer is extremely common; for every cancer patient there is at least one (and often many more) weary and under-supported loved one. Betty is working to make that experience much easier! To learn more about Betty's books and caregiver support resources, visit her website at *www.Caregivers4cancer.com*.

Twenty

Christi Rae Hart the First

Author: Toni Hart

Christi Rae Hart the first. That is what I called her when she was in trouble. Otherwise she was known as Tootsie or Toots. When she was small, she would do a somersault and then excitedly tell me she had been a "Tootsie Roll."

I don't know how to write this. I've often told my friends that I only write checks, and now that we have debit cards, it is even easier. How do I begin writing my thoughts about the life and death of my child and dearest friend? Christi's life was full of adversity and triumph as she fought, and beat, cancer three times as a young woman. She wrote her story for her children and others a few years before she passed away unexpectedly; and so I will allow her to tell it for me:

How Cheerleading Saved my Life?!?

When I was 14 years old, I was much like any other girl. I went to school, struggled to know who I was, did homework and chores (whether I wanted to or not) and talked for hours on the phone with my friends. I had been going to private school and was getting ready to start high school the following fall. I wanted to try out for sophomore cheerleading, and while I had years of dance lessons, my tumbling skills were terrible. At our school, you pretty much had to be able to do a back handspring to make the squad, because they frequently went to National competitions. I really hated back handsprings, but my desire to be a cheerleader won out—so I practiced them—a lot. My older brother, Gerry, was a gymnast and we went down to the school each morning at 6:00 a.m. to practice. He would stand at my side and spot me with his arm behind my back. Well, the cheerleading clinics began and I was pretty excited, but I started having a lot of pain in my back. My mom took me to a chiropractor, but he couldn't help. By the next day, every time I took a breath the pain shot through my chest. The chiropractor knew this was not a back problem and I was taken to the Emergency Room. I remember blacking out during x-rays.

We discovered that I had a tumor on my rib, right in the place Gerry's fist had been when he spotted me! That friction made my lung fill up with blood—causing all of the pain. That night they tapped my lung and drained over five pounds of blood from it. I have always been amazed and grateful the back handsprings, which were so hard for me, turned out to be such a blessing. If not for the dreaded practicing (and Gerry's right fist) the tumor would have gone undetected for much longer.

Obviously, I missed the cheerleading tryouts! Instead, I was taken by ambulance to LDS Hospital for surgery. My surgeon was a funny guy. He did a lot to make me feel special (even smuggled me a set of hospital greens—a big no-no!)

My friends had given me a t-shirt that looked like human anatomy, with the bones and muscles of the chest depicted. Before surgery, we laid it over me with an arrow in the right spot saying "cut here." The surgery went well and when they wheeled me back, they had placed a great big bandage over the spot that said "OUCH!"

During the surgery, three ribs and the lower lobe of my right lung were removed. Sometimes ignorance is bliss. When the doctors told me that the tumor was "malignant"—I was thinking "stagnant" or dirty—so I took the news better than my parents! It didn't take long, though, to know that "malignant" means cancer.

Many friends and family supported me. They had moved my bed into my parent's room and there was a long "get well soon" banner, and lots of cards and letters. About 18 months of chemotherapy followed. I would go to the hospital two days every three weeks. The medicine the first day didn't make me very sick, but the medicine the next day was almost unbearable. Sometimes I would be throwing up before we even got home, and it would be five to seven days before I could keep anything down. The second week, I would feel all right and eat normally, and the third I would eat a lot in anticipation of the next chemo. At the time, they said to give me anything I wanted to eat, and I really liked yogurt and Chef Boyardee Raviolis. I can eat raviolis again now, but still have a hard time eating yogurt!

I remember how Gerry's friend, Ron, came with us to the hospital and about turned green at the sight of the needles. I kind of liked being tough when he couldn't even watch what they did to me. The sight of Primary Children's Hospital would make me ill and many times I just wanted to run far away on chemo days. As you receive more chemotherapy, your veins get smaller and harder because of scar tissue. Sometimes they would have to "stick" me eight-nine times in a visit. I never let the same person try more than twice. My medical experiences certainly taught me to be assertive!

Hair

Being 14-15 is rough. Doing it bald presented additional challenges. Losing my hair was horrible. I really cried about it. I had this one lock that lasted longer than the rest and I tried to make it stay. Of course, it didn't. I had taken this modeling/poise class before this all happened and I had just done a big hair show for *Sebastian* a couple of weeks prior to my surgery. We did have a good laugh when they called me back the next year to do another hair show, we told them I would love to, but that I didn't currently have any! I used to say that it was great because I could put my hair in rollers—then get in the shower!!! It was a trial though, and I always had a knit cap on when I took off my wig—I never looked at myself in the mirror bald, not even once.

A friend of mine's mother was a nurse. She came to the hospital at first, I'm sure to try to cheer me, but kept talking about how "funny" it would be to lose eyelashes and eyebrows. She was trying to make it seem all right—but before that, I didn't have any idea that I would lose that hair too. Going to the wig shop was an experience as well. My head is smaller than most and I had to crisscross the elastic straps underneath to make the wig fit snuggly. But, in the end, I looked all right.

Wig Mishaps

Most importantly, my spirits were good. I was truly blessed with perspective and hope. It never occurred to me that I wouldn't get better, just that this was a trial for me to learn what I needed in this life. Believe it or not, I tried out for JV cheerleader the next year (even though I wore a wig and was still having chemotherapy) and made it!

Well, wearing a wig sometimes caused "technical difficulties." At one cheerleading practice, someone was climbing on my shoulders and stood on my hair and it slid to the side, then stepped on the other side and it slid that way! Oh my.

That wasn't too bad, but another time I was at a church dance. Being 14, it was pretty cool to finally be old enough to attend the dances. My friends and I had gone on the stage to talk to the DJ. One friend jumped off, then I did, then another friend jumped down. The problem was that the hand of the friend behind caught my wig and it came off—completely!!! Well, my friends all jumped to cover me and get it back in place—but needless to say, I no longer felt "cool." I was rather devastated and cried a lot. We all left the dance and went to one friend's home and talked. They really helped me feel better—especially when one told a story of trying to catch a cute lifeguard's eye at the water park. She had gone down the water slide and at the bottom, lost her two front false teeth, and had to ask him to help her find them!!! We laughed pretty hard about both experiences.

Nothing compared though to what happened at Gerry's graduation pool party. I was with my friends and we felt pretty "awesome" getting to be at the "Senior's" party when we were only Sophomores. I was strutting a bit and went to take off my swimsuit cover-up by crisscrossing my arms at my waist to reveal wonderful me—except, off came my wig with the cover-up! Definitely not good. My friends rallied again and quickly covered me, but I was mortified. I was again able to leave with my friends. Good friends have a way of making it all seem better.

When my wig got worn looking and needed to be replaced, it was fun to get the comments about how great my hair looked or being asked if I got some kind of hot oil treatment. They probably thought I was hiding beauty secrets, when I smiled and said I hadn't. I guess overall, the wigs didn't look too bad. I even had another modeling agency call after seeing my photo in the yearbook, but modeling was definitely not for me!

Gone Today, Hair Tomorrow!

I started growing hair back after about a year of chemo, but there was no guarantee that it would stay until treatments were over. During this time, my family went to Disneyland. I had very short hair and decided to go without my wig. That was interesting. I felt so exposed—like I was walking around in my undies! It was a good way to beat the heat though—wigs could be so hot and itchy! A few months later, about the time I turned 16, I did finish chemotherapy. My hair had grown in darker and curlier than before. I was a nervous wreck the first time I went to school without my wig. When friends would say, "You cut and colored your hair!" inside, I was thinking, "Well, actually, no," But I would just smile. We had a great time thinking of lines to say, like, "No, I haven't had my hair cut in a couple of years" or "Thomas O'Brien (my oncologist) does my hair." After all, if you can't laugh at yourself, then you're sunk!

Again

I had regular checkups and all appeared well for a couple years. I graduated and attended my first year of college at BYU. My family moved to Minnesota, and I took a semester off school so I could travel to Ecuador with my parents when Gerry completed his time there as a missionary. What an amazing trip!

Many miracles happened over this period of time. My dad had been commuting to Minnesota for work with Northwest Airlines, but it took a bit of convincing (like the neighbor boy setting five fires in our backyard) to relocate the family. My dad was working as a consultant and no one in my family had health insurance—except me. I had gotten a job at Laura Ashley as the office manager and they had great insurance for employees, starting very soon after being hired (quite unusual for a retail shop.) We made arrangements for my checkup and tests right after I became eligible. In the time right before my appointment, I was starting to get worried something was wrong. When I walked up stairs, my heart raced and I would get dizzy. I even blacked out at work. My doctor called me at work after my scans to tell me that my cancer had returned. They thought the tumor was about the size of an orange.

I was much more afraid this time, probably because I knew exactly all the hardships that would follow. However, I still had faith that this was just another trial for me, that the Lord was in charge, and that I would be fine.

When they did the surgery, it turned out to be much more serious than they had expected. The tumor was very large—about the size of a honeydew melon or a small watermelon—and it was pressing on my heart. The surgery was long. They had to use lasers to cut it off my heart, rebuild my heart sac with parts of my diaphragm and remove another lobe of my right lung along with more rib. It turned out that my surgeon was one of only a couple in the country that could have performed the surgery I needed.

Suddenly, our move to Minnesota, my time off of school, and my health insurance seemed part of a much larger plan. I was exactly where I needed to be. Another 18 months of chemotherapy followed. Each month I would spend one week in the hospital for treatments. Several times I got sick when my blood counts were low and had to go back for another week of IV antibiotics.

During this time, I still worked at Laura Ashley. They were so understanding and even brought me work to do at the hospital sometimes. I loved working there. I especially loved the Home Furnishings section and learned a lot about working with fabric and wallpaper.

Things were going all right, I had completed my six weeks of radiation—that was weird, kind of like getting a severe sunburn from the inside out—when they found a mass in my chest cavity and decided they needed to investigate. Unfortunately, the only way to do that was another thoracotomy. To make matters worse, the mass turned out to be extra sludge from the previous surgery that had collected because they had pulled my chest tubes too early. This additional surgery was very hard to recover from, both physically and emotionally; physically, because my body was worn down from the chemo, radiation, and the past surgery earlier that year; emotionally, because it was unnecessary and could easily have been prevented. Each of these surgeries took a minimum of six weeks to begin to recover.

I naturally have a low temperature, low heart rate, low blood pressure, etc. Well, this isn't any problem normally, but it did make my oxygen monitors unhappy! After surgery, when I would go into a deeper sleep, my oxygen level would drop and set off the monitor—it happened frequently. I got used to hearing the alarm, then waking and taking several deep breaths. Well, once when I hadn't been home long from the hospital, I fell asleep on the couch watching a movie. While asleep there, I heard an alarm, woke and started my deep breaths—only the alarm wouldn't stop. It turned out to be my brother's alarm clock in the next room!

Faith to Continue On...

Sometimes I would feel very low—being isolated from friends who were off at college doing what I wanted to be doing. I prayed much through this time, and it brought some amazing experiences. One night, I was feeling so lonely and sad, and I truly prayed that I could feel the Lord's love for me. After many tears, I could almost see myself in my mind. I was so tired, weak and overwhelmed that I couldn't bear any more and I felt myself collapsing. But just when I started to fall, I felt the arms of Christ catch me from behind, comforting me and holding me up to bear more than I could have on my own. It is such a sweet memory for me. It felt so tangible and real. I still am amazed at the experience.

Another time I again had been praying for help and comfort at night in my bed. My room was in the basement, separated from the main areas of the house. At the end of my prayer, both of my parents came down to check on me. I know this might not sound very amazing to most, but it is the only time they ever came to check on me, together, after I had already gone to bed. I believe they were prompted to come see me, because the Lord often answers our prayers through others; this time my parents brought me the love and concern He wanted me to feel.

I received a blessing from Elder Russell M. Nelson, a leader in my church. I was told that my life would not be one day shorter than it was meant to be. At the time, I was looking for a little more hope and promises of healing in the blessing, but later I realized how amazing it is to know that my life would be according to the Lord's will for me, and that even if my life was shortened, it would be enough. I am so grateful for the many spiritual blessings I received from my trials. Because I turned to the Lord in my need, I was truly blessed with strength and increased faith.

One of the benefits about having *Ewing's Sarcoma* is that it is considered a childhood cancer, so I was always on the children's wing of the hospital. Since I was usually the oldest patient around, I developed camaraderie with the nurses. They would hang out in my room to do their charting. I tried a few times to reach out to the younger patients by painting their fingernails or talking with them. Sadly, most were extremely sick.

There was a boy with leukemia who pretty much lived at the hospital. He recently had a bone marrow transplant that had not gone well. His family life was terrible and no one ever came to visit him. A few times he got a day pass and his mother was supposed to come take him on a date, but she never showed up. It was heartbreaking. I know a couple of the nurses would take him to see a movie or on another outing, and they would play video games with him too. I hope I never know what desperate situation would cause a mother to neglect her child when he was so ill. There were so many tragedies. Such as another teenager, who suffered through countless thoracotomies and still didn't make it, or sharing a room with little children who went home without hope.

Drugs definitely mess with your mind, even if they are prescribed for you! One time, while still on strong painkillers, I remember just crying because Gerry hadn't come to watch a movie with me when he said he would. My Mom assured me that he had come, we had watched the movie together, and he had even rested on my bed with me! Later, I had taken a shower and Mom said my hair looked greasy afterwards. She asked if I had washed it, I said I thought I had, and then she asked if I had washed out the shampoo—apparently not! Another time I was home from the hospital and realized, looking down, that I had only shaved one leg, not the other. Now I understand why they caution you not to operate heavy machinery while on some meds!

Oh the Things People Say!

There were two memorable moments with young missionaries from my church. The first was at the hospital following a surgery. One missionary had some slight disability and certainly lacked "people skills." He was quiet at first during the visit, then commented, "My Dad had cancer... he died... but it was all right, because he lived in California and we didn't see him much anyway." His companion was so embarrassed. The conversation resumed, then later he spoke up again and said, "I had a friend in high school who had cancer... he died too... but it was OK because I heard him give his testimony of faith before he died." At this point his companion was about dying and said they had to leave. After they left, Mom and I burst out laughing—even though it hurt my incision so much! It was just too funny!

Another missionary moment was at our house over dinner. At the time, the Irish singer Sinead O'Connor was popular, she was also bald. Well, during dinner we were discussing her when one of the newer missionaries said, "She'd be good looking if she weren't BALD!" Obviously he didn't know anything about me—especially since I had my wig on at the time. The whole family just about croaked and looked at me. I simply got up and went to the kitchen to get more food—and brought it back—without my wig on! We all burst out laughing and he kept apologizing. Poor guy!

My extended family was always so supportive. One year they all pitched in so I could go to a seminar by Dr. Bernie Segal in Chicago. The seminar and his books were helpful to me, including visualizations to help me heal. But I think the best part about it was feeling the love of my family and knowing they were there for me. At a family reunion they presented me with a framed poem they had written for me. I was so touched and grateful for them.

At the end of my chemo, I had a "small" procedure to remove my permanent IV line and harvest bone marrow. It was traumatic. In pre-op, when they were reviewing the procedure, they asked if I was there to have a line installed in my neck. Panicked, I said "NO, I was there to have my line removed!" Since my veins had grown so small and tough throughout my treatments and I knew it would be difficult to find a spot for the IV, I asked that they please put me under first with gas, and then put in the IV. At the end of all my treatments, I didn't think I could take even one more needle poke. I had horrible hallucinations from the gas, and then when I awoke, I felt something on my neck and feared they really had installed another line! I was assured it was just my IV. After trying eleven times to start an IV in my arms, they had installed one in my jugular vein. I naturally coughed coming out from the anesthesia and quickly felt my throat closing and couldn't breathe! It turned out that they had also "missed" the first time they tried to install the IV in my neck. When I coughed, it dislodged the clotted vein from the first attempt and it was swelling in my neck. We got the internal bleeding to stop, finally, so I could breathe, but I had a bruise that covered my neck and chest for about five weeks. Unfortunately this included the time I was a bridesmaid for a good friend—lovely! Oh, I was so glad to be done at last.

Finally, I was through with treatments and able to return to school. Hooray! Happy day!!! But at the same time, it was hard to think about studying something as trivial as French when I had just been given another chance at life. Shouldn't I be trying to save the world or doing some great deed? I finally conceded that studying French would open my eyes to understanding other cultures and was therefore worthwhile.

College Bound—A Joyful Return!

I returned to school with a vengeance. I took a heavy load of classes, worked as a custodian from four to eight am in the Tanner Building, and volunteered in student government as the Program Director for Handicapable Week (10-15 hours a week)—as well as acting as the campus liaison for the American Cancer Society.

It was crazy busy, but felt I had to make up for lost time. Every few months, I would travel home for scans via the *Corporate Angels*, a network of corporations that would transport cancer patients to medical care when they had extra spots in their private planes. I usually had to drive to Denver to catch a plane, but it made it possible for me to have scans where I had medical insurance!

Handicapable Week was a wonderful venture. It was a week of activities focused on disability awareness for the whole student body at Brigham Young University. I learned so much, and after months of planning, the time finally came.

We kicked off the week with a Handicapped Technology and Awareness Fair at University Mall. We had about 20 corporations come show their products and services for the disabled. We had advertised in newspapers and on radio and had a good turnout. We hosted a variety of participants, from a van with a wheelchair lift to a disabled children's performing group, from sport wheelchairs to the Arthritis Foundation. One company "New Outlook" would go around to homebound patients and teach them to paint. We were able to vote on favorite artwork, and I bought one painted by a woman who holds her paintbrush between two knuckles and guides it with her mouth! I was amazed at her talent.

The entire week we sponsored "DARE" booths around campus, daring students to experience a disability for a day. They were awarded a free t-shirt for participation. We also held an "Exploratorium" in the Wilkinson center, with a series of obstacle courses and challenges geared toward disability awareness. Monday we had Peter Jeppson share his experiences. He was badly burned in a car accident when he was 19 and had undergone 48 major surgeries since then to correct the damage. On Tuesday, we had Ray Smith speak on his experiences with polio and post-polio syndrome. It was the first time he had ever spoken of his experiences in public, and it came right from his heart.

Tuesday night the Utah State University's Theater for the Deaf performed with the Utah Valley Youth Sign Language Choir. The theater was packed with people sitting in the aisles!

My hair was growing in again too. I wrote this in my journal, "It's fun having my own hair again, not just for vanity's sake; it was a whole mindset. It was always a worry when anyone suggested a pillow fight or sledding or skiing or sports or most fun active activities. I always felt like a wet blanket. I had to hold my head just so, and it interfered with my dance classes. And now it is gone. I feel like I can be alive now—it is a sort of freedom not many appreciate."

The school year ended soon afterwards and I was preparing for my Internship in Switzerland. I was to work at a retail store in Neuchâtel and speak only French! I had an amazing time—but that is a tale for another storybook. Unfortunately, my cancer story continued when I returned.

I had felt so good, hiking in the mountains, working and traveling. I was home for just four days, had my scans and flew to my brother Gerry's wedding, planning to stay in Utah to attend school again. However, my scans revealed two new tumors, on my left lung this time. To say I was devastated is an understatement. When I reluctantly returned to Minnesota, I even had them repeat the scans before consenting to surgery, hoping that the prayers and blessings I received would have made the tumors disappear. They hadn't. The surgery was performed, but there was no more chemo to give me. I had already had it all, yet the cancer had returned.

A Journey towards Understanding

That fall was the darkest period of my life so far. I had been so sure I understood the Lord's will for me. Now I was in confusion and felt lost. I wrote, "I feel isolated—from my dreams, from my friends, from life. I've enjoyed this time with my family, but have been so self-focused that I haven't taken advantage of it. I only wish I could feel the Lord closer to me, or rather me closer to Him. Then I'd feel like I had more direction and not so in limbo."

"I've been trying hard and don't seem to be getting anywhere... I don't know why I can't get out of myself lately. Not even to you dear journal. These past months have been—that's just the problem, I can't figure out what they've been or what I'm feeling most of the time. I've felt different and without direction. I feel I'm not doing a very good job at life lately. I feel like I should be handling things better. Maybe I'm just disappointed. I felt I had worked out so many things in Europe. I felt I knew where I was going and why. I thought I knew who I was. Then the carpet was ripped out from under me and I suppose I'm still sitting on the floor feeling hurt and bruised." When I got sick again, I was so stubborn and closed with the Lord. I hadn't realized that at the same time I had closed a large part of myself.

In January I was able to return to school, and to slow down a bit. I no longer had so much to prove to myself or anyone else and I was more open to being taught by the Lord. In my journal I wrote, "I have been trying a lot harder to be closer to the Lord lately and I feel my mind and heart reopened and flooded with thoughts and feelings. I felt so empty before. I love the Lord and the gospel with all my heart and I'm so grateful for my Mom, Melanie and my family. I feel I can start progressing again. I'm so glad."

For some wonderful reason, even though the odds were overwhelming that the cancer would return, 14 years later, it never has. Maybe I finally learned what the Lord was trying to teach me with this trial, or maybe He just had other directions for my life. My years fighting cancer are largely the story of how I became who I am, and of how my faith developed. I still don't have it all figured out, but at least I learned this much: The Lord knows who I am. He wants me to become more like Him. He loves me and wants me to be happy. He has a plan for me and for each of us. If I trust in Him, I will become more than I could imagine on my own. I don't have to understand it all right now; I am led day by day. My experiences have helped me to empathize with others through their trials. I am so grateful for all I was taught through these years. My journey has brought a depth of understanding I have taken with me as my path continues on.
—*Christi*

More from Christi's Mother, Toni Hart:

Today is exactly one month until the first anniversary of Christi's death. I just bought my Christmas tree. We always buy our tree in time to have it decorated by December second. That is Christi's birthday and a family tradition since her birth.

For the last two weeks I have been in a terrible depression. I have felt as if my face belonged to one person, and my shattered heart belonged to another. Life appears normal for the face person, but the other one feels nothing.

I have been terrified of facing this final month of memories. The "this time last year we did this, or talked about this" days are ending and I have felt a panic that a flood of pain would engulf me, and I might not survive it. As a response, I've gone numb.

I have been praying to *feel* again. I've felt so detached from Christi. My eyes cry when I see her pictures or I am reminded of some memory, but it doesn't reach my heart. She is fading away.

As I have been pondering and pleading with the Lord to open the pathway to my soul again, I have come to realize that moments of hurt are worth any price in order to stay emotionally, and spiritually, connected with my daughter.

Miraculously, I just recently came across a note Christi wrote on my 60th birthday:

Dear Mom,

I hardly know where to begin. You mean so very much to me. When I think of all you have taught me, I am humbled. I have learned about being a good Mother, how to tackle projects, studying the scriptures, always striving to be a more Christ-like person, creativity, loving fine things, sharing love with others, pursuing interests, reading, being open minded, preserving traditions and so much more. Thank you for all of it.

Forgive my selfish desire, but I hope we will always be on earth together. I can't imagine being here without you. I lean on you for so much strength and understanding. I know at times you do not feel the strength of our love. I hope today you feel both loved and honored.

Thank you for being my kindred spirit. Thank you for the services you have given so constantly. Thank you for being my children's Grandma. Thank you, Angel Mother. (When my children were small, I always tried to get them to say I was their "Angel Mother." I couldn't even bribe them into it and it was a family joke)

Always,

C

I pray that I will never again drift from the love and bond that I have with Christi. But, if for what-ever reasons I do, I know that a loving God will find a way, some miracle, some memory, some story, that will testify to me that my family is forever.

Behind the Story

Christi (Hart) Hales is my oldest, dearest friend. She is the kind of companion you have only once in your life, if you are lucky. The friend who knows you sometimes better than you know yourself; who is familiar with all your weaknesses and loves you in spite, and sometimes because, of them. When at times it felt like no one understood me, when I would doubt myself, she always knew just what to say to lift my spirits and make the world "right" again. You often hear great tributes given to those who have passed on, and sometimes we wonder if there isn't some "aggrandizement" happening now that the person is no longer here. In the case of Christi, there is no praise given which isn't fully deserved. I think the story she wrote for her children, and which has been shared in these pages, naturally shows the greatness of her spirit.

I met Christi my freshman year of high school, shortly after she was first diagnosed with cancer. We were inseparable ever after; at least in spirit, as we eventually lived miles apart. Christi and I went to college together; she even paid for her space in our apartment during her third bout with cancer, ensuring she had a place to "come home to" when the battle was won. That is how we felt as we lived together in those university years... that we created a home away from home. Christi's side of the room being empty during those cancer-filled months made it very lonely at times.

What a fighter, and survivor, Christi was as she returned "home" victorious for the third time! Together we met and courted our husbands and married just days apart in the summer of 1994. Then we had our children at the same time: first a boy, then a girl, and then when Brynn was born, Christi gave birth to spontaneous triplets. Her children are a miracle as she was never supposed to become pregnant after all that chemo and radiation!

About four years ago, it was Christi who introduced me to the profession of story preservation. She was passionate and together we built a business helping people write their stories and publish beautiful storybooks to strengthen their families and pass wisdom on to posterity. I owe all I am doing now to her leadership.

In December of 2008, on a Sunday afternoon, I came home from church to hear to a voice message from Robert, Christi's husband. He said that something had happened to Christi and I should call him as soon as I can.

He ended the message by saying "I love you." We had a good friendship, but he had never told me that... so I knew something was very wrong!

It was just a week previous that I last spoke with Christi. She had a terrible virus (turns out pneumonia) and called to hear a friendly voice as she laid on the couch trying to prepare crafts for her children's Christmas party. I told her "Christi, you sound awful!" and gave her the chastisement only a good friend can for not resting more. The conversation was short. It is natural to wish I knew it would be the last time we would talk. There are so many more things I would have said instead of giving her a bad time!

Christi's lungs were to fill with blood the following Friday night (possibly a weakness from her lung surgeries and cancer) and she would collapse into her husband's arms while the ambulance was on its way. Robert later told me that, as this happened, he felt a sense of calm and a message that everything would be alright. Christi spent a few days in the hospital on life-support and everyone hoped for recovery, though there was little-to-no brain activity. It was finally realized that Christi would need to be removed from life-support and plans were made for this to happen just after Christmas. But it seemed that Christi was in control of the timing and was not having her family suffer through Christmas Day with this looming sorrow; so just after the family visited with her on the 23 of December, she quickly passed.

I was able to travel to Christi's funeral with my family shortly after Christmas. At the viewing the night before, I had a full half-hour alone with Christi. My husband took all of her children and ours to ice cream; Robert waited in the lobby for guests; and I truly had some quiet time alone with her. I feel certain Christi arranged this... that's the kind of friends we were.

I had a great conversation with Christi as I stroked her beautiful long hair while she lay in the coffin. I sensed her near and could see an image in my mind of her glorious, smiling face... literally beaming, with a glint of "knowing" as she had progressed beyond me now and was finding some mirth in this situation. I told her how wonderful she looked and that there is some benefit to dying young... she was a true sleeping beauty! We talked and laughed about all the things we had hoped for or been afraid of in the future. I observed that she didn't have to worry about growing old after all. As I spoke with Christi, I felt a great warmth and calm that all was *right*, and everything will yet be *right*. This was her time, she was ready, and I sensed her joy.

As I returned home from the funeral, I had the oddest experience. I could clearly feel my muscles flexing and stretching with each movement. I felt more healthy and alive than I can ever remember. It was an unusual awareness and struck me profoundly how strange it is that I should feel so alive, and excited to live, as I left the funeral of my best friend. What I clearly sensed is that I have more living to do, and there is purpose in life. I also had a "knowing" that Christi is somehow part of my life's purpose. She was always an especially compassionate, comforting person. It was a natural result of all she went through. I have an impression that she is still part of the healing and story preservation work we do, only from "the other side."

Christi is part of my life's mission in many ways, from her influence throughout my life, the financial contributions of her husband towards my grief work on her behalf (using her life insurance money!), and the presence I sense as I move forward.

As I end the **Behind the Stories** sections, and complete this book, I would like to highlight the last lines of the story Christi wrote. It was the message printed at her funeral and is remarkably insightful to her existence then, now, and for us all:

"My experiences have helped me to empathize with others through their trials. I am so grateful for all I was taught through these years. My journey has brought a depth of understanding I have taken with me as my path continues on." –Christi Hales

Melanie and Christi in college

Melanie and Christi receiving awards for their work in story preservation

Stories Are Our Triumph

The silhouette on the cover of this book represents the value of our stories. We stand, elevated on a winner's platform, holding our wisdom high above our heads, saying to the world as we do, "This is my greatest gift!" Stories are the substance of life. Our sojourn on this planet is short; after we are gone, our stories are what remain. By sharing our unique experiences—something we *ALL* can do—we leave a significant mark on the planet. Our stories can transcend the influence of today and become the material which guides future generations.

Whatever our experiences, whatever our endeavors, if we recognize the opportunity found in deliberately and carefully recording our life wisdom, we may actually make a much bigger difference in the world than we ever imagined. *Story* is the universal thread that binds us together. It weaves the joy and pathos of the human experience here and now, and of all humanity from the dawn of time to eternity. It is through story that we know each other, learn from each other, avoid mistakes and make progress.

Telling story is a primitive and most basic human need. Before the wheel, stories existed. They were told around campfires, as petro glyphs on cliff walls, painted on Polynesian Tapa cloths and depicted on the lodges, teepees, totem poles, and other central structures of a society where the stories, and their importance, could be ever present. Among people with no written language, the storyteller was the most revered member.

Beyond the historical and current need to share and hear stories is the additional benefit of storytelling as a vital part of healing. In their landmark book, *On Grief and Grieving*, Elizabeth Kübler-Ross and David Kessler write of the importance of storytelling in the healing process. They share that telling your story is primal to the grieving process and that storytelling allows you to open your confusion and cover ground that needs exploring. They warn that not telling our stories, but holding them in, takes a huge amount of effort and is unnatural.

In the opening section of this book, *Tragedy to Triumph*, I explained that the purpose of *The Triumph Book* is to show—through the stories of those who have "been there"—that it is possible to overcome grief, feel joy and discover purpose after tragedy. Often, simply sharing our stories is the way we find our purpose, as they serve to uplift and assist others through their hardships and give hope when it is hard to be found in the midst of suffering. The joy and catharsis which came to each author featured in this book as they wrote of their experiences were powerful and real. The hope we have that this collection will reach and help countless others magnifies the significance of our stories and increases our sense of purpose for going through these hardships.

The opportunity to share stories and uplift others through the storytelling process is available to everyone. Very often we fail to share our life stories with one another out of the fear we may come across as conceited or prideful. We may doubt if our stories are actually interesting and worthwhile, or, most frightening of all, we fear that our stories might demonstrate that we are, in truth, much more valuable or powerful than anyone knows.

As I have gone through the process of searching for stories, I've come to recognize that *EVERYONE* has a powerful and important story to share. While many of the stories in this book were found by following a trail of bread crumbs from one author or acquaintance to another, I also located a powerful story literally up the hill and another which came from a friend I had known for years, yet never fully knew the depth of her life's challenges which brought the inner strength she possesses.

In the process of compiling this book, I have learned that we are living among Giants. There has yet to be a person who has shared their story with me that hasn't touched me in some profound way. I now view each of them with much greater respect and appreciation than before. These Giants are not the few whose story is "good enough" to be preserved on the pages of a book for all to read. They are the people you know, work with or wave to as you drive down the street. The person whose story is most meaningful of all is *yours*!

Your individual story matters. There are future generations, especially among your own posterity, who will find *your* story extremely interesting and important. Here is an example: In an old miners shack, high in the Sierra Nevadas, a journal was found. The first few pages were missing, but the rest of the book was intact. The book was eventually published and sold at the souvenir shops in the tourist stops throughout the area. It is called *The Diary of a Forty-Niner.*

It is a fascinating book. A man who lived through the gold rush accounts the day-to-day life of the time. I am sure the events he chronicled seemed normal and ordinary to him, but to those of us who did not live through that era it is intriguing. There was a sweetheart he left behind in the east when he traveled west for the Gold Rush. Reading his journal, you find yourself rooting for them to get together. You hope he will find gold and not be killed by the drunken miners around him. You mourn the tragedies he records, which occur all too often to the people in his life; and you feel empty when the journal ends and you don't know how things turned out or if he ever struck gold!

The publisher of the book could only guess, with some historical research, the identity of the author; and yet you are riveted by his life experiences, his desires, hopes and dreams. It doesn't matter whether his identity is correct or not, the history he records and the human sympathy we feel makes this book important. Do you know that the purchase price of a paperback copy of this book today starts at $150? It is out of print and has become valuable.

If an old journal found in a shack can become that valuable to people who don't even know the author, imagine how precious YOUR stories will be to future generations and especially your own posterity.

We are all living lives of great importance. We have experiences and learn great truths which, if recorded and shared, can strengthen our future generations. It is vital that we don't take these stories to our graves without helping the world be a better, more loving and peaceful place because of the hard-earned knowledge we have gained.

Most, if not all, of us have read or at least heard of the story written by a young girl hiding in an attic from the Nazis during World War II. Anne Frank's story was, unfortunately, not an uncommon one. There were many children in hiding during this time, but because she took the time to write her experiences down, they have become a source of inspiration for literally millions of people, with thousands of visitors traveling every year to witness this little hiding place.

You also have experiences in your life which may seem common and ordinary, but if you take the time to preserve them, you could find that your experience is actually extraordinary and valuable. For example, I had the privilege of being a tour guide in Yellowstone National Park for three summers. The first summer I was there was 1989. This was one year after the Great Fires of Yellowstone. In the summer of 1988, the fires were a huge controversy because they raged all summer and burnt much of the park. The Park Service had previously adopted a "let-burn" policy which allowed fires to burn naturally when not accidentally started by men, in an effort to return Yellowstone to its primitive, natural and original state (in truth, most of the fires that summer were man-caused and we did fight them, however the very existence of this policy during such a crisis brought tremendous criticism).

There were places in the park where the fire burned so hot that nothing grew there the next year. Often, when I started my tours, we drove through a few of these places and the tourists became very upset, even enraged at times, when they saw what looked like devastation. It was my job to explain how fires are a natural and important part of the Yellowstone ecosystem. Eighty percent of the trees in Yellowstone are called Lodgepole Pine trees. Lodgepoles renew themselves through fire. They have a serrotenous pine cone, or fire activated pine cone, which is covered in a glue-like sap that melts away during a fire, allowing the pine cone to spring open, planting new and healthier trees. Without fire, these trees become unhealthy and die without being replanted. The areas where the fire burnt the hottest, and left the ground barren, are the places where previous fire had not come and cleared the way for healthy trees.

Throughout most of the park, however, the fires burnt just enough to create incredibly fertile soil and the most vibrant, beautiful plants and flowers grew there the summer of 1989. The color of the flowers was intense with an especially brilliant variety called *fireweed* which grew profusely all through the fire-charred places of the park. Yellowstone in 1989 was the place to be! It was a window in time when nature was exceptionally glorious.

Thousands of people visited Yellowstone that summer, but I wonder how many captured this phenomenon. I wonder how many were able to tell the story the way I could. Fortunately, this was a time before the internet and cheap long-distance, so I wrote all of my memories in letters to my mother. She compiled them for me and now I have a story full of the splendor of Yellowstone in 1989-1991. I was able to write a storybook which captured a window in time that may never be quite the same again.

You also have experiences in your life which, like the gold miner's story, may seem ordinary in the present, but will be fascinating to your descendants and anyone else who reads it. Your story may inspire your future granddaughter to be courageous and brave, because *you* were in the face of *your* challenges. Or you may teach a grandson that it is alright if things don't go as you'd hoped or planned, and that you can find success in unexpected places. You may become an inspiration to a much larger group of people, to a nation or to the world; just as young Anne Frank's story has been read or told to millions.

As you conclude reading this book, I hope you place it on the shelf (or pass it along to a friend) with a deeper sense of your own purpose. May you view your own life with a greater awareness of the Triumph inherent in all you endure, and the knowledge that your suffering is as valuable as your pleasure in the grand scheme of existence. I hope you see the experiences, hardships and tragedies you have endured, or are in the midst of, as something of greater meaning than you might have before reading these stories... more than a severe pain or nuisance you've had to put up with, more than something you are grateful to have "over with," more than a challenge you face currently with the persistent question "Why me?!!!"

Maybe you have learned in this book from Laura Pasley to instead ask, "Why not me?" or from Nancy Hopps that "...what to the ego may look like failure or tragedy, may on the soul level be revealed as Divine Perfection." Perhaps you will remember the message from Nick Wells, "Everything that happens to us in our lives is meant to be a positive learning experience; EVERYTHING!" Or you may recall the communication from Terry Thomas, *"Feel gratitude.* When things go badly, even tragically, find a way to express gratitude. It will change your life." You may be deeply impressed by the example of forgiveness from Cammy Wilberger towards the rapist and murderer of her beautiful daughter. You might find courage to endure when life's adversities seem to pile up, as Veronica Lowery did. Her story shows it is possible to live through multiple tragedies and still have joy and hope.

Many of these ideas and kernels of wisdom may be part of you already, and reading this book confirmed what you've felt and experienced in your own life. Or you might have gained more insights than you expected at the start of the book. Whatever the messages, wisdom, life-lessons or confirmations you gained from this reading, I hope you will collect them into your own story of triumph.

To borrow the words from Christi Hart Hales once again: "May *your* journey bring a depth of understanding *you* take with *you* as *your* path continues on." Thank you for sharing this part of the journey with me.

Preserve and Share your Triumph Story

Throughout this book I have made mention of the bereavement program I created as an answer and purpose to my tragedy, which helps people to write, preserve and share their stories. It was often through the contacts I made while developing this bereavement program that many of the stories for *The Triumph Book* were found.

During the course of compiling these stories, I reworked this original bereavement program into one which addresses the grief and pain which comes from all forms of tragedy, in addition to death-loss. While reading the wisdom of the authors of this book, and struggling through additional challenges, these ideas have been channeled into what is called *The Triumph Program*, which is a process for discovering, writing and sharing your Triumph Story.

The Triumph Program is available as a tangible workbook or an on-line course. It can be used individually with success as you read the "food for thought" and complete the activities in each section at your own pace, following the simple instructions provided.

However, this program can also be a vehicle which reaches wider expanses through the support and community of a group setting. The group discussion and exercises at the end of each section allow for greater insight, sharing and epiphanies while giving each participant a true understanding that they are not alone in their suffering, or in their growth. Groups can be conducted in churches, by bereavement counselors, in locations for grief support, and among friends. *The Triumph Program* can also unite and increase family solidarity when used in the home.

Upon completion of the program, participants will have the opportunity, if they desire, to submit their Triumph Stories to be considered for future books in the *Triumph Series* and can be shared in the on-line community.

There is also a publishing resource available for preserving the stories and corresponding pictures in a beautiful storybook.

You can learn more about the program at:

www.TheTriumphBook.com

Tune in to The Triumph Hour Podcasts

Listen to the authors of *The Triumph Book*, and other Courageous Survivors, share insights and wisdom gained through life's profound, and often costly, experiences. You can also submit to be a guest and share your Triumph Story in an upcoming show.

www.TheTriumphHour.com